Inspired by Charles Tilly's brilliant insights, Ernesto Castañeda has assembled a superb roster of scholars to explore links between migration and the creation and persistence of inequality. Timely and engaging, *Immigration and Categorical Inequality* makes a novel contribution to scholarly debates. It will also interest a broad audience eager to understand migration.
—**Viviana Zelizer**, *Princeton University*

Ernesto Castañeda's introductory tribute to the broad sweep of Charles Tilly's scholarship, along with studies of migrant categorization, networks, and inequality, insightfully illuminate the relational processes of social closure based on nationality, race, and ethnicity. It is a "must read" for those interested in social exclusion mechanisms.
—**Hilary Silver**, *George Washington University*

Drawing on Charles Tilly's foundational theorizing on migration and social boundaries, the chapters in *Immigration and Categorical Inequality* draw on an array of methods and contexts to show how categories of race and nation become reified, reinterpreted, redrawn. The authors in this volume stand on the shoulders of a social science giant in Tilly to help us see further into how migration shapes life across the globe.
—**Tomás R. Jiménez**, *Stanford University*

Tilly's relational perspective on human migration offers a fresh approach to understanding a social phenomenon affecting communities across the globe. The edited collection not only introduces Tilly's relational approach to migration scholars but also offers new theoretical and empirical insights into contemporary processes of immigrant incorporation, social networks, group boundaries, and inequality. Castañeda's collection successfully demonstrates the continued vitality of Tilly's scholarship for contemporary and future migration scholars.
—**Ali Chaudhary**, *Rutgers University*

IMMIGRATION AND CATEGORICAL INEQUALITY

Immigration and Categorical Inequality explains the general processes of migration, the categorization of newcomers in urban areas as racial or ethnic others, and the mechanisms that perpetuate inequality among groups. Inspired by the pioneering work of Charles Tilly on chain migration, transnational communities, trust networks, and categorical inequality, renowned migration scholars apply Tilly's theoretical concepts using empirical data gathered in different historical periods and geographical areas ranging from New York to Tokyo and from Barcelona to Nepal. The contributors of this volume demonstrate the ways in which social boundary mechanisms produce relational processes of durable categorical inequality. This understanding is an important step to stop treating differences between certain groups as natural and unchangeable. This volume will be valuable for scholars, students, and the public in general interested in understanding the periodic rise of nativism in the United States and elsewhere.

Ernesto Castañeda is Assistant Professor of Sociology at American University in Washington, DC. He is the author of *A Place to Call Home: Immigrant Exclusion and Urban Belonging in New York, Paris, and Barcelona* (Forthcoming Stanford University Press, 2018), coeditor with Cathy L. Schneider of Collective Violence, Contentious Politics, and *Social Change: A Charles Tilly Reader* (Routledge, 2017), and coauthor with Charles Tilly and Lesley Wood of *Social Movements 1768–2018* (Forthcoming Routledge, 2018). He has published articles on social movements, immigration, borders, and homelessness. He holds a Ph.D. in sociology from Columbia University.

IMMIGRATION AND CATEGORICAL INEQUALITY

Migration to the City and the Birth of Race and Ethnicity

Edited by Ernesto Castañeda

Routledge
Taylor & Francis Group
NEW YORK AND LONDON

First published 2018
by Routledge
711 Third Avenue, New York, NY 10017

and by Routledge
2 Park Square, Milton Park, Abingdon, Oxon, OX14 4RN

Routledge is an imprint of the Taylor & Francis Group, an informa business

© 2018 Taylor & Francis

The right of Ernesto Castañeda to be identified as the author of the editorial material, and of the authors for their individual chapters, has been asserted in accordance with sections 77 and 78 of the Copyright, Designs and Patents Act 1988.

All rights reserved. No part of this book may be reprinted or reproduced or utilised in any form or by any electronic, mechanical, or other means, now known or hereafter invented, including photocopying and recording, or in any information storage or retrieval system, without permission in writing from the publishers.

Trademark notice: Product or corporate names may be trademarks or registered trademarks, and are used only for identification and explanation without intent to infringe.

Library of Congress Cataloging-in-Publication Data
A catalog record for this book has been requested

ISBN: 978-1-138-10717-5 (hbk)
ISBN: 978-1-138-29541-4 (pbk)
ISBN: 978-1-315-10037-1 (ebk)

Typeset in Minion
by Apex CoVantage, LLC

Visit the eResources: www.routledge.com/9781138295414

 Printed in the United Kingdom by Henry Ling Limited

This book is dedicated to Charles Tilly, an extraordinary scholar, mentor, and human being.

CONTENTS

1 **Understanding Inequality, Migration, Race, and Ethnicity from a Relational Perspective**   1
 Ernesto Castañeda

2 **Migration and Categorical Inequality**   26
 Douglas S. Massey

3 **Immigration or Citizenship? Two Sides of One Social History**   44
 Josiah Heyman

4 **Stigmatizing Immigrant Day Labor: Boundary-Making and the Built Environment in Long Island, New York**   65
 Ernesto Castañeda and Kevin R. Beck

5 **Migration-Trust Networks: Unveiling the Social Networks of International Migration**   83
 Nadia Y. Flores-Yeffal

6 **Ethnic Weddings: Reinventing the Nation in Exile**   99
 Randa Serhan

7 **Trust Networks and Durable Inequality among Korean Immigrants in Japan**   121
 Hwaji Shin

8   **Ethnic Centralities in Barcelona:
    Foreign-Owned Businesses between
    "Commercial Ghettos" and Urban
    Revitalization**   140
    Pau Serra del Pozo

9   **Remittance-Driven Migration in Spite
    of Microfinance? The Case of Nepalese
    Households**   171
    Bishal Kasu, Ernesto Castañeda, and Guangqing Chi

About the Contributors   197
Index   199

1

UNDERSTANDING INEQUALITY, MIGRATION, RACE, AND ETHNICITY FROM A RELATIONAL PERSPECTIVE

Ernesto Castañeda

This book analyzes the impact that migration,[1] particularly cumulative long-distance migration into urban areas, has in the creation of categories of people often referred to as immigrant nationalities, ethnicities, or races. Based on social science studies, this book sees "race" not as a natural category but as something socially constructed, with a history to be explored and mechanisms that make it salient as something to be explained (Golash-Boza 2016; Morning 2011).

> *More than 100 years ago, American sociologist W.E.B. Du Bois was concerned that race was being used as a biological explanation for what he understood to be social and cultural differences between different populations of people. He spoke out against the idea of "white" and "black" as discrete groups, claiming that these distinctions ignored the scope of human diversity.*
>
> (Gannon 2016)

Race is not a biological fact but rather the result of social categorizations (Bonilla-Silva 2006; Yudell et al. 2016). Categorization aids human cognition by providing decision-making shortcuts (see Massey in this volume). Nominal categories group people in mutually comprehensive ways. Persistent categories, such as those framed around race, ethnicity, or nationality, tend to naturalize historical access to resources and social status over time. Categorical groups become part of a hierarchy with those with more power and resources at the top. Symbolic differences and unequal distribution of resources among social groups create and reproduce categorical inequalities.

Most academic and folk theories about what causes inequality focus on individual barriers and opportunities. In contrast, this book shows how persistent and unquestioned inequality are created and justified by social boundaries between certain groups (Tilly 1998). In the next pages, I introduce Charles Tilly's work on migration and inequality. I then discuss the work of other relevant authors and different approaches to the issue, including social boundary theory, categorical inequality, social psychological approaches, and theories of race and ethnicity. Finally, I discuss the chapters in this volume and the overall contribution to a growing approach to study the creation and reproduction of inequality.

Tilly's Contribution to Our Understanding of Migration, Ethnicity and Categorical Inequality

The sociologist Charles "Chuck" Tilly is renowned for his work on revolutions, war, state formation, social movements, and contentious politics (see Castañeda and Schneider 2017). Tilly preferred relational accounts, theoretical and empirical work focused on concrete ties, relations, trading, communication, and interactions between specific individuals and social sites forming networks with emergent properties (Diani 2007; Mische 2011). Tilly was a pioneer in the theorizing of social boundaries and categorical inequality through relational processes among networks of historically marginalized groups, such as migrants or the descendants of slaves. Tilly's theorizing helps us understand why it is misguided to treat immigration as extraordinary, as a social problem, or as an exception to a world neatly organized in nation-states (Tilly 1984).

Charles Tilly published insightful empirical and theoretical pieces on migration: he was one of the first social scientists to document the important role that social networks play in migration. He described how chain migration results in the concentration of immigrants in certain localities (Tilly and Brown 1967; Tilly 1990). Tilly pointed out how remittances—the money sent by workers abroad to their family in the hometown—are a way to fulfill family obligations, demonstrating the importance of social relations despite distance (Castañeda 2013; Zelizer and Tilly 2006).

Tilly was a student of migration and published on the topic throughout his career. His work relies on migration data and methodologies from historical sociology, demographic, life stories, and ethnographic research. Tilly was part of a collaborative project comparing French immigrants from Lyon who monopolized the silk industry in Paterson, New Jersey, in the nineteenth century and immigrants from Frosinone, Italy, living in Mamaroneck, New York, in the twentieth century (Tilly 2008:127). Reminiscent of Thomas and Znaniecki (1918), the project included looking at letters and photos sent by migrants across the Atlantic as well as many oral history interviews (Castañeda 2009; Castañeda 2017). Unfortunately, Tilly and his coauthors never published the results of that study. Nonetheless, Tilly learned much about migration from these interviews and primary sources.

While Tilly pioneered the quantification of historical events, he also theorized using historical secondary sources as well as qualitative data and ethnographic observations. While Tilly was not an ethnographer, he had a great sense of what good ethnography entailed thanks to his many ethnographer colleagues and his having been a mentor to dozens of students conducting ethnographic studies. He was also familiar with the complexities involved in writing ethnographic findings. He became very interested in ethnography as a privileged method to understand social processes (Auyero 2006; Smith 2006; Tilly 2006).

Migration Networks

In the same way that Tilly foreshadowed the importance of social networks in facilitating immigration, he also wrote about themes later documented and detailed by other migration scholars. Tilly had a good grasp of the big picture regarding migration processes and ethnic identification.

Tilly explains why migration is not the movement of individuals—as it is commonly understood—but the movement of families, townships, and trust networks. His work corrects the popular but limited understanding of international migration simply as an issue of labor supply and demand based on neoclassical economics (Todaro 1969). For example, after discussing the proletarianization of former European peasants who moved into industrializing centers within Europe, he then discussed the attractiveness of relatively high wages in North America, which encouraged them to leave their place of birth to cross the Atlantic.

> *Not that the smoothly rational operation of an open, competitive, international labor market characterized by wage differentials accounts for the rhythm and timbre of American immigration. At the very least we need to recognize two facts about that immigration. First, it was and is extraordinarily selective by origin and type of migrant. Second, it usually did not draw on isolated individual decision makers but on clusters of people bound together by acquaintance and common fate. Nor were [the] clusters mere categories—skilled or unskilled, Jew or Gentile, Greek or Italian. To be sure, individuals did migrate to the United States, and sometimes alone. But they did so as participants in social processes that extended far beyond them. Of course, members of different categories of the European population migrated to the United States (and, for that matter, returned to Europe) at spectacularly different rates. But the categories we ordinarily apply to those differences poorly describe the actual groups that lived and organized transatlantic migration.*
>
> (Tilly 1990:83; all emphases added by me)

In the quote, Tilly proposes why a relational theory of migration is superior to a neoclassical one (Castañeda 2013). He also talks about how the categories that are used by others to describe migrants in American cities are often not the ones that migrants used before they left their homelands. For example in the United States, Sicilians became "Italians," Mayas become "Latino," Galician Polish peasants became "Slavs" in Cleveland, and Albanians passed as Italians in the Bronx's Little Italy (Cornelius, FitzGerald and Lewin Fischer 2007; Hammack, Grabowski and Grabowski 2002; Kosta 2014; Thomas and Znaniecki 1918).

Tilly also underlined early on the specific ties between sending and receiving networks. Though he did not explicitly use the term "transnational," he had a transnational network conception of migration (Basch, Glick Schiller and Szanton-Blanc 1994):

> *We need a rough distinction between sending and receiving networks. The connections among people at a given point of origin constitute the sending networks; those among people at the destination, the receiving networks. The knitting together of the two creates new networks that span origin and destination. The distinction can only be rough because many people make multiple moves, and because once a migration system starts operating, the line between "origin" and "destination" begins to blur. Nevertheless, the distinction makes sense because the characteristics of the new networks depend on the pairings that occur at the junction of origin and destination.*
>
> (Tilly 1990:86)

I observed these transnational dynamics while conducting ethnographic work in migrant circuits connecting Mexico to New York, Algeria to Paris, and Morocco to Barcelona (Castañeda 2013), and much has been written about the features of migrant transnationalism in recent decades (Glick Schiller, Basch and Blanc-Szanton 1992; Waldinger 2015).

Tilly saw several problems with theories that assumed assimilation to one mainstream culture. He reminded us that assimilation is not fully the result of individual migrants. It is influenced by existing hierarchies in the places of destination (Portes and Zhou 2003):

> *The network structure of migration makes implausible several standard ways of analyzing immigration: an assimilation of individuals to a dominant culture, as individual status-striving, or as the wholesale transplantation of preexisting groups. "Assimilation" becomes implausible because the paths of change vary enormously from stream to stream of migration, because the process is collective rather than individual, and because the network structure multiplied, contradicts the idea of a single*

dominant pattern to which people might approximate themselves. *Individual status-striving, although it surely occurs, accounts poorly for group changes after immigration because it misses the centrality of interpersonal connections to the fate of any particular group. Wholesale transplantation badly describes a process in which people greatly transform their social relations, and often create new group identities. Instead of a series of individual transformations in the direction of a dominant American culture, migration involves negotiation of new relationships both within and across networks. Instead of individual status-striving, collective efforts to cope. Instead of wholesale transplantation, selective re-creation of social ties.* Once we recognize the network structure of migration, some of the old, standard questions stop making sense. It is idle, for example, to ask whether in general migrants are smarter, braver, or more desperate than nonmigrants; some systems of social ties select in one direction, some in another. It is not very useful to classify migrants by intentions to stay or to return home, because intentions and possibilities are always more complex than that—and the migrants themselves often cannot see the possibilities that are shaped by their networks. . . . *The decisive, recurrent regularities concern the structures of migration networks themselves.*

(Tilly 1990:87–88)

While much of the migration literature is influenced by classic and neoclassical economic assumptions and emphasizes individual rational choice theory, Tilly instead offers a relational perspective. Tilly arrived at these conclusions through demographic and community studies in Delaware (Tilly 1965), which he conducted through the relational understanding of network theory as proposed by Harrison White, as well as through oral histories and historical cases.

Another popular misunderstanding is that every migrant in the world was to go to the United States or to the global north, but Tilly looks at the historical record to qualify this notion:

With respect to wealth, education previous work experience, and region of origin, the 2.3 million Italians who migrated to Argentina between 1860 and 1914 resembled the 4.1 million who migrated to the United States. What is more, the great majority of both groups seem to have arrived via chain migration, with the idea of earning enough to return home. Immediately on arrival in the new land, both groups moved chiefly into unskilled labor. But Italians came to occupy much more prominent positions in Argentina (and especially Buenos Aires) than in the United States (and especially New York). Two factors made a large difference: first, investment opportunities for workers who saved money were greater in Argentina than in the United States; second, it was easier to

> *move from unskilled to skilled jobs in Argentina. Both factors gave Italian immigrants who worked hard and saved in Argentina stronger reasons for remaining in their adopted country.*
>
> (Tilly 1968:87)

As we see throughout Tilly's work, he is interested not only in the particularities of each case but also in looking at patterns and similar mechanisms across cases in different locations and historical periods. The importance of networks to propel and sustain migration (Massey et al. 1987; Massey 1990; Massey et al. 1993; Menjívar 2000) and of transnational connections between receiving and sending communities is much more widely accepted and appreciated today (Castañeda, Morales and Ochoa 2014; Levitt 2001; Mouw et al. 2014; Snel, Hart and Van Bochove 2016). However, important insights about the historical relevance of cities as destinations of migrants and as "factories of ethnicity" remain understudied. It is thus useful to reintroduce Tilly's argument about cities and the manufacturing of ethnicity.

Cities and Migration

Historically, cities were born because of rural-urban migration (Castañeda 2012a; Castañeda 2012b; Castles and Davidson 2000; Weber 1958). Public areas in cities are places where strangers meet to trade without sharing kinship, religion, or language (Simmel 1971). Since the industrial era, cities have needed a constant infusion of new inhabitants to function, prosper, and compete with other cities (Tilly 1978). International migration is key in repopulating, industrializing, and revitalizing American cities (Tilly 1970).

Tilly (1976) discusses the unique "love-hate" relationship between cities and migrants. While the textile, manufacturing, construction, and service industries are always in need of new labor, some of the people already living in the city may see migrants as a threat to their employment, economic stability, and culture. This is a recurrent process that has been present since people founded cities. Tilly provides some examples:

> *By the early 19th century, evolving capitalist economic and property relations—notably the spread of wage labor, the separation of households from the means of production, and the rising productivity of commercial agriculture—had combined with diminishing land resources and an expanding demand for labor in urban-industrial areas to make long-distance migration a logical choice for many Europeans. Recent scholars of European emigration generally agree that local conditions, including land-tenure patterns, agricultural requirements, and resource management, profoundly influenced rates of emigration and return as well as the kinds of people who emigrated. Those from regions,*

> such as certain parts of southern Italy, where land ownership was still possible hoped to use American wages to purchase land upon their return. The sons of west Norwegian cattle farmers, shut out from ownership, along with fairly-well-off farmers seeking larger farms, also left Europe.
>
> (preview Tilly 1990)

As the summary above shows, Tilly's work takes into account the role of material history and regular people in his approach to social history. The advantage of having a historical understanding of the rise of particular nation-states is that Tilly is not limited to national histories or to studying populations only within fixed political boundaries or from the point of view of loyalties to elites or governments (Castañeda and Schneider 2017). Thus, Tilly avoids "methodological nationalism" (Wimmer and Glick Schiller 2002) by not taking for granted current international borders and political units. Cities are a better site to study concrete immigration processes than only looking at population movement between present-day nation-states.

Chain Migration and the Manufacturing of Ethnicity in Destination Cities

Migrants often engage in temporary and "circular migration," splitting time between their hometown and a faraway workplace (Massey et al. 1987; Tilly 1990). Part-time city residents go home and bring family members and friends back with them, leading some to settle permanently in the city. This starts the process of chain migration from particular places: migrants bring another person similar in origin to them and the new individual may do the same and so on (MacDonald and MacDonald 1964). Chain migration results from migrants' pre-migration links. New immigrants support the newer wave of family, friends, and hometown acquaintances. They often live close by and work together or in similar industries. Having family, friends, and even acquaintances in cities with jobs makes it easier for prospective migrants to find work and shelter in unfamiliar cities.

Chain migration makes it easier for newcomers to find themselves among people who came from their area and share a common culture (Tilly and Brown 1967). The networks, opportunities, and comfort zones that the migrants create may produce segregation (see Shin in this volume). Strong bonds form between people who have already settled in a city and the migrants coming from the same area; they often cluster spatially or socially in categorical networks or catnets, concrete social groups that share belonging to the same social category (Tilly 1984). Furthermore, working-class migrants often have limited time and opportunity to socialize beyond their community.

Cities and migrants have a "love-hate" relationship because economic forces push people out of rural areas and pull them into cities, where labor is in demand and where immigrants are necessary for economic growth. Yet, established city residents—the result of previous migrations—begrudge the newcomers as interlopers (see Heyman in this volume). Tilly presents concepts that help us better understand how cities and migrants interact, including the middle-range theory of cities as factories of ethnicity (Tilly 2010). Once spatial segregation and concentration in jobs occur, ethnicity is born through internal and external processes. This manufacturing of ethnicity or *ethnitization* can be detected by the construction of institutions formed around that community such as mutual aid societies, clubs, drinking halls, and minority churches (Castaneda 2017; Castañeda 2012a; Moya 2005). Those who are not members of these categorical networks name these groups with derogatory terms or religious, geographical, or national markers (Catholics, Sicilians, Irish). Natives assign stereotypical attributes to the whole group, as many chapters in this book describe. These processes create an increasingly visible new categorical group in a city. This manufactured ethnicity is reinforced by the way that migrant groups settle in different parts of the city and move within it as jobs and opportunities change. Cities are "ethnic factories" because they encourage visible concentration and stratification into groups along ethnic, race, and religious lines (Tilly 1976).

Early-twentieth-century American migration scholars framed migrants as uprooted (Handlin 1951) and thus prone to immoral and disorderly behavior. This botanical analogy had an elective affinity with the Chicago School of Sociology's ecological model (Park 1915; Park 1950). It was common to talk about transplanted villages as urban ethnic villages. Tilly corrects this approach by writing about transplanted networks rather than transplanted villages. He did not blame immigrants' patriotism or intellect for their failure to assimilate quickly but rather was able to see the structural and organizational arrangements that caused migration and favored ethnic relations over individual immersion into majority networks.

The processes described here are most common for large groups of displaced farmers and industrial and low-skilled workers. The less skilled or educated migrants are, the more they depend on their friends, family and co-ethnics. "Unskilled" laborers who become labeled as ethnic are under the threat of being seen as perpetually different, are given fewer opportunities, and are more likely to be stuck in undesirable jobs. Tilly contrasts this with another migration ideal type that he calls "career migration." Career migration describes the mobility of professionals seeking job opportunities in their fields of knowledge far from where they currently reside (Tilly 1978). Professionals are relatively less dependent on co-ethnic networks when their skills and abilities are valued. Immigrant professionals are more likely to work with members of the majority group and are more likely to be seen as individuals rather than as "ethnics"—as exceptions to the rules.

Categorical Inequality

So far the concept of categorical inequality has been best described in sociological books including Tilly's *Durable Inequality* (1998) and Douglas Massey's *Categorically Unequal: The American Stratification System* (Massey 2007). Pierre Bourdieu has a parallel analysis in his book *Distinction: A Social Critique of the Judgement of Taste* (1984 [1979]). Along with other publications, this work underlines how inequality is reproduced and justified (Bourdieu 1996 [1989]; Bourdieu and Passeron 1990; Massey 2007; Massey and Sanchez 2010; Tilly 1998). Rogers Brubaker and Patrick Weil show the historical contingencies and arrangements that created physical borders and discourses around nationality and ethnicity as well as citizenship laws (Brubaker 1992; Brubaker 1996; Brubaker 2004; Brubaker et al. 2006; Brubaker 2012; Weil 2005; Weil 2008). All of these works share a relational understanding of inequality. They understand life chances and socioeconomic status as not only resulting from personal traits and virtues but also arising from structural arrangements that work at the group level rather than individually. These works underline historical trends and economic contexts along with socio-psychological dynamics.

The work of Richard Alba agrees with the epistemological reality of the phenomena and the mechanisms described by Tilly and others. Yet, Alba uses the historical cases of Irish, Italians, and other "ethnic whites," as well as demographic trends such as the diminishing numbers of WASPS and whites in general, and presents optimistic outlooks for Latinos and Asians (Alba 2009). Studies of New York (Kasinitz et al. 2008) tend to also paint an optimistic picture for many ethnic groups that have the prospect of forming what I would call a "rainbow upper class"—with top jobs filled by members from diverse backgrounds. These authors also point to the changing and expanding definition of who is considered white through time. Groups formerly seen as inferior and racially different later become white as their children intermarry and experience upper social mobility.

Social Boundaries

Other publications by Tilly as well as by other sociologists, anthropologists, and political scientists frame categorical inequality in terms of symbolic and social boundaries (Barth 1969; Lamont and Molnar 2002). Clearly, boundaries are permeable and open to change after time (Tilly 2004). Aristide Zolberg, a scholar of immigration to Europe and the United States and Tilly's New School colleague, applies social boundaries to discuss immigrant inclusion (Zolberg and Woon 1999),

> *Immigration leads inevitably to heated discussions about how boundaries between "us" and "them" might be drawn or erased. On one side of the*

> *Atlantic, the passions awakened by the Rushdie affair in the United Kingdom (in February 1989) and the "headscarf" affair in France (in September 1989) denote a simmering confrontation between "Christian" Europe and "intruding" Islam. On the other side, the heat generated by the English-only movement and the referendum on bilingual education in California (June 1998) point to an equally dramatic clash between "Anglo-America" and the "invading" Spanish language. As major foci of tension and contention, Islam and Spanish are metonyms for the dangers that those most opposed to immigration perceive as looming ahead: loss of cultural identity, accompanied by disintegrative separatism or communal conflict.*
>
> (Zolberg and Woon 1999:5)

While the particular examples and the year of publication may feel dated, the analysis about the popular discourses of the threats of Spanish and Muslims immigrants is unfortunately still current. Then, Zolberg and Woon masterfully dissect the social construction of the "Hispanic" ethnic label in the United States:

> *While Mexico has clearly held the lead with regard to immigration since 1960, followed by more recent flows from the Caribbean—Cuba and the Dominican Republic—the major source of Hispanics is in fact the United States itself, including not only the island of Puerto Rico, which was acquired in 1898 and whose natives subsequently became U.S. citizens, but also the borderlands of the Southwest. Conquered from Mexico in the middle of the nineteenth century, the latter have experienced sustained immigration since the turn of the twentieth century, so that most of their Hispanics have been U.S. citizens by virtue of jus soli for several generations.*
>
> *Yet here also, in the eyes of the hosts, this highly disparate population has acquired an essentialized unified identity. This has been reified by way of the institutionalization of Hispanics as one of five categories in the US census defining mutually exclusive population groups—at least for the time being. Singled out as the source of the group's unity is the fact of sharing Spanish—not necessarily as a first language, but as a tongue present in the home alongside English, or yet as the language of their forbearers. The oddness of this construct is highlighted by the fact that whereas the other four categories reflect traditional American constructions of races founded on color, Hispanics can be of any race, including white and black Cubans, light and dark Puerto Ricans, mestizo, Indio, or even thoroughly "Europeo" Mexicans. By an ironic twist, one essentialism overrides another, as one word of Spanish provides an escape from the categorization of a person as black by virtue of the "one drop of blood" rule.*
>
> (Zolberg and Woon 1999:6–7)

Zolberg and Woon then discuss how in some cases skin color defines race and becomes the master category, while for others language trumps skin color as marking categorical belonging for the individual, the U.S. Census Bureau, and others who witness the person speaking.

> *Seen in that perspective, Spanish bears a family resemblance to Islam in Europe: as the common speech of an expanding population, spatially concentrated in urban and rural colonies insulated from mainstream societal disciplines, it feeds fantasies of a malignant growth that threatens national unity.*
>
> (Zolberg and Woon 1999:7)

Zolberg and Woon make the analogy between Spanish and Islam, not because religion and language are ontologically the same but because, in their respective contexts, they are the attributes that determine a contested belonging and are the basis of categorization and exclusion by others. However, Zolberg acknowledged that the analogy between Spanish and Islam is imperfect because while one can speak many languages, religious affiliation is mutually exclusive between religious faiths. Still, the processes of boundary-making around them are similar:

> *[T]he emergence of particular elements of culture as the focal points of contentious debates provides an entry point into the dynamics of inclusion and exclusion more generally. At the heart of all debates about incorporation are the twin questions: how different can we afford to be, and how alike must we be? Negotiations about these matters in turn center on identity issues: who can become a member of society, and what are the conditions for membership? Although collective identity formation is commonly conceptualized as a self-referential process, it usually also involves self-conscious efforts by members of a group to distinguish themselves from whom they are not, and hence it is better understood as a dialectical process whose key feature is the delineation of boundaries between "us" and "not us." The process of incorporation can be thought of as the negotiations in which hosts and immigrants engage around these boundaries.*
>
> (Zolberg and Woon 1999:8)

Zolberg proposes three boundary-spanning processes:

1. **Individual boundary crossing,** *without any change in the structure of the receiving society and leaving the distinction between insiders and outsiders unaffected. This is the commonplace process whereby immigrants change themselves by acquiring some of the attributes*

of the host identity. Examples include replacing their mother tongue with the host language, naturalization, and religious conversion.

2. **Boundary blurring,** *based on a broader definition of integration—one that affects the structure (i.e., the legal, social, and cultural boundaries) of the receiving society. Its core feature is the tolerance of multiple memberships and an overlapping of collective identities hitherto thought to be separate and mutually exclusive; it is the taming or domestication of what was once seen as "alien" differences. Examples include formal or informal public bilingualism, the possibility of dual nationality, and the institutionalization of immigrant faiths (including public recognition, where relevant).*

3. **Boundary shifting,** *which denotes a reconstruction of a group's identity, whereby the line differentiating members from nonmembers is relocated, either in the direction of inclusion or exclusion. This is a more comprehensive process, which brings about a more fundamental redefinition of the situation. By and large, the rhetoric of pro-immigration activists and of immigrants themselves can be read as arguments on behalf of the expansion of boundaries to encompass newcomers, while that of the anti-immigrant groups can be read as an attempt to redefine them restrictively in order to exclude them.*

Boundary shifting can occur only after substantial boundary crossing and boundary blurring have taken place; however, it does not necessarily follow in their wake because of the possibility of negative reactions, as noted. Negotiations under way in the Netherlands today might eventually result in a shift of the boundary of recognized religious pillars to include Islam. Paralleling this, the contemporary spread of Spanish in some regions of the United States may prepare the way for a more explicit reconfiguration of these regions into bilingual entities, at least in some aspects of daily life.

(Zolberg and Woon 1999:9)

Zolberg then talks about the incorporation of outsiders and the possible backlashes, the relational or conversational nature of the integration process, and the negotiation of difference:

Both boundary crossing and boundary shifting involve an in-between phase, occasionally fraught with awesome tension because it involves an "unnatural act"—the transformation of strangers into members, of the not us into part of us. Thus, an acceleration of boundary crossing and of boundary shifting can provoke negative reactions on the part of the hosts, leading to a crystallization of boundaries, the imposition of conditions that render crossing more difficult and blurring impossible, and perhaps even a redefinition of the host identity amounting to a shift of the boundary in a more exclusive direction. Concomitantly, some of the newcomers may react to increased boundary-crossing opportunities by resisting any sort of identity change. Though incorporation is an interactive process, involving both hosts and newcomers, the actors are not equal: since the negotiations take place in the host country, power relationships are generally asymmetric in favor of the host majority, which naturally has the upper hand. In the cultural realm, host values and traditions are firmly implanted and benefit from institutional support, while the immigrant minorities, who may differ initially with regard to a variety of cultural elements deemed significant by the hosts—notably, religion and language— are at best in a liminal situation with regard to formal and informal membership in the host society, as well as institutional recognition. Though in the main, boundary crossings are the actions of immigrant newcomers, the emergence of fusion in music, food, art, dress, and even speech and manners point to boundary crossings on the part of individuals from the host majority. This may contribute to the incorporation of immigrants in general by creating buffer zones of indifference to elements of imported culture formerly thought unacceptable, and some of these elements may even come to be positively valued and celebrated.

(Zolberg and Woon 1999:9–10)

Zolberg agrees with commentators claiming that immigrants should want to integrate, but he also clarifies that integration does not happen in a vacuum or solely of the migrants' own accord. The willingness to integrate may increase in a receptive context and a welcoming host society (Castañeda, Morales and Ochoa 2014). The host society is key for successful immigrant integration and peaceful cohabitation:

though boundary shifts and blurrings of host structures have the most wide-ranging effects on immigrant incorporation, as pro-active and creative actors, immigrants do not only passively react to host decisions about structures of most relevance to them, but their views of how boundaries should be drawn, crossed, shifted, or blurred are part of the negotiations about boundaries. Though their voice might be muted as a function of their marginal position, the reinforcement of the rights of persons in liberal democracies, both as the result of internal political struggles and the spread of universal human rights, bolsters the legitimacy of the aspirations of immigrant newcomers; consequently, their views on issues involving their welfare carry greater weight in negotiations. Boundary dynamics vary also as a function of the nature of different components of culture.

(Zolberg and Woon 1999:10)

As Zolberg and Woon write, immigrant integration happens in a larger cultural and political context. Immigrants have agency advocating for themselves. Boundary dynamics may impede their ability to enjoy the same political rights and opportunities as the majority group.

Normally, social boundaries are porous. Some individuals from subordinate categories advance to ostensibly superior categories and profit from access to previously hoarded skills, knowledge, and opportunities. However, when there is no mobility or integration and boundaries are activated, social relations polarize along a given us/them boundary, and collective violence becomes more likely. Tilly (2003) made boundary activation, as well as mechanisms such as brokerage (uniting the members of several categories, violent entrepreneurs, and violent specialists against a rival coalition), central to understanding a wide array of violent conflicts. Tilly describes how nation formation, the decrease of civil wars and internal violence, and the consolidation of democracy occurred through the integration of *trust networks* into governing coalitions (Castañeda and Schneider 2017).

Trust Networks

In his later work, Tilly argues that it is not general categorical labels (e.g., working-class, Italian, black, woman) that matter for individuals but rather their specific networks, which may or may not be categorical. Chain migration, ethnic organizations, niche employment, opportunity hoarding (Tilly 1998; Tilly 2005b), and political claim-making create "trust-networks"—groups of like-minded people who, for the most part, benefit members and fend them off from outside threats (and opportunities).

Individual migration may lead to family reunification in faraway cities. Chain migration reunites friends, former neighbors, and acquaintances. Yet, as the networks expand, they also bring together countrymen who have never before met each other. They must consciously and actively construct associations, exchange favors, and invest in relations rather than purely exploit newcomers (Mahler 1995; Menjívar 2000; Tilly 2007). Tilly introduces the concept of trust networks in this way:

> *"Interpersonal trust networks" may strike you as a mysterious term. Out of all the various networks that connect people, it helps to single out those that involve unusual amounts of mutual trust. People rely especially on those networks when they are carrying on long-term, crucial enterprises such as procreation, child rearing, religious or political commitment, long-distance trade, and, of course, migration. In those networks, members bet valued outcomes on the likelihood that other people will meet their responsibilities competently. Trust networks include some religious communities, political conspiracies, webs of ethnic traders, and kinship groups. For thousands of years,*

trust networks have performed an enormous range of political, economic, and spiritual work for human beings, especially those human beings who could not rely on governments to provide them with sustaining services. But here we concentrate on trust networks' place in long-distance migration.

(Tilly 2007:5)

Migrant streams attached to trust networks are concentrated in specialized economic, geographic, and social niches and may confine members and limit opportunity. They prosper and linger when they corner profitable markets or economic sectors. However, trust networks are also important to maintain solidarity between origin and destination (see Flores-Yeffal in this volume). Trust networks entail rights and obligations, social insurance, and social control; therefore, they require certain self-segregation to persist in the long-term. Trust networks may slow assimilation because they depend on us/them social boundaries (Tilly 2007), which can cause problems in later generations, as categorical membership in the ethnic group may result in more drawbacks than advantages (see Shin in this volume).

Relations and Categories

A relational approach brings a sociological understanding to moral, political, and economic issues, where social relations are paramount to understanding actual practices (Zelizer 2012). Tilly and his coauthor, the economic sociologist Viviana Zelizer, describe how social relations, boundary work, and categorical groups help explain economic transactions such as alternative currencies and migrant remittances. As they write:

> *Local money provides just one example of a much more general process. In a wide variety of situations, people engaged in everyday social interaction establish boundaries between insiders and outsiders that sustain crucial social activities. Those boundaries then create consequential connected categories—not only insiders and outsiders but also us and them, worthy and unworthy, intimate and impersonal, congenial and threatening. To be sure, general cognitive processes affect perception and use of those categories. But the categories themselves emerge from social interaction, and their contents depend on social interaction (Tilly 2005b; Zelizer 2005). . . . Immigrant remittances provide a doorway into related phenomena, in this case still mainly monetary, but now involving long-distance and long-term creation of categories through complex social interaction.*
>
> *From immigrant remittances we turn to other forms of category creation in which money occupies a less central place: interpersonal networks*

of trust and relations between nationalism and citizenship. Each case illuminates a different aspect of a general argument:

- *Social interaction generates, informs, and then responds to a significant set of connected categories.*
- *Those categories depend on interaction among three elements: (1) socially maintained boundaries, (2) relations within the boundaries, and (3) relations across the boundaries.*
- *They regularly involve mental accounting systems, of which short-term quid pro quo exchanges constitute only one special type.*
- *People complement mental accounting systems with earmarking practices; they establish subdivisions within ostensibly homogeneous money and other media by signaling commitment of media segments to distinct relations and transactions.*
- *Relational work—the effort of establishing, terminating, negotiating, and transforming interpersonal relations—goes on continuously, shaping boundaries, accounting systems, and categories.*

By the end we hope to have established not that all categories result from interpersonal interactions, much less that all categories are somehow essentially social, but that coherent social processes regularly generate, deploy, and alter an important set of human categories.

(Zelizer and Tilly 2006:2-3)

Zelizer and Tilly write from the perspective of economic sociology about how social practices both create and draw social meaning from categories. Immigrant remittances provide a special example, wherein money is not just money but represents love, sacrifice, and commitment to emigrants' family members "left behind" in their place of origin (Castañeda and Buck 2011; Castañeda and Buck 2014).

Race

Tilly's writings on migration mainly focused on European historical migrations and contemporary Latin American migration, yet Tilly understood the arrival of people from Africa as forced migration, as well as a textbook example of categorical inequality: the combination of policed social boundaries and labor exploitation. Race in America has historically depended on boundary-work dividing "black" and "white" populations. While slavery eventually ended, categorical disadvantage for blacks continues to this day. Race is an odiously durable form of ethnicity connected to having "dark" skin.

Tilly wrote about the great migration of southern blacks from the South to northern cities known as the First Great Migration of 1916–1930 as well as the even larger Second Great Migration of 1940–1970:

> *[T]he situation in the city, rather than the fact of moving, shook Negro family life in the time of the great northward migration. The distinction may seem academic: the impact of any move on the individual always includes the differences in living conditions between the origin and the destination. Yet it matters a great deal. For in the one case we might conclude that as migration slowed down and the immediate shock of moving faded, the troubles of Negro families would disappear. In the other case, we could hardly expect much improvement until the opportunities open to Negro men and women in the big city changed.*
>
> (Tilly 1968:146)

Tilly writes that the move presents a shock for all immigrants, especially for those coming from rural areas. For blacks, the issue of race and integration does not disappear after they settled north; racism traveled north with them. Furthermore, Tilly directed the dissertation of Joe R. Feagin, who became an influential race scholar, and coauthored a book on the effects of housing subsidies on poor, mainly black families in Boston (Feagin, Tilly and Williams 1972).

Book Contributions

This book shows how a theoretical relational approach to migration and categorical inequality is useful to study different cases and periods; using methods ranging from ethnography and interviews to archival research, social network analysis, and geospatial mapping. All of these original chapters discuss the causes and consequences of group inequality. The chapters in this volume are in conversation with parts of Tilly's work. The chapters build on one another and provide an overall theoretical framework to think about inequality. Yet each of the chapters stands alone. Each describes particular case studies, mechanisms, and histories surrounding the creation and maintenance of categorical inequality. All of the chapters are theoretical and empirical, yet with different emphases. The first chapters are more theoretical, the middle chapters are qualitative, and the last two use quantitative methods. They all look at processes of stratification mainly in metropolitan areas and their suburbs; the last chapter discusses migrant-sending regions in Nepal.

In Chapter 2, "Migration and Categorical Inequality," the sociologist and demographer Douglas Massey explains the relationship between the process of categorization and the effect that it has on immigrants. Massey draws on decades of pioneering work regarding migration from Mexico to the United States, his influential work on black/white urban segregation, and social psychology literature to give an overview of the historical and contemporary processes that generate categorical inequality. He explains how different sectors of the population from three different Caribbean sites (Puerto Rico, Cuba, and the Dominican Republic) were more likely to emigrate and how this shaped different integration experiences in the United States along national-origin lines.

In Chapter 3, "Immigration or Citizenship? Two Sides of One Social History," the border scholar Josiah Heyman discusses the role of capital and industrial processes in drawing workers to cities. Heyman connects Tilly's work on migration and nation formation to social history and the work of the historical anthropologist Eric Wolf. This chapter includes a powerful theory about the formation of insider/outsider boundaries and the historical formation of the concept of citizenship. It discusses the process through which city inhabitants stopped seeing internal migrants as strangers, while international immigrants were further highlighted as different and problematic.

In Chapter 4, "Stigmatizing Immigrant Day Labor: Boundary-Making and the Built Environment in Long Island, New York," Kevin Beck and I discuss an empirical case study that illustrates specific mechanisms that draw social boundaries between groups and the consequences they have for those whose labor is categorized as "disposable." Citizen employers are in a position of power to stigmatize and exploit day laborers. They further rationalize withholding pay because "illegals" work off the books. This chapter discusses boundary-making practices that marginalize Latino day laborers and result in the internalization of illegality: the construction of day labor spaces as dangerous, flash hirings, and wage theft. Our findings reveal that day laborers once tolerated in Huntington Station, Long Island, became framed as a threat, leading to conflict over a hiring site. We propose the concept of "flash hiring" to explain a hiring practice we observed that demonstrates the simultaneous stigmatization of people, spaces, and day labor. Finally, we draw attention not only to the material loss incurred by wage theft but also to the ways in which workers internalize the effects of wage theft and come to understand themselves as outsiders in their community.

In Chapter 5, "Migration-Trust Networks: Unveiling the Social Networks of International Migration," Nadia Y. Flores-Yeffal, author of a book-length treatise on the subject, applies Tilly's concept of trust networks to explain the social process of migration and survival of undocumented migrants. She concentrates on the enabling aspects of trust networks and how crucial they are for vulnerable individuals, such as undocumented Mexicans.

In Chapter 6, "Ethnic Weddings: Reinventing the Nation in Exile," sociologist Randa Serhan astutely describes a particular migrant trust network as it materializes in important social gatherings: the weddings of its members.

Serhan shows how ethnic weddings represent and reproduce trust among kin and co-ethnic networks, and reinforce nationalism even for a group in a tense political situation of exile and without the immediate possibility of return to the homeland. Serhan shows how trust networks among Palestinians in the East Coast facilitate cultural maintenance, marriage markets, and no-interest credit to afford weddings and the formation of new households, and how wedding parties are a true celebration of the bonds that bring a group together.

In Chapter 7, "Trust Networks and Durable Inequality among Korean Immigrants in Japan," the sociologist Hwaji Shin presents the fascinating case of how Japanese society categorizes Korean immigrants and their offspring. As Shin summarizes, the postwar state incorporated Japanese colonial trust networks but categorically excluded Korean colonial trust networks in various ways. Had these Koreans been included and incorporated socioeconomically and legally, we would have seen Koreans in Japan developing a hyphenated identity ("Korean-Japanese"). Today, instead we have the "Zainichi Korean"—culturally assimilated, but legally not incorporated, who still heavily need to rely on their own trust networks. This is similar to post-colonial Britain and France where the former colonial subjects became racially marginalized as they were not well incorporated into their post-colonial state or economy. This case shows the general application of some of Tilly's concepts and the role of trust networks in helping immigrants. It also shows the limits of co-ethnic solidarity.

In Chapter 8, "Ethnic Centralities in Barcelona: Foreign-owned Businesses between 'Commercial Ghettos' and Urban Revitalization," the Catalan geographer Pau Serra del Pozo intervenes in an important debate about whether ethnic businesses help in fostering or stalling urban economic development. He uses geospatial analyses to present immigrant concentration and diffusion of businesses and to establish benchmarks to discuss the different types of ethnic business concentrations in particular neighborhoods and economic sectors. This study shows some of the points that Tilly made about the importance of networks to migration, opportunity hoarding, and niche specialization, which forge the way for ethnic stereotypes and socioeconomic standing.

In Chapter 9, "Remittance-driven Migration in Spite of Microfinance? The Case of Nepalese Households," Bishal Kasu, Guangqing Chi, and I show how, despite the rhetoric that celebrates their economic development potential, microfinance and remittances are often not enough to escape poverty. A popular approach frames international migration as a way for economic actors to get access through credit. However, the interactions we discover between poverty, caste, remittances and microfinance show that the New Economics of Labor Migration (NELM) theory has serious limitations and some faulty assumptions.

Together these chapters show how social boundaries and mechanisms explain relational processes of durable categorical inequality and constitute a powerful middle-range theory applicable from New York to Barcelona and from Mexico to Nepal. Specifying these mechanisms shows how inequality is socially constructed. This understanding in itself could be an important step to stop thinking of categorical inequality as natural and unchangeable.

Acknowledgments

Mathew Marquez, Jonathan Klassen, and Erasmo Noguera helped with administrative tasks. Maura Fennelly, Christopher Perl, Heather Rosoff, Daniel Oshiro, Hannah McNamara, Casey Chiappetta, Kathryn Whelan, and Genae Hatcher helped with editing.

I deeply thank Dean Birkenkamp for supporting this project from the beginning. Thanks to Amanda Yee and the production team at Routledge. For their encouragement on this project, I want to thank Craig Calhoun, Viviana Zelizer, Sid Tarrow, Marco Giugni, Mario Diani, the late Aristide Zolberg, Alexandra Delano, Randa Serhan, Andreas Koller, Robert Smith, Lesley Buck, and many others. Errors and omissions are my own.

Note

1. The term "migrant" is the general term. It includes the process of emigrating (leaving) and immigrating (arriving) without putting the emphasis on only one side of the same coin. Most people move with the intention of returning to the hometown. Some settle permanently in their new homes, but many, if not most, will return to the sending community. The word "migrant" is advantageous because it accurately describes people's trajectories, often consisting of multiple stops and multiple moves within the life course.

References

Alba, Richard D. 2009. *Blurring the Color Line: The New Chance for a More Integrated America*. Cambridge, MA: Harvard University Press.

Auyero, Javier. 2006. "Introductory Note to Politics under the Microscope: Special Issue on Political Ethnography I." *Qualitative Sociology* 29:3 Special Issue: Political Ethnography I www.springerlink.com/content/xl0867087510146h/fulltext.pdf.

Barth, Fredrik. 1969. *Ethnic Groups and Boundaries: The Social Organization of Culture Difference*. London, UK: George Allen and Unwin.

Basch, Linda, Nina Glick Schiller and Cristina Szanton-Blanc. 1994. *Nations Unbound: Transnational Projects, Postcolonial Predicaments and the Deterritorialized Nation-State*. Langhorne, PA: Gordon & Breach.

Bonilla-Silva, Eduardo. 2006. *Racism without Racists: Color-Blind Racism and the Persistence of Racial Inequality in the United States*. Lanham, MD: Rowman & Littlefield Publishers.

Bourdieu, Pierre. 1984 [1979]. *Distinction: A Social Critique of the Judgement of Taste*. Cambridge, MA: Harvard University Press.
Bourdieu, Pierre. 1996 [1989]. *The State Nobility: Elite Schools in the Field of Power*. Oxford, UK: Polity Press.
Bourdieu, Pierre and Passeron, Jean Claude. 1990 [1970]. *Reproduction in Education, Society, and Culture*. London: Sage Publications.
Brubaker, Rogers. 1992. *Citizenship and Nationhood in France and Germany*. Cambridge, MA: Harvard University Press.
Brubaker, Rogers. 1996. *Nationalism Reframed Nationhood and the National Question in the New Europe*. Cambridge, UK: Cambridge University Press.
Brubaker, Rogers. 2004. *Ethnicity without Groups*. Cambridge, MA: Harvard University Press.
Brubaker, Rogers. 2012. "Categories of Analysis and Categories of Practice: A Note on the Study of Muslims in European Countries of Immigration." *Ethnic and Racial Studies* 36(1):1–8. doi: 10.1080/01419870.2012.729674.
Brubaker, Rogers, Margit Feischmidt, Jon Fox and Liana Grancea. 2006. *Nationalist Politics and Everyday Ethnicity in a Transylvanian Town*. Princeton, NJ: Princeton University Press.
Castañeda, Ernesto. 2009. "Charles Tilly: Connecting Large Scale Social Change and Personal Narrative." *Sociological Research Online* 14(5):24.
Castañeda, Ernesto. 2012a. "Urban Citizenship in New York, Paris, and Barcelona: Immigrant Organizations and the Right to Inhabit the City." Pp. 57–78 in *Remaking Urban Citizenship: Organizations, Institutions, and the Right to the City* Vol. 10, *Comparative Urban and Community Research*, edited by M. P. Smith and M. McQuarrie. New Brunswick, NJ: Transaction Publishers.
Castañeda, Ernesto. 2012b. "Places of Stigma: Ghettos, Barrios and Banlieues." Pp. 159–90 in *The Ghetto: Contemporary Global Issues and Controversies*, edited by R. Hutchison and B. D. Haynes. Boulder, CO: Westview Press.
Castañeda, Ernesto. 2013. "Living in Limbo: Transnational Households, Remittances and Development." *International Migration* 51(s1):13–35. doi: 10.1111/j.1468-2435.2012.00745.x.
Castañeda, Ernesto. 2017. "The Organizational Ecology of Immigrant and Ethnic Associations in America and Europe: The Importance of Urban Contexts, and Their Role in Immigrant Integration." *Working Paper*.
Castañeda, Ernesto and Lesley Buck. 2011. "Remittances, Transnational Parenting, and the Children Left Behind: Economic and Psychological Implications." *The Latin Americanist* 55(4):85–110. doi: 10.1111/j.1557-203X.2011.01136.x.
Castañeda, Ernesto and Lesley Buck. 2014. "A Family of Strangers: Transnational Parenting and the Consequences of Family Separation Due to Undocumented Migration." Pp. 175–202 in *Hidden Lives and Human Rights in America: Understanding the Controversies and Tragedies of Undocumented Immigration*, edited by L. A. Lorentzen. Santa Barbara, CA: Praeger.
Castañeda, Ernesto, Cristina Morales and Olga Ochoa. 2014. "Transnational Behavior in Comparative Perspective: The Relationship between Immigrant Integration and Transnationalism in New York, El Paso, and Paris." *Comparative Migration Studies* 2(3):305–34.

Castañeda, Ernesto and Cathy Lisa Schneider. 2017. *Collective Violence, Contentious Politics, and Social Change: A Charles Tilly Reader*. New York: Routledge.

Castles, Stephen and Alastair Davidson. 2000. *Citizenship and Migration: Globalization and the Politics of Belonging*. New York: Routledge.

Cornelius, Wayne A., David FitzGerald and Pedro Lewin Fischer. 2007. *Mayan Journeys: U.S.-Bound Migration from a New Sending Community*. Boulder, CO: Lynne Rienner.

Diani, Mario. 2007. "The Relational Element in Charles Tilly's Recent (and Not So Recent) Work." *Social Networks* 29(2):316–23.

Feagin, Joe R., Charles Tilly and Constance W. Williams. 1972. *Subsidizing the Poor: A Boston Housing Experiment*. Lexington, MA: DC Heath.

Gannon, Megan. 2016. "Race Is a Social Construct, Scientists Argue." February 4. *Live Science*. (www.livescience.com/53613-race-is-social-construct-not-scientific.html).

Glick Schiller, Nina, Linda Basch and Cristina Blanc-Szanton. 1992. "Transnationalism: A New Analytic Framework for Understanding Migration." *Annals of the New York Academy of Sciences* 645(1):1–24. doi: 10.1111/j.1749-6632.1992.tb33484.x.

Golash-Boza, Tanya. 2016. "A Critical and Comprehensive Sociological Theory of Race and Racism." *Sociology of Race and Ethnicity* 2(2):129–41. doi: 10.1177/2332649216632242.

Hammack, David C., Diane L. Grabowski and John J. Grabowski. 2002. *Identity, Conflict, and Cooperation: Central Europeans in Cleveland, 1850–1930*. Cleveland, OH: Western Reserve Historical Society.

Handlin, Oscar. 1951. *The Uprooted: The Epic Story of the Great Migrations That Made the American People*. Boston, MA: Little, Brown.

Kasinitz, Philip, John H. Mollenkopf, Mary C. Waters and Jennifer Holdaway. 2008. *Inheriting the City: The Children of Immigrants Come of Age*. New York & Cambridge, MA: Russell Sage Foundation; Harvard University Press.

Kosta, Ervin. 2014. "The Immigrant Enclave as Theme Park: Culture, Capital, and Urban Change in New York's Little Italies." Pp. 225–243 in *Making Italian America: Consumer Culture and the Production of Ethnic Identities*, edited by S. Cinotto. New York: Fordham University Press.

Lamont, Michèle and Virag Molnar. 2002. "The Study of Boundaries in the Social Sciences." *Annual Review of Sociology* 28:167–95.

Levitt, Peggy. 2001. *The Transnational Villagers*. Berkeley, CA: University of California Press.

MacDonald, John S. and Leatrice D. MacDonald. 1964. "Chain Migration Ethnic Neighborhood Formation and Social Networks." *The Milbank Memorial Fund Quarterly* 42(1):82–97. doi: 10.2307/3348581.

Mahler, Sarah J. 1995. *American Dreaming: Immigrant Life on the Margins*. Princeton, NJ: Princeton University Press.

Massey, Douglas S. 1990. "Social Structure, Household Strategies, and the Cumulative Causation of Migration." *Population Index* 56(1):3–26.

Massey, Douglas S. 2007. *Categorically Unequal: The American Stratification System*. New York: Russell Sage Foundation.

Massey, Douglas S., Rafael Alarcon, Jorge Durand and Humberto González. 1987. *Return to Aztlan: The Social Process of International Migration from Western Mexico*. Berkeley, CA: University of California Press.

Massey, Douglas S., Joaquín Arango, Grame Hugo, Ali Kouaouci, Adela Pellegrino and J. Edward Taylor. 1993. "Theories of International Migration: A Review and Appraisal." *Population and Development Review* 19(3):431–66.

Massey, Douglas S. and Magaly R. Sanchez. 2010. *Brokered Boundaries: Creating Immigrant Identity in Anti-American Times*. New York: Russell Sage Foundation.

Menjívar, Cecilia. 2000. *Fragmented Ties: Salvadoran Immigrant Networks in America*. Berkeley, CA: University of California Press.

Mische, Ann. 2011. "Relational Sociology, Culture, and Agency." Pp. 80–97 in *The Sage Handbook of Social Network Analysis*, edited by J. S. a. P. Carrington. London: Sage Publications.

Morning, Ann. 2011. *The Nature of Race: How Scientists Think and Teach About Human Difference*. Berkeley, CA: University of California Press.

Mouw, Ted, Sergio Chavez, Heather Edelblute and Verdery Ashton. 2014. "Binational Social Networks and Assimilation: A Test of the Importance of Transnationalism." *Social Problems* 61(3):329–59. doi: 10.1525/sp.2014.12192.

Moya, Jose C. 2005. "Immigrants and Associations: A Global and Historical Perspective." *Journal of Ethnic and Migration Studies* 31(5):833–64. doi: 10.1080/13691830500178147.

Park, Robert Ezra. 1915. "The City: Suggestions for the Investigation of Human Behavior in the City Environment." *American Journal of Sociology* 20(5):577–612.

Park, Robert Ezra. 1950. *Race and Culture*. Glencoe, IL: The Free Press.

Portes, Alejandro and Min Zhou. 2003. "The New Second Generation: Segmented Assimilation and Its Variants." *Annals of the American Academy of Political and Social Sciences* 530:74–96.

Simmel, Georg. 1971. "The Metropolis and Mental Life." Pp. 324–339 in *Georg Simmel on Individuality and Social Forms*, edited by D. N. Levine. Chicago, IL: The University of Chicago Press.

Smith, Robert C. 2006. *Mexican New York: Transnational Lives of New Immigrants*. Berkeley, CA: University of California Press.

Snel, Erik, Margrietha T. Hart, and Marianne Van Bochove. 2016. "Reactive Transnationalism: Homeland Involvement in the Face of Discrimination." *Global Networks*: 16(4):413–550. doi: 10.1111/glob.12125.

Thomas, William Isaac and Florian Znaniecki. 1918. *The Polish Peasant in Europe and America: Monograph of an Immigrant Group*. Chicago, IL: The University of Chicago Press.

Tilly, Charles. 1965. *Migration to an American City*. Newark, DE: Department of Agriculture.

Tilly, Charles. 1968. "Race and Migration to the American City." Pp. 135–57 in *The Metropolitan Enigma: Inquiries into the Nature and Dimensions of America's Urban Crisis*, edited by J. Q. Wilson. Cambridge, MA: Harvard University Press.

Tilly, Charles. 1970. "Migration to American Cities." Pp. 171–86 in *Toward a National Urban Policy*, edited by D. P. Moynihan. New York: Harper.

Tilly, Charles. 1976. "Cities and Migration: Interview Script." in *Television Series 'Culture, Community and Identity: An Ethnic Perspective'*. Wayne State University.

Tilly, Charles. 1978. "Migration in Modern European History." Pp. 48–74 in *Human Migration: Patterns, Implications, Policies*, edited by W. McNeill and R. Adams. Bloomington, IN: Indiana University Press.

Tilly, Charles. 1984. *Big Structures, Large Processes, Huge Comparisons*. New York: Russell Sage Foundation http://deepblue.lib.umich.edu/bitstream/2027.42/51064/1/295.pdf.

Tilly, Charles. 1990. "Transplanted Networks." Pp. 79–95 in *Immigration Reconsidered: History, Sociology, and Politics*, edited by V. Yans-McLaughlin. Oxford, UK: Oxford University Press.

Tilly, Charles. 1998. *Durable Inequality*. Berkeley: University of California Press.

Tilly, Charles. 2003. *Politics of Collective Violence*. Cambridge, UK: Cambridge University Press.

Tilly, Charles. 2004. "Social Boundary Mechanisms." *Philosophy of the Social Sciences* 34(2):211–36.

Tilly, Charles. 2005a. "Chain Migration and Opportunity Hoarding." Pp. 153–170 in *Identities, Boundaries, and Social Ties*, edited by Charles Tilly. Boulder, CO: Paradigm Press.

Tilly, Charles. 2005b. *Identities, Boundaries, and Social Ties*. Boulder, CO: Paradigm Publishers.

Tilly, Charles. 2006. "Afterword: Political Ethnography as Art and Science." *Qualitative Sociology* 29(3 Special Issue: Political Ethnography I):409–12 www.springerlink.com/content/w82q65u8r7527880/fulltext.pdf.

Tilly, Charles. 2007. "Trust Networks in Transnational Migration." *Sociological Forum* 22(1):1–25.

Tilly, Charles. 2008. *Explaining Social Processes*. Boulder, CO: Paradigm Publishers.

Tilly, Charles. 2010. "Mechanisms of the Middle Range." Pp. 54–62 in *Robert K. Merton: Sociology of Science and Sociology as Science*, edited by C. Calhoun. New York: Columbia University Press.

Tilly, Charles and Harold C. Brown. 1967. "On Uprooting, Kinship, and the Auspices of Migration." *International Journal of Comparative Sociology* 8(2):139–64.

Todaro, Michael P. 1969. "A Model of Labor Migration and Urban Unemployment in Less Developed Countries." *American Economic Review* 59(1):138–48.

Waldinger, Roger David. 2015. *The Cross-Border Connection: Immigrants, Emigrants, and Their Homelands*. Cambridge, MA: Harvard University.

Weber, Max. 1958. *The City*. Glencoe, IL: Free Press.

Weil, Patrick. 2005. *La République Et Sa Diversité: Immigration, Intégration, Discriminations*. Paris: Éditions du Seuil.

Weil, Patrick. 2008. *How to Be French: Nationality in the Making since 1789*. Durham, NC: Duke University Press.

Wimmer, Andreas and Nina Glick Schiller. 2002. "Methodological Nationalism and Beyond: Nation State Building, Migration and the Social Sciences." *Global Networks: A Journal of Transnational Affairs* 2(4):301–34.

Yudell, Michael, Dorothy Roberts, Rob DeSalle and Sarah Tishkoff. 2016. "Taking Race out of Human Genetics." *Science* 351(6273):564–65. doi: 10.1126/science.aac4951.

Zelizer, Viviana A. 2005. *The Purchase of Intimacy*. Princeton, NJ: Princeton University Press.

Zelizer, Viviana A. 2012. "How I Became a Relational Economic Sociologist and What Does That Mean?" *Politics & Society* 40(2):145–74. doi: 10.1177/0032329212441591.

Zelizer, Viviana A. and Charles Tilly. 2006. "Relations and Categories." Pp. 1–31 in *The Psychology of Learning and Motivation*, Vol. 47. Categories in Use, edited by A. Markman and B. Ross. San Diego, CA: Elsevier.

Zolberg, Aristide R. and Long Litt Woon. 1999. "Why Islam Is Like Spanish: Cultural Incorporation in Europe and the United States." *Politics and Society* 27(1):5–38.

2

MIGRATION AND CATEGORICAL INEQUALITY

Douglas S. Massey

Migration is a fundamental feature of the human condition. Human beings emerged in Africa some 150,000 years ago, and within a very short time (geologically speaking) they spread out to occupy the entire globe. They reached Asia approximately 100,000 years ago, Australia 50,000 years ago, the Americas 15,000 years ago, and the outer islands of Polynesia 2,000 years ago (Goldin, Cameron and Balarajan 2011). The progressive expansion of the human population outward from Africa was accomplished through geographic mobility, showing that migration has always been critical for human adaptation (Coale 1974; McNeil 1979). In response to changing material conditions people historically have moved with the goal of improving their circumstances (Cavalli-Sforza and Cavalli-Sforza 1995). Homo sapiens is the only species that has been able to inhabit virtually every ecological niche on the planet, a feat accomplished through the uniquely human strategy of combining migration with cultural adaptation (Massey 2005).

Since the earth was fully settled around two millennia ago, the natural tendency of humans to migrate has inevitably brought different peoples and cultures into contact with one another. This is related to another fundamental proclivity: the imperative to classify people socially (Fiske 2003). Unlike computers, human beings think not in bit strings or linear chains of logic but in terms of categories that are socially constructed through learning and imbued with explicit and implicit meanings (Macrae and Bodenhausen 2000). In our minds we divide the perceptual world into conceptual categories. We respond to changing conditions encountered in the environment based on our understandings of these categories. We often fall back on cognitive shortcuts known as heuristics and routinized patterns of behavior, habits, or schemas (Fiske 2003; Kahneman 2011).

Migration and Social Cognition

The most important environment for human beings is the social environment, and social cognition is a critical capability for people (Fiske and Taylor 2007). We are programmed to cognitively arrange the social world into categories and then to allocate people to cells within the resulting categorical structure (Fiske 2003). It is a universal human tendency to classify people on the basis of age, sex, and kinship (Macrae and Bodenhausen 2000). However, as human societies have increased in size, density, and complexity, many other categories have been created such as income, wealth, skill, occupation, education, location, and power, along with myriad other human characteristics (Massey 2007).

Migration presents human beings with an immediate psychological and social challenge: how to allocate new arrivals into the categorical structures we carry around in our heads. Recent work has shown that when it comes to classifying other people, human social cognition is characterized by two fundamental dimensions: warmth and competence (Fiske et al 2002). Warmth is shorthand for a person's likeability, trustworthiness, approachability—ultimately whether a person's intentions toward us are benign or hostile. Competence refers to a person's instrumental ability to act on the basis of these intentions and the skill and power he or she possesses to do so (Cuddy, Fiske and Glick 2008). Whenever we engage with an unknown human being, we seek to place the person cognitively within a social space defined by these two dimensions (Cuddy et al. 2009). Once the person is defined within this categorical space, we employ various learned scripts and attributions to deal with him or her.

These learned scripts and attributions cluster to form stereotypes, which may be classified into four ideal types (Fiske, Cuddy and Glick 2007). Those high in both warmth and competence are perceived as being just like us—members of our own group or other groups similar to us. This includes all of the positive traits, attributions, and sentiments we associate with in-group membership. In-group membership is also associated with positive emotions such as pride, esteem, and respect (Fiske, Cuddy and Glick 2002).

The remaining combinations of warmth and competence yield three different kinds of out-groups (Fiske, Cuddy and Glick 2007). Those high in competence and low in warmth are seen as envied out-groups, whose members are readily recognized as having power, agency, and skill but who are not seen as very amiable, trustworthy, or approachable. They are not well liked but are respected because they have power and skill. These groups are often associated with emotions such as envy, jealousy, and, when misfortune befalls them, schadenfreude—pleasure derived from their misfortune (Cikara and Fiske 2012). Under circumstances of societal breakdown they may even become victims of ethnic cleansing or genocide (Harris and Fiske

2011). Classic examples of envied out-groups are middleman minorities such as Asians in the United States, Chinese in Malaysia, or Indians in East Africa (Lin et al. 2005; Cuddy et al. 2009).

The combination of high warmth and low confidence defines pitied out-groups such as the aged, the infirm, the mentally disabled, and the physically handicapped. People in these categories are perceived as human beings, but, through misfortunes or other forces outside their control, they are to a lesser or greater degree seen as incapacitated, lacking agency and active ability. Rather than being envied, they are targets of pity, sympathy, and pathos (Fiske, Cuddy, and Glick 2007). Under normal circumstances, they are protected and often not treated as equal, but under conditions of societal disorder they may be abandoned.

The final pairing of low warmth and low competence is reserved for despised out-groups such as drug addicts, drug dealers, the homeless, prostitutes, and other societal outcasts. Lacking both warmth and competence, members of envied groups are perceived not as fully human but instead as depersonalized objects, tantamount to animals, or social actors to be ignored, exploited, or disposed of, if necessary (Harris and Fiske 2007, 2009). The relevant emotions are scorn, contempt, and derision.

Like any other social actor, migrants who arrive in a new destination are inevitably classified cognitively by natives who draw upon this two-dimensional scheme, which has become known as the BIAS (Behavior from Intergroup Affect and Stereotypes) map of the stereotype content model (Cuddy, Fiske and Glick 2007). The arrival of a few migrants does not present much of a challenge socially or psychologically. In the absence of extant group labeling and categorical attributions, a few new strangers will tend to be treated as individuals, albeit strange ones, and classified socially as specific persons to be located in social cognition on the basis of experience and interaction. However, once a critical mass of migrants has accumulated in a given area, natives increasingly come to view them not as individuals but as members of a categorical group located on the BIAS map and associated with stereotypical behaviors and characteristics. Once such categorical distinctions are reified in social cognition, natives fall back on the associated stereotypes in dealing with migrants, especially during times of stress and uncertainty.

Social labeling and cognitive categorizations happen to all migrants, but for internal migrants, persons moving within the confines of a single nation state, the process of stereotyping is muted and categorical distinctions are usually less reified. Internal migrants have an easier time working their way into the favored category of esteemed in-group if they speak the same language and share a common national culture, though this is not always the case. For example, during the great twentieth-century internal migrations, poor white populations that had migrated to cities such as Chicago and Detroit were singled out and labeled stereotypically as "hillbillies" and "white trash," but their children generally lost the markers of rural southern origins and later came to occupy a position in the BIAS map as members of the white in-group. In contrast, black migrants from the rural South were severely stigmatized, ostracized, and segregated, and residential segregation persisted no matter how many generations their descendants spent in the city or what socioeconomic status they had achieved (Massey and Denton 1993).

With the exception of black movement into cities during the twentieth century, internal migration in the United States has generally not posed serious challenges to social classification. In contrast, the arrival of large numbers of foreigners immediately raises issues of social perception and classification, for they generally bear a different culture, speak a different language, and display unfamiliar cultural markers and distinctive phenotypes that contrast with those in the host population. The result is the systematic stereotyping of immigrants based on national origin, which over time and across the generations yields ethnic and racial stereotypes. These stereotypes may be more or less durable depending on the degree to which markers of foreign origin can be shed by immigrants and their descendants and the degree to which social boundaries with natives are blurred or brightened by social structures and interpersonal practices in the host society (Alba and Nee 2003; Massey and Sánchez 2010).

Boundaries and Categories

There is nothing inevitable about the location that a particular immigrant-origin group comes to occupy in a society's BIAS map. Indeed, immigrants of the same nationality may occupy very different locations in different countries and at different points in time. Perceptions about the warmth and competence of immigrants—and thus the stereotypes attributed to them—depend on three basic factors: (1) the traits and resources that the immigrants bring with them when they arrive in the host country; (2) how those traits and resources relate to existing cognitive structures that predate the arrival of the immigrants; (3) and the social structures that exist or evolve to govern interactions between natives and immigrants after their arrival (Portes and Zhou 1993; Portes and Rumbaut 2006; Massey and Sánchez 2010).

Immigration is always a selective process. Hence, one can generally assume that those who arrive as immigrants in a country of destination are not a random cross-section of the population of origin (Jasso and Rosenzweig 1990). An immigrant group's eventual location in the BIAS map—and consequently the stereotypes that ultimately apply to it—are thus heavily dependent on the specific processes and procedures by which individuals are selected to become immigrants in the first place. The selection of immigrants occurs at both origin and destination and takes a variety of forms that vary widely from group to group.

People virtually always migrate with a motivation to improve their circumstances, either by evading threatening or unrewarding conditions at origin or by gaining access to better conditions abroad or both (Massey et al. 1998). With respect to the decision to depart, one may distinguish, conceptually if not always in practice, among three basic kinds of immigrants: economic migrants, family migrants, and refugees. Whereas economic migrants are motivated to move in order to improve their material circumstances, family migrants generally move to achieve family reunification or take advantage of family ties, and refugees generally depart countries of origin to escape circumstances that pose an immediate threat to individual or group well-being.

In general, we may expect economic migrants to be positively selected on the basis of unobservable traits such as ambition, motivation, and aspiration as well as on observable traits such as education, skill, and health. The degree of selection depends on the cost and difficulty of the move—the higher the cost and difficulty, the more highly selected immigrants can be expected to be (Massey and Aysa-Lastra 2011). In contrast, migrants moving for purposes of family reunification are generally less selected with respect to unobservable traits such as ambition and motivation. To the extent that homophily prevails, however—that is, the degree to which relatives share similar social and economic characteristics—family migrants tied to economic migrants also can be expected to be selected for traits such as skill and education, though generally not to the same degree as the original immigrant.

The direction and degree of selectivity among refugees depends very much on the reason for their need to flee (Chiswick 1979). Refugees from natural disasters, war, and civil violence are generally the least selected with respect either to observable or unobservable characteristics. Their emigration is compelled by a serious and very immediate threat to well-being, which prompts a mass exit of people without regard to personal characteristics or ambitions. The sole goal of movement is often survival, the most fundamental and indiscriminate of human motivations. Refugees escaping ethnic violence and genocide are unselected with respect to individual characteristics, but they are highly selected with respect to any characteristics correlated with group membership. If the persecuted minority is well educated, then on average refugees will likewise be well educated.

Political refugees are generally highly selected, but the nature and direction of the selection depends on the political goals and practices of the regime that people are seeking to escape. Those seeking to escape a socialist revolution from below are generally persons connected to or members of the ruling elite and often possess high levels of human and financial capital. In contrast, those seeking to escape a right-wing putsch are often from the peasant or working classes and lack either human or financial capital, though the outflows may also include intellectuals who possess high levels of education.

Whatever their motivation for leaving, emigrants generally face an additional level of selection imposed by the country of destination, and this selection itself depends on the economic goals, political objectives, and enforcement practices of the government in power at the time of emigration. Most countries in the developed world seek to attract immigrants on the basis of economic and human capital and so define preferred categories of entry for people with skill, education, and money while imposing restrictions on those who lack these resources. Most nations also seek to facilitate family reunification and set aside visas for relatives of people already in the country of destination. Countries of destination also establish certain categories of people who are permitted to enter on humanitarian grounds or for political reasons. Virtually all nations impose qualitative restrictions based on health (such as excluding the sick and infirm), mental capacity (excluding the retarded and mentally handicapped), and morality (excluding criminals and those of questionable character, such as prostitutes).

The particular combination of selective processes in play at origin and destination determines the specific set of traits and characteristics brought into the receiving country by any group of immigrants at any point in time; these, in turn, help condition the stereotypes that are ultimately attributed to the immigrant group. The way in which different selection processes combine across different places of origin and destination to produce contrasting immigrant streams is well illustrated by late-twentieth-century immigration to the United States from the Spanish-speaking Caribbean. Puerto Rico, the Dominican Republic, and Cuba were all colonized by Spain as slaveholding plantation societies and thus share many elements of culture and history. If emigrants from each country were simply selected at random, the resulting immigrant streams would probably not differ much from one another. However, the vagaries of history yielded very different selection processes that generated contrasting populations of migrants.

The first group members to arrive were the Puerto Ricans, who began migrating *en masse* during the 1950s when a crash modernization program sought to transform the island from an agrarian to an industrial economy, thus setting off mass migration from the countryside (Fitzpatrick 1971; Jackson 1984). Some migrants relocated to urban centers such as San Juan and Ponce, bringing about the urbanization of Puerto Rico, but, as occurred in Europe during its industrialization, Puerto Rican cities could not generate enough employment to absorb all those displaced from the countryside. Consequently, the surplus emigrated abroad, in this case to the United States and more particularly New York. Puerto Ricans were simultaneously pushed by land consolidation and mechanization in communities of origin and by the lure of steady jobs and higher wages in the continental United

States (Maldonado 1976). Corresponding to these selective forces, Puerto Rican emigrants came predominantly from the peasant and working classes; because they were U.S. citizens and flights were cheap, there was little or no selection on the receiving side. Most immigrants went to work in the industrial and service sectors of the New York urban area (Sánchez Korrol 1994), where they were segregated residentially on the basis of skin color (Denton and Massey 1989).

After 1970, when factory jobs diminished in number and unemployment rates rose, Puerto Ricans were eligible for the full array of social benefits and protections open to other U.S. citizens. Like most lower-class people from the Caribbean region, Puerto Ricans brought with them a matrifocal family pattern characterized by low rates of marriage, high rates of unwed childbearing, high rates of marital disruption, and a predominance of female-headed households (Barrow 1996). As a result, Puerto Ricans disproportionately ended up in single-parent, welfare-dependent families (Bean and Tienda 1988) and came to be stereotyped as lazy, dependent, promiscuous lower-class people who preferred handouts to work—very similar to the invidious stereotyping of African American women as welfare queens (Gilens 1999).

At the other extreme of the socioeconomic distribution are emigrants from Cuba, who left for the United States *en masse* in response to the consolidation of Fidel Castro's socialist regime in the early 1960s. In contrast to the situation in Puerto Rico, this structural transformation displaced the elite of Cuban society—first the political leadership and then in succession the entrepreneurial class, the professional class, the middle class, and, only relatively late in the game, the working class (Portes and Bach 1985; Grenier and Pérez 2002). In the context of the Cold War, the Cuban émigrés were admitted with open arms as refugees from communist tyranny. They were provided with generous public support and small-business loans to facilitate integration and lauded publicly as heroes in the fight against Soviet imperialism (Masud-Piloto, 1995). As a result, Cubans in the United States became stereotyped as politically conservative entrepreneurs and business leaders with stable families who not only lived up to but also exemplified the "American dream" of socioeconomic success.

In between the extremes set by Puerto Ricans and Cubans were immigrants from the Dominican Republic. During the dictatorial regime of Rafael Trujillo, Dominicans were largely prohibited from leaving for purposes of nation building (instead, Trujillo encouraged immigration from Europe). However, his assassination in 1961 ushered in a period of political instability, civil conflict, and a tilt leftward that was arrested by U.S. occupation in 1965 (Grasmuck and Pessar 1991). Much of the leftist agitation came from middle-class students and professionals who had been frustrated by the restrictions on freedom during the Trujillo era. In order to defuse political tensions, the U.S. ambassador was instructed to offer legal residence visas generously and widely in order to induce such people to exit the country (Martin 1966). The economic and political elite remained in place to enjoy the fruits of the U.S. intervention; meanwhile, the lower classes had no means to emigrate. Thus, immigration from the Dominican Republic was predominantly legal and middle class (Riosmena 2010). As a result, in the United States Dominicans came to be perceived as stable, striving, and hardworking, and while they suffered some of the same tribulations as Puerto Ricans, they generally managed to move ahead.

These three contrasting stereotypes have nothing to do with the culture prevailing on the islands or characteristics intrinsic to people of Puerto Rican, Cuban, or Dominican origin. Instead, they follow primarily from the contrasting selection processes that brought each group to the United States, the context of the reception group members experienced upon arrival, and the subsequent treatment they encountered in markets and social settings. Immigration from the Spanish Caribbean also serves to illustrate the importance of preexisting cognitive structures in shaping the social perception of new immigrant groups, for the Caribbean is a racially diverse region in which conceptions of race and racial identity are quite different from those in the United States. This often leads to a mismatch between the racial identities held by many Latino immigrants and those imposed by natives of the United States.

The historical taxonomy of race in the United States has evolved to conceive of race as dichotomous and characterized by a "one-drop rule" wherein any African blood or ancestry renders one black rather than white (Sweet 2005). In contrast, throughout the Caribbean race is conceptualized as a continuum ranging from white to black with many intermediate categories, and, rather than being ascribed strictly on the basis of appearance, identities are also contingent on socioeconomic status, with income, wealth, and social standing having a whitening effect (Telles and Sue 2009). Many Latino immigrants who consider themselves unambiguously "white" in their country of origin are clearly perceived as "black" according the standards of the United States. Likewise, many people who define themselves in Spanish using *mestizo*, a term connoting "mixed" racial origins, would not have such a classification recognized by most white Americans.

As a result, no matter what darker-skinned Caribbean immigrants may think about themselves, they tend to be perceived as "black" in the United States and treated accordingly—subject to the same prejudices, discrimination, and mistreatment as African Americans (Frank and Akresh 2010). Over time Caribbean origin Latinos have thus tended to move in two different directions depending on skin color and phenotype, with African-looking, dark-skinned persons experiencing higher levels of segregation, lower wages, and greater discrimination than their light-skinned counterparts after controlling for other social and economic characteristics (Denton and Massey 1989; Telles and Murguía 1992; Gomez 2000; Hersch 2011). In American social cognition, skin color and other African phenotypical markers tend to trump language, class, and national origins in defining the categorical position of immigrants in U.S. society.

Creating Categorical Inequality

As the foregoing example of skin color discrimination clearly illustrates, an immigrant's categorical position in American society is not merely psychological but also fundamentally social and conditioned by host-country practices of segregation and discrimination. Immigrants are not only classified cognitively within the perceptual space defined by warmth and competence but located socially in structural positions defined by the institutions and normative practices of the host society, yielding social categories in society that roughly parallel those in social cognition (Massey 2007). Social categories may be nominal—simply dividing people into discrete groups that imply no rank ordering or differential access to resources—but in stratified societies, social categories tend to be ordinal and entail divergent access to status, prestige, income, and wealth, thus producing categorical inequality.

Social categories come to exist through processes of boundary formation and reification, which serve either to enhance or impede the flow of ideas, resources, and people between the categories that constitute a society's social structure (Massey and Sánchez 2010). The fundamental mechanisms of stratification are exclusion and exploitation (Tilly 1998; Massey 2007). Exclusion is brought about by social mechanisms that prevent out-group members from accessing societal resources while facilitating access by in-group members. Exploitation is achieved through social means that compel out-group members to work for less than the full value of their labor while remunerating in-group members in ways that better reflect their contribution to the final value of the service or product.

The most extreme system of stratification is slavery, where members of the enslaved group are forced to work for no more than the food, lodging, and clothing necessary to keep them fit to work. They are denied access to virtually all material, symbolic, and emotional resources in society (Massey 2007). In the United States, the enslavement of persons of African origin was ended by the Emancipation Proclamation and the Thirteenth Amendment to the U.S. Constitution. It was replaced by a new system of racial subordination known as Jim Crow in which African Americans were relegated to menial occupations, paid less than whites doing the same work, and barred from using superior facilities set aside for whites (Packard 2002). This de jure system of segregation prevailed throughout the South until the civil rights era of the 1960s (Massey 2007), whereas in the North de facto practices of segregation and discrimination achieved much the same result (Massey and Denton 1993).

Aside from Africans imported during the slave trade, immigrants to the United States have not generally been subject to slavery or de jure segregation. Historically, however, they *have* been subjected to a variety of forms of de facto segregation and discrimination. Over the years many immigrant groups—the Irish, Chinese, Japanese, Poles, Italians, Jews, and Mexicans—have been subject to myriad informal processes of exclusion and exploitation in American labor and housing markets. They have also had to endure being paid less than white Anglo-Saxon Protestants for the same work and have been ostracized from WASP neighborhoods, jobs, networks, and social organizations (Massey 1985, 2009). Numerous examples of exclusion and exploitation stain the history of American immigration, ranging from advertisements stating that "Irish Need Not Apply" to deed restrictions prohibiting the transfer of property to members of the "Hebrew Race." Other examples include covenants forbidding the rental or sale of housing to persons of African origin, the use of Slavs as low-wage strikebreakers, the internment of Japanese Americans, and the exclusion of Italians from elite professions. Out-groups have also been subjected to a widespread use of pejorative labels such as "paddy," "dago," "wop," "hunky," "polack," "kike," "nigger," "spic," and many, many others (Higham 1955; Jacobson 1999; Roediger 1991).

Prior to the civil rights era of the 1960s, discriminatory behaviors, exclusionary practices, and derogatory epithets were in common usage. Indeed, discrimination on the basis of national origin was widespread, and exclusionary mechanisms were built into American society at virtually all levels. For most of the twentieth century, such discrimination and exclusion were perfectly legal and not only tolerated but expected in many circles (Massey 2011). Since the passage of landmark civil rights legislation in the 1960s and 1970s, however, most overt practices of exploitation and exclusion have been declared illegal, and for the most part explicit prejudicial language is no longer tolerated in public discourse (Massey 2011). Racial prejudice did not disappear in the post-civil rights era, but appeals to racial animus were expressed symbolically using coded terms and loaded concepts such as "welfare queen," a modality that came to be known as "dog-whistle politics" (López 2014), though in his presidential campaign Donald Trump apparently threw away the dog whistle.

Neither did the passage of civil rights legislation end discrimination and segregation. Members of advantaged groups naturally resist the redistribution of resources implied by the prohibition of historical mechanisms of exploitation and exclusion. Loss aversion is a basic human motivation, making it very painful for people to give up resources they once possessed or controlled (see Tversky and Kahneman 1991). Instead, they tend to invent new mechanisms to preserve their privileged status in society (Massey 2011). Thus, discrimination and segregation persist in the United States, but they are achieved by processes and practices that are clandestine rather than overt (Pager and Shepherd 2008). The older, cruder mechanisms of exploitation and exclusion that were once applied to earlier waves of immigrants from Europe cannot be visited upon today's immigrants from Africa, Asia, and Latin America. Like African Americans, however, contemporary immigrants nonetheless continue to experience subtle forms of segregation and discrimination in a variety of settings, especially if they have dark skins. As Mason (2004:817) concluded from his detailed examination of the economic consequences of race for Hispanic immigrants, "neither the abandonment of Spanish nor the abandonment of a specifically Hispanic racial self-identity is sufficient to overcome the penalties associated with having a dark complexion and non-European phenotype."

Although informal processes of exclusion and exploitation continue to operate in subtle but powerful ways to undermine the socioeconomic status and well-being of immigrants in the United States, in recent years the immigration system itself has emerged as a critical agent of stratification in American society (Massey 2012; Massey and Pren 2012a). Immigrants from Latin America have been particularly affected by U.S. immigration policies and enforcement practices. They represent a majority of all immigrants present in the United States and the majority of those present without documents.

Owing to mass immigration over the past four decades, Latinos have come to compose the largest minority group in the nation. Whereas in 1970 the Latino population stood at just 9.6 million people and made up only 4.7 percent of the U.S. population, by 2010 these figures had risen to 50.5 million people and 16.3 percent of the population (Ennis, Ríos-Vargas and Albert 2011). From 1970 to 2010 some 11.5 million Latin Americans entered the country as legal immigrants, and net unauthorized migration is estimated to have been in the neighborhood of 9 million (Massey and Pren 2012a). Whereas in 1970 nearly three-quarters of Latinos were native born, by 2010 the share had dropped to around 60 percent (Acosta and de la Cruz 2011).

The national origins of Latinos have also shifted markedly. In 1970 the top three groups were Mexicans (60 percent of the total), Puerto Ricans (15 percent), and Cubans (7 percent), compared with just 6 percent from Central or South America. By 2010, however, Puerto Ricans and Cubans had declined to 9 percent and 4 percent of the Latino population, respectively, while Mexicans represented to 63 percent and Central and South Americans, 13 percent. By the mid-2010s, more than three-quarters of all Latinos traced their origins to Mexico, Central America, or South America, whereas just 15 percent were from the Caribbean (Ennis, Ríos-Vargas and Albert 2011).

In addition, whereas Cubans, Puerto Ricans, and Dominicans tend to be legal residents or U.S. citizens, large numbers of Mexicans and Central or South Americans are noncitizens, and a substantial share lack documents entirely. As a result, legal status has become a primary dimension of categorical inequality among Latino immigrants in the United States. According to estimates from the U.S. Department of Homeland Security, 58 percent of Mexican immigrants are present without authorization, compared with 57 percent of Salvadorans, 71 percent of Guatemalans, and 77 percent of Hondurans (Hoefer, Rytina and Baker 2010). Undocumented migrants are no longer a small share of Latino immigrants in the United States. Among Mexican and Central Americans, they constitute the majority of all those born abroad; even when one considers national origins as a whole, the undocumented constitute 21 percent of all persons of Mexican origin, 38 percent of those of Salvadoran origin, 50 percent of those of Guatemalan origin, and 52 percent of those of Honduran origin. Never before have so many people found themselves outside the law, nor have the undocumented been so concentrated into such a small number of national origins.

As a result, Latino immigrants are now the most vulnerable of all of America's disadvantaged populations. No other group—black, white, or Asian—contains such a large fraction of unauthorized and hence exploitable people. The rising share of undocumented migrants among Latin American immigrants in particular and Latinos more generally is critical to understanding categorical inequality in the United States today (Massey and Pren 2012a). Although Latinos may be a protected U.S. category under civil rights legislation, undocumented migrants are not. Indeed, U.S. immigration law encourages and often compels employers, landlords, and service providers to discriminate against the undocumented even as civil rights law requires them to affirmatively protect the rights of Hispanics and not to discriminate on the basis of national origin.

The remarkable rise in the number of Latino individuals out of status has implications that extend far beyond the undocumented themselves. In addition to the 1.5 million undocumented children living in families with an unauthorized parent, there are around 4 million U.S.-born citizen children, whose progress in society is held back by the very real fears of their undocumented family members. These numbers do not take into account the millions of other older children and more distant relatives of undocumented migrants.

The rise of illegal migration can be traced back to 1965 when Congress amended the Immigration and Nationality Act to impose numerical limits on immigration from the Western Hemisphere (Massey and Pren 2012b). Whereas entries from Latin America were not subject to quota limitations prior to this date and some 50,000 migrants in fact, entered each year from Mexico alone, over the next decade a new system was phased in that ultimately limited legal residence visas to 20,000 per country per year. In the same year, Congress terminated a guest worker program with Mexico that had been in place for twenty-two years and which, up to then, had made as many as 450,0000 temporary work visas available to Mexicans each year. As a result, Mexico went from having access to a half-million legal visas per year in the late 1950s to having access to just 20,000 visas in the late 1970s. Since then, illegal migration has begun its inexorable rise.

By the end of the 1970s, the circular flow of workers between Mexico and the United States had been reestablished under undocumented auspices (Massey and Pren 2012a). Between 1965 and 1985 the number of undocumented entries was massive; however, so was the return migration, and an estimated 85 percent of undocumented entries were offset by departures, yielding only modest growth in the resident undocumented population (Massey and Singer 1995). Nonetheless, the rise of illegal migration provided enterprising politicians, bureaucratic entrepreneurs, and media moguls with a golden opportunity to mobilize voters, secure agency resources, and boost circulation and ratings by demonizing Latin American immigrants as a grave threat to the nation, leading to the rise of the "Latino threat narrative" in public discourse (Chavez 2001, 2008). Illegal migrants are by definition criminals and lawbreakers, and in American social cognition they soon came to occupy the perceptual space reserved for despised out-groups such as drug addicts and the homeless, a perception that soon generalized to Latin American immigrants generally (Lee and Fiske 2006).

The growth in undocumented entries between 1965 and 1979 inevitably produced a rising tide of border apprehensions, which provided ongoing concrete evidence of an "alien invasion" of the country, thus pushing American public opinion in an increasingly conservative direction to support the implementation of more restrictive immigration and border policies. This ultimately resulted in a dramatic expansion of the size and budget of the U.S. Border Patrol (Massey and Pren 2012a). The end result was a self-perpetuating cycle in which rising border apprehensions produced a conservative reaction that demanded more enforcement measures, which in turn produced more apprehensions, which then produced more conservatism and calls for harsher enforcement measures, which generated more apprehensions (Massey and Pren 2012b)

Given this powerful feedback loop, border apprehensions continued to rise long after the undocumented inflow had stabilized (Massey and Pren 2012b), and the resulting militarization of the border had the perverse effect of discouraging return migration (Massey, Durand and Malone 2002). As crossing the border without authorization became more difficult and costly, migrants responded by curtailing border crossing. Instead of staying home in sending communities, they remained in the United States, avoiding the even higher costs and risks of crossing at some future date (Redburn, Reuter and Majmundar 2011). This dynamic was given an exogenous boost by terrorist events in the 1990s and 2001, which resulted in the enactment of laws and enforcement operations that not only accelerated border enforcement but also dramatically increased deportations from within the United States while curtailing the rights and liberties of noncitizen foreigners (Massey and Pren 2012b).

As rates of return migration plummeted, net immigration rose, and the undocumented population growth accelerated to record levels (Massey and Pren 2012b). Meanwhile, the concentration of enforcement resources in San Diego diverted flows away from California to make Latin American immigration a truly national phenomenon for the first time (Massey and Capoferro 2008). Mexican immigration, in particular, was transformed from a circular flow of male workers going to three states into a settled population of families living in all fifty states, which further exacerbated anti-immigrant, anti-Latino sentiment throughout the nation (Massey, Durand and Malone 2002; Massey and Pren 2012a).

In forty years, Latinos in the United States went from being a regionally isolated and ethnically segmented populations of Mexicans, Puerto Ricans, and Cubans composed overwhelmingly of native-born citizens and legal resident aliens to being a national population of Mexicans and South and Central Americans who were mostly foreign-born and illegal. As the share of illegal migrants in the population rose, and as harsher laws and policies were implemented to exclude and punish those without documents, the socioeconomic status of Latin American immigrants steadily deteriorated. Increasingly, Latinos have slid downward to join African Americans at the bottom of the U.S. class distribution (Massey 2007; Massey and Gelatt 2010; Massey and Sánchez 2010; Massey and Gentsch 2011; Massey and Pren 2012a). Illegality has become part of the stereotype of Mexicans in the United States and aids in their categorical exclusion from mainstream American society. Tilly's conception of durable inequality is useful to understand the popular descriptions of Hispanics and their low status. The future of Latinos will partly depend on whether or not this categorical group can gain in likability and perceived competence and thus move closer to the in-group.

References

Acosta, Yesenia D., and G. Patricia de la Cruz. 2011. *The Foreign Born from Latin America and the Caribbean: 2010 American Community Survey Briefs*. Washington, DC: U.S. Bureau of the Census.

Acosta-Belen, Edna, and Carlos E. Santiago. 2006. *Puerto Ricans in the United States: A Contemporary Portrait*. New York: Lynne Rienner Publishers.

Alba, Richard, and Victor Nee. 2003. *Remaking the American Mainstream: Assimilation and Contemporary Immigration*. Cambridge, MA: Harvard University Press.

Barrow, Christine. 1996. *Family in the Caribbean: Themes and Perspectives*. Kingston: Ian Randle and James Curry Publishers.

Bean, Frank D., and Marta Tienda. 1988. *The Hispanic Population of the United States*. New York: Russell Sage Foundation.

Cavalli-Sforza, Luigi Luca, and Francesco Cavalli-Sforza. 1995. *The Great Human Diasporas: The History of Diversity and Evolution*. Cambridge, MA: Perseus Books.

Chavez, Leo R. 2001. *Covering Immigration: Popular Images and the Politics of the Nation*. Berkeley, CA: University of California Press.

Chavez, Leo R. 2008. *The Latino Threat: Constructing Immigrants, Citizens, and the Nation*. Stanford, CA: Stanford University Press.

Chiswick, Barry R. 1979. "The Economic Progress of Immigrants: Some Apparently Universal Patterns." Pp. 357–99 in William Fellner, ed., *Contemporary Economic Problems, 1979*. Washington, DC: American Enterprise Institute.

Cikara, Mina, and Susan T. Fiske. 2012. "Stereotypes and Schadenfreude: Behavioral and Physiological Markers of Pleasure at Others' Misfortunes." *Social Psychological and Personality Science* 3(1):63–71.

Coale, Ansley J. 1974. "The History of the Human Population." *Scientific American* 231(3):15–28.

Cuddy, Amy J. C., Susan T. Fiske, and Peter Glick. 2007. "The BIAS map: Behaviors from Intergroup Affect and Stereotypes." *Journal of Personality and Social Psychology* 92:631–648.

———. 2008. "Competence and Warmth as Universal Trait Dimensions of Interpersonal and Intergroup Perception: The Stereotype Content Model and the BIAS Map." Pp. 61–149 in M. P. Zanna, ed., *Advances in Experimental Social Psychology* Vol. 40. New York: Academic Press.

Cuddy, Amy J., Susan T. Fiske, Virginia S.Y. Kwan, et al. 2009. "Is the Stereotype Content Model Culture-Bound? A Cross-Cultural Comparison Reveals Systematic Similarities and Differences." *British Journal of Social Psychology* 48:1–33.

Denton, Nancy A., and Douglas S. Massey. 1989. "Racial Identity among Caribbean Hispanics: The Effect of Double Minority Status on Residential Segregation." *American Sociological Review* 54:790–808.

Ennis, Sharon R., Merarys Ríos-Vargas, and Nora G. Albert. 2011. *The Hispanic Population: 2010 Census Brief*. Washington, DC: U.S. Bureau of the Census.

Fiske, Susan T. 2003. *Social Beings: A Core Motives Approach to Social Psychology*. New York: Wiley.

Fiske, Susan T., Amy J. Cuddy, and Peter Glick. 2002. "Emotions Up and Down: Intergroup Emotions Result from Perceived Status and Competition." Pp. 2247–64 in D. M. Mackie and E. R. Smith, eds., *From Prejudice to Intergroup Emotions: Differentiated Reactions to Social Groups*. Philadelphia, PA: Psychology Press.

———. 2007. "Universal Dimensions of Social Perception: Warmth and Competence." *Trends in Cognitive Science* 11:77–83.

Fiske, Susan T., Amy J.C. Cuddy, Peter Glick, and Jun Xu. 2002. "A Model of (Often Mixed) Stereotype Content: Competence and Warmth Respectively Follow from Perceived Status and Competition." *Journal of Personality and Social Psychology* 82:878–902.

Fiske, Susan T., and Shelly Taylor. 2007. *Social Cognition: From Brains to Culture*. New York: McGraw-Hill.

Fitzpatrick, Joseph P. 1971. *Puerto Rican Americans: The Meaning of Migration to the Mainland*. Englewood Cliffs, NJ: Prentice Hall.

Frank, Reanne, and Ilana Redstone Akresh. 2010. "Latino Immigrants and the U.S. Racial Order How and Where Do They Fit in?" *American Sociological Review* 75(3):378–401.

Gilens, Martin. 1999. *Why Americans Hate Welfare: Race, Media, and the Politics of Anti-Poverty Policy*. Chicago: University of Chicago Press.

Goldin, Ian, Geoffrey Cameron, and Meera Balarajan. 2011. *Exceptional People: How Migration Shaped Our World and Will Define Our Future*. Princeton, NJ: Princeton University Press.

Gomez, Christina. 2000. "The Continual Significance of Skin Color: An Exploratory Study of Latinos in the Northeast." *Hispanic Journal of the Behavioral Sciences* 22:94–103.

Grasmuck, Sherri, and Patricia R. Pessar. 1991. *Between Two Islands: Dominican International Migration*. Berkeley: University of California Press.

Grenier, Guillermo J., and Lisandro Pérez. 2002. *The Legacy of Exile: Cubans in the United States*. New York: Allyn & Bacon.

Harris, Lasana T., Mina Cikara, and Susan T. Fiske. 2008. "Envy, as Predicted by the Stereotype Content Model: A Volatile Ambivalence." Pp. 131–47 in R. Smith, ed., *Envy: Theory and Research*. New York: Oxford University Press.

Harris, Lasana T., and Susan T. Fiske. 2007. "Social Groups That Elicit Disgust are Differentially Processed in mPFC." *Social Cognitive and Affective Neuroscience* 2:45–51.

———. 2009. "Dehumanized Perception: The Social Neuroscience of Thinking (or Not Thinking) about Disgusting People." *European Review of Social Psychology* 20: 192–31.

———. 2011. "Dehumanized Perception: A Psychological Means to Facilitate Atrocities, Torture, and Genocide?" *Zeitschrift für Psychologie* 219(3):175–81.

Hersch, Joni. 2011. "The Persistence of Skin Color Discrimination for Immigrants." *Social Science Research* 40(5):1337–49.

Higham, John. 1955. *Strangers in the Land: Patterns of American Nativism, 1860–1925*. New Brunswick, NJ: Rutgers University Press, 1955.

Hoefer, Michael, Nancy Rytina, and Bryan C. Baker. 2010. "Estimates of the Unauthorized Immigrant Population Residing in the United States: January 2009." Vol.? Washington, D.C.: Department of Homeland Security, Office of Immigration Statistics.

Jackson, Philip. 1984. "Migration and Social Change in Puerto Rico." Pp. 195–213 in C. Clarke, D. Ley and C. Peach, eds., *Geography and Ethnic Pluralism*. London: Allen and Unwin.

Jacobson, Matthew F. 1999. *Whiteness of a Different Color: European Immigrants and the Alchemy of Race*. Cambridge, MA: Harvard University Press.

Jasso, Guillermina, and Mark R. Rosenzweig. 1990. *The New Chosen People: Immigrants in the United States*. New York: Russell Sage Foundation.

Kahneman, Daniel. 2011. *Thinking Fast and Slow*. New York: Farrar, Straus and Giroux.

Lee, Tiane L., and Susan T. Fiske. 2006. "Not an Outgroup, Not Yet an Ingroup: Immigrants in the Stereotype Content Model." *International Journal of Intercultural Relations* 30:751–68.

Lin, Monica H., Virginia S.Y. Kwan, Anna Cheung, and Susan T. Fiske. 2005. "Stereotype Content Model Explains Prejudice for an Envied Outgroup: Scale of Anti-Asian American Stereotypes." *Personality and Social Psychology Bulletin* 31:34–47.

López, Ian Haney. 2014. *Dog Whistle Politics: How Coded Racial Appeals Have Reinvented Racism and Wrecked the Middle Class*. New York: Oxford University Press.

Macrae, C. Neil, and Galen V. Bodenhausen. 2000. "Social Cognition: Thinking Categorically About Others." *Annual Review of Psychology* 51:93–120.
Maldonado, Rita. 1976. "Why Puerto Ricans Migrated to the United States in 1947–1973." *Monthly Labor Review* 99(9):7–18.
Martin, John B. 1966. *Overtaken by Events: The Dominican Crisis from the Fall of Trujillo to the Civil War*. New York: Doubleday.
Mason, Patrick L. 2004. "Annual Income, Hourly Wages, and Identity Among Mexican-Americans and Other Latinos." *Industrial Relations* 43:817–26.
Massey, Douglas S. 1985. "Ethnic Residential Segregation: A Theoretical Synthesis and Empirical Review." *Sociology and Social Research* 69:315–50.
_____. 2005. *Strangers in a Strange Land: Humans in an Urbanizing World*. New York: W.W. Norton Publishers.
_____. 2007. *Categorically Unequal: The American Stratification System*. New York: Russell Sage Foundation.
_____. 2009. "Racial Formation in Theory and Practice: The Case of Mexicans in the United States." *Race and Social Problems* 1:12–26.
_____. 2011. "The Past and Future of American Civil Rights." *Daedalus* 140(2):37–54.
_____. 2012. *Immigration and the Great Recession*. Stanford, CA: Stanford Center on Poverty and Inequality.
Massey, Douglas S., Joaquín Arango, Graeme Hugo, Ali Kouaouci, Adela Pellegrino, and J. Edward Taylor. 1998. *Worlds in Motion: International Migration at the End of the Millennium*. Oxford: Oxford University Press.
Massey, Douglas S., Jorge Durand, and Nolan J. Malone. 2002. *Beyond Smoke and Mirrors: Mexican Immigration in an Era of Economic Integration*. New York: Russell Sage Foundation.
Massey, Douglas S., and Maria Aysa-Lastra. 2011. "Social Capital and International Migration from Latin America." *International Journal of Population Research* Volume 2011, Article ID 834145, 18 pages. www.hindawi.com/journals/ijpr/2011/834145/
Massey, Douglas S., and Chiara Capoferro. 2008. "The Geographic Diversification of U.S. Immigration." Pp. 25–50 in Douglas S. Massey, ed., *New Faces in New Places: The Changing Geography of American Immigration*. New York: Russell Sage Foundation.
Massey, Douglas S., and Nancy A. Denton. 1993. *American Apartheid: Segregation and the Making of the Underclass*. Cambridge, MA: Harvard University Press.
Massey, Douglas S., and Julia Gelatt. 2010. "What Happened to the Wages of Mexican Immigrants? Trends and Interpretations." *Latino Studies* 8:328–54.
Massey, Douglas S., and Kerstin Gentsch. 2011. "Labor Market Outcomes for Legal Mexican Immigrants under the New Regime of Immigration Enforcement." *Social Science Quarterly* 92(3):875–93.
Massey, Douglas S., and Karen A. Pren. 2012a. "Origins of the New Latino Underclass." *Race and Social Problems* 4(1):5–17.
_____. 2012b. "Unintended Consequences: Explaining the Post-1965 Surge in Latin American Immigration." *Population and Development Review* 38(1):1–29.
Massey, Douglas S., and Magaly Sánchez R. 2010. *Brokered Boundaries: Creating Immigrant Identity in Anti-Immigrant Times*. New York: Russell Sage Foundation.

Massey, Douglas S., and Audrey Singer. 1995. "New Estimates of Undocumented Mexican Migration and the Probability of Apprehension." *Demography* 32:203–13.

Masud-Piloto, and Feliz Roberto. 1995. *With Open Arms: Cuban Migration to the United States*. Lanham, MD: University Press of America.

McNeill, William H. 1979. "Historical Patterns of Migration." *Current Anthropology* 20(1):95–102.

Packard, Gerald M. 2002. *American Nightmare: The History of Jim Crow*. New York: St. Martin's Press.

Pager, Devah, and Hana Shepherd. 2008. "The Sociology of Discrimination: Racial Discrimination in Employment, Housing, Credit and Consumer Markets." *Annual Review of Sociology* 34:181–209.

Portes, Alejandro, and Robert L. Bach. 1985. *Latin Journey: Cuban and Mexican Immigrants in the United States*. Berkeley: University of California Press.

Portes, Alejandro, and Rubén G. Rumbaut. 2006. *Immigrant America: A Portrait*, 3rd Edition. Berkeley: University of California Press.

Portes, Alejandro, and Min Zhou. 1993. "The New Second Generation: Segmented Assimilation and Its Variants." *Annals of the American Academy of Political and Social Science* 530:74–96.

Redburn, Steve, Peter Reuter, and Malay Majmundar. 2011. *Budgeting for Immigration Enforcement: A Path to Better Performance*. Washington, DC: National Academies Press.

Riosmena, Fernando. 2010. "Policy Shocks: On the Legal Auspices of Latin America— U.S. Migration." *Annals of the American Academy of Political and Social Science* 630(1):270–93.

Roediger, David R. 1991. *The Wages of Whiteness: Race and the Making of the American Working Class*. New York: Verso Books.

Sánchez Korrol, Virginia E. 1994. *From Colonia to Community: The History of Puerto Ricansin New York City*. Berkeley: University of California Press.

Sweet, Frank W. 2005. *Legal History of the Color Line: The Rise and Triumph of the One-Drop Rule*. Palm Coast, FL: Backintyme Press.

Telles, Edward E., and Edward Murguía. 1992. "The Continuing Significance of Phenotype among Mexican-Americans." *Social Science Quarterly* 73(1):120–122.

Telles, Edward E., and Christina Sue. 2009. "Race Mixture: Boundary Crossing in Comparative Perspective." *Annual Review of Sociology* 35:129–46.

Tilly, Charles. 1998. *Durable Inequality*. Berkeley: University of California Press.

Tversky, Amos, and Daniel Kahneman. 1991. "Loss Aversion in Riskless Choice: A Reference Dependent Model." *Quarterly Journal of Economics* 106:1039–61.

3

IMMIGRATION OR CITIZENSHIP?

Two Sides of One Social History

Josiah Heyman

Introduction

Drawing on Charles Tilly's seminal work on citizenship, I propose that we refocus our approach to immigration by combining in one single view the historical development of nation-state membership (termed "citizenship") and internal and international migration.[1] I argue that the characterization of newly arriving outsiders ("immigrants") makes sense only in contrast to the gradual definition and clarification of insiders ("citizens"). I am thus critical of social, economic, and political accounts that focus only on immigrants or only on citizens, without seeing them as outcomes of simultaneous if contrastive processes. These social positions are partly a result of the gradual rise of nation-states, which is obvious, but they are also affected directly and indirectly by capitalism, including the attraction of immigrant populations into growth centers, the movement of capital to new sites of production (sometimes glossed as globalization), and the decline of old sites of capital investment. State formation is likewise funded by revenues from the capitalist economy. I thus suggest we need to envision three interweaving processes: human migration, internal and international; nation-state consolidation and the rise of citizenship regimes; and capital mobility, accumulation, and withdrawal.

I draw my inspiration from Tilly's concept of dual processes shaping the modern world, capitalism and nation-state formation (Tilly 1984, 1992).[2] "Immigrant" is an emergent outcome of the intersection of those processes. I also draw on his analysis of the history of citizenship, including the state-population relationship developed around taxation, military service, political inclusion, and rights (Hanagan and Tilly 1999; Tilly 1996). While immigration has attracted widespread scholarly and political attention (an important synthesis is Massey et al. 2009), the production of insider roles and identities has received much less attention (though certainly there are outstanding works besides Tilly, some of which I cite later in the text). This is because we often assume the unconscious stance of normal insiders while seeing immigrants as strange outsiders. We need to break those assumptions by problematizing all sides of the history.

My argument has four parts:

(1) Immigration (in particular the targets I frame here, immigration politics and host-immigrant relations) should not be considered mainly in terms of immigrants and their effect on the receiving society. We also should consider the long-term development of citizenship, both generally and in specific national histories. We should define the core subject as the dual emergence of insiders and outsiders across social and political history.
(2) Polities (states and political arrangements) aim to stabilize around particular formations of who is included as a citizen. Yet these formations are continuously disrupted by capital's abandonment of older, better-established labor with stronger rights and organizations and by the recruitment of new pools of migrant, relatively exploitable labor. Neither of those is directly a political process, but the former pressures existing citizens' sentiments and behaviors, while the latter brings new populations into the societal mix.
(3) Internal and international migration need to be viewed together, in a single processual history. Only over time does the internal/international distinction emerge, as bounded nation-state identities strengthen. The dynamic capitalist search for new labor sources and new production sites stimulates both internal and international migration.
(4) My inquiry aims not at immigration or international borders alone but at inside-outside boundaries (Tilly 2005) within modern states. This includes citizenship and host/newcomer distinctions, which intersect other social boundaries such as race, internal region, and so forth (Fassin 2011). My immediate agenda within insider/outsider politics is how the frame of contentious "immigration politics" emerges and evolves over time and the processes and results of demands for inclusion by immigrants and especially their descendants as citizens.

To illustrate these points, I begin with an ideal-type model of the interactions among the three processes of capitalism, labor migration, and state formation. With this simplification, it is easier to envision the complex dynamics. I then explore this approach more deeply with a case study of U.S. internal and external migration history. The U.S. case has a rather complicated history, with reversions between internal and external labor sources, and likewise internal and external relocations of capital investment. I do not provide a systematic debate with other views of immigration or citizenship and likewise do not provide a thorough comparative analysis needed to clinch the argument; that remains for future work.

An Ideal-Type Model of State Formation, Capitalism, and Migration

I begin with an ideal-type model. Ideal types, following Weber (1949:89–99), involve abstraction from actual details. They are useful in developing and communicating key concepts but are not realistic themselves. In developing the model, I draw on two key analyses by Tilly. The first states that in the modern era citizenship is a contract-like arrangement between members of a population and a government, mainly large territorial states. These arrangements emerge over time as a result of social struggle and bargaining, though such "bargaining" rarely constitutes negotiations between equals. Tilly foregrounds instances of states bargaining citizenship to populations in exchange for mass military service and direct taxation, but a wider variety of struggles and bargains can be identified, including political cohesion being exchanged for mass political participation and symbolized feelings of belonging. Second, Tilly sees such formations of citizenship not just as inclusive but also exclusive, giving rise to social boundaries of insider and outsider.

To supplement Tilly, I have added Eric Wolf's synthetic history of the assembling of working classes (1982:352–83). Capitalist recruitment is a dynamic force, continually arranging and rearranging various subordinate classes. This has been a subordinate thread in immigration studies, where several scholars (Krissman 2005; Piore 1979) have pointed to deliberate initiation of migratory flows by employers seeking inexpensive and bountiful labor. Once such flows are initiated, network dynamics reproduce and gradually modify them. Key capitalist processes include both new moments of bringing workers in, and also moments of movement of capital outward to production sites offering fresh supplies of workers. Both instances, quite clearly, are "spatial fixes" for increases in the price of labor in David Harvey's conceptualization (1982).

In these fixes, what is being sought? Whether moving capital out or workers in, employers escape experienced laborers and entrenched social settings (as well as old technologies and infrastructures), seeking workers with relatively limited knowledge of wage rates, working conditions, and organization of formal and informal labor resistance. Besides escaping established workers, employers also seek new labor pools during periods of rapid expansion due to exhaustion of existing supplies. They soak up the migration-available population in a catchment area and then begin to move further afield. In either moving outward to fresh workers or encouraging in-migration, employers characteristically seek particular kinds of workers: peasants and artisans "freed" from old ties by collapsing and/or

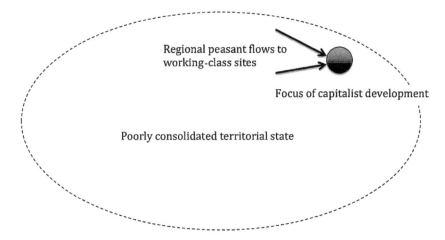

Figure 3.1 Initial stage of "immigration": short-distance internal flows.

transforming economies, increasing populations, and so forth. I refer to them as peasant-workers, allowing for greater complexity of actual sources and labor relations.

In Figure 3.1, we see an ideal-type of the early stages of capitalist development based on regional peasant-worker migration within an early forming nation-state.

Such workers later on may socially become insiders of the same state as the early capitalist core, but initially they are strange, migrant outsiders, with distinct regional, often rural ways of life. Gradually, capitalist revenues fund states that consolidate around military and other elite political projects, as well as bargains needed to include (as citizens) the restive new working masses.

These historical moments of migratory initiation/transformation are especially interesting because the move to import new masses of labor (or to transfer production) challenges existing socio-political-spatial arrangements. Newcomers arrive, unaccounted for in existing political bargains. Political arenas then undergo contentious processes, with both reactionary and progressive responses to the newcomers. Citizenship almost always lags the radical moves of capitalism, so that citizenship-immigration politics can be seen as a repeatedly disrupted and repaired bargaining to cope with such unforeseen changes (Figure 3.2).

With the unceasing drive of capital accumulation, existing production sites expand or decline in the face of new competition. Seeking spatial fixes for aging investments and increasingly experienced and demanding workers, investors open up new sites of production, which in turn induce novel migration flows from their own rural hinterlands or international sources, as seen in Figure 3.3.

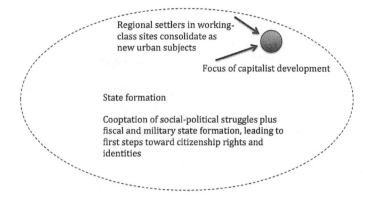

Figure 3.2 Beginning of shift in identity from stigmatized urban marginal (ex-migrants) to national citizens.

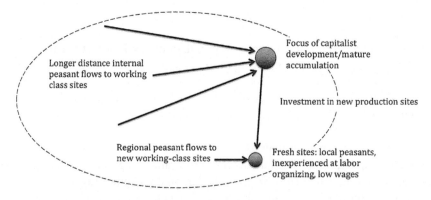

Figure 3.3 Wider peasant-worker migrant recruitment region. Movement of capital to new production sites.

Revenue from capital accumulation funds state consolidation, but the dynamic spatial movement of capital and workers continues to challenge political arrangements, as seen in Figure 3.4.

A notable change is the gradual emergence of administered external borders with respect to migration–previous border addressed resource claims, customs tariffs, and military presence (McKeown 2008). International immigrants begin to separate as a social category from citizens, even internal migrants (often with the distinction publicly phrased as race, ethnicity, and/or religion).

Over time, these processes expand and deepen to take the forms of international migration, border enforcement, citizenship politics, and capitalist globalization with which we are familiar in the present day. We model this first in terms of economics in Figure 3.5, then politics in Figure 3.6.

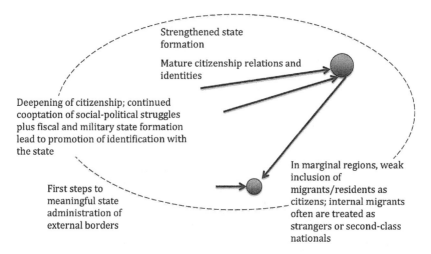

Figure 3.4 Emergence of strong territorial state; internal deepening processes (administration, education/socialization); beginning of meaningful external borders; citizenship, belonging, patriotism become major social identity set. International becomes a meaningful contrast to internal.

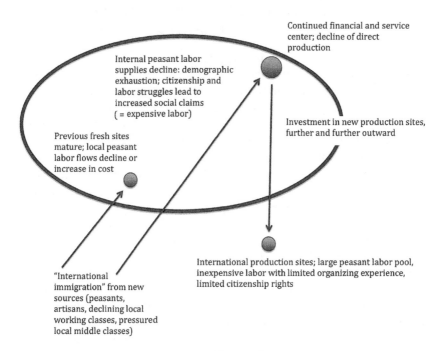

Figure 3.5 Emergence of contemporary "binaries" in economy: inward immigration flows; outward capital flows and globalization of production.

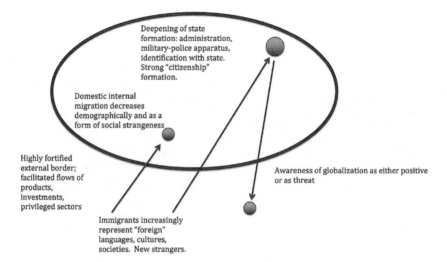

Figure 3.6 Emergence of contemporary "binaries" in society/politics: international versus domestic. Migrants as salient social subjects no longer include internal migrants but only international migrants. Reactive citizenship politics.

U.S. History: Citizenship, Workers, Migration
Part One: 1800–1965

The United States is a vast country, and its economic and migration histories are enormously complex. It is likewise challenging to offer a coherent chronological narrative when many simultaneous processes occur in economic, demographic, and political domains. In this part, I provide a selective narrative, one that addresses three themes: (1) the expansion of U.S. capitalism and its search for new pools of labor, domestic and international, focusing on the textile and garment industries; (2) U.S. state formation and citizenship from the early industrial period starting in 1790 through the mid-1960s, with specific reference to the inclusion of internal and external migrants; and (3) the antecedents of the current (post-1965) immigration formation, in particular the rise and decline of the so-called Great Migration, the flow north and west of southern whites and blacks in the first half of the twentieth century. The following part addresses Mexican (and more generally Latin American, Caribbean, and Asian) immigration since the late nineteenth century, with an emphasis on the period from 1965 to the present. Here, I draw on several works of historical synthesis, notably Gordon, Edwards, and Reich (1982), and the American Social History Project (2008a, 2008b). I am inspired by Herbert Gutman's seminal essay "Work, Culture, and Society in Industrializing America" (1976), which views U.S. history through the prism of waves of new proletarians entering but also resisting industrial discipline.

Important studies by Jane Collins (2003) and Jefferson Cowie (1999) inform my account of internal and international spatial fixes and movement of capital. Higham's (1955) is an important work of the history of immigration and citizenship politics, updated by Calavita (1984), Massey, Durand, and Malone (2002), Zolberg (2008), and Ngai (2004), while Omi and Winant (1994) is a less labor-oriented but helpful source on U.S. racial and ethnic formations.

Here I use textile and garment manufacturing as a leading indicator of capitalist recruitment of labor forces and spatial relocation of production, a role it played until the 1970s; obviously, this results in underplaying other important sectors, such as mining, railroads, steel manufacturing, automobile manufacturing, animal slaughter/packing, construction, services, and so forth. When necessary, I mention other sectors, but, even when they are not discussed, their story is broadly the same. Textile and garment manufacturing (with the former in the lead) in the United States started in the early nineteenth century in New England and in the Philadelphia and Baltimore areas. The initial workforce was young women from rural families in the immediate hinterlands of the new industry, who lived in corporate dormitories. By such work, they were able to supplement increasingly fragile rural family economies by bringing in wage incomes and also to accumulate dowry funds for marriage, which had long been an activity of unmarried daughters through domestic service (Dublin 1979). This novel migrant work force is, then, an illustrative example of how dynamic capital seeks "freed" labor from declining agricultural districts.

The textile mill workforce changed quickly, however. Northeastern farm families, including their children, had other production and employment options in the expanding Midwestern frontier. New England women workers rebelled against wage cuts, drawing in no small part on their identity as quintessential Americans, freeborn populations of English, Protestant descent from the original colonies (the very first version of symbolic claims to citizenship in the new nation). They were quickly replaced by Irish immigrants, again young people made available by a collapsing rural economy, but one geographically outside the United States. In the Irish case, workers were more likely to migrate or eventually reunite with natal and procreative families, rather than living as temporary migrants in dormitories (Dawley 1976). Both processes are depicted in Figure 3.7.

The Irish persisted as the core of the textile mill workforce well into the twentieth century, though from the late nineteenth through the twentieth century the Irish were supplemented by French Canadians and southern and eastern Europeans. Comparable immigrant workforces, with specific source and target patterns (such as the Chinese in West Coast rail construction), were drawn into the extraordinarily rapidly growing U.S. economy. Workers from the Protestant parts of the British Isles were drawn early into expanding

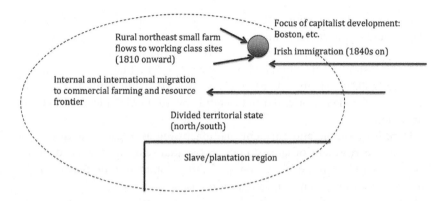

Figure 3.7 U.S. case: initial stage of "immigration": short-distance internal flows; rapid change to international Irish immigration; relatively strong state from beginning but violent regional division. Official borders set into place vs. Great Britain (Canada), Mexico, Native Americans by war, theft, and diplomacy.

U.S. capitalism, especially when providing specific industrial skills (Cornish and Welsh miners, northern British iron puddlers, and so forth). But they were included relatively quickly into workplace and wider societal hierarchies above the other immigrants, because of their specific labor roles, because of their religion, and because they meshed with the dominant ideology of the freeborn American (e.g., see Wallace 1987 on Welsh versus Irish coal miners in Pennsylvania).

The Irish and, to a lesser extent, Germans, arriving at the same time, did not fit so well. Many were Catholic, and the Irish in particular were sharply divided from the English and Scots with whom the formative American republic identified. The early thrust of anti-immigrant politics was a mixture of hostility to Catholicism, temperance (because these new immigrant populations were associated with drinking), and a patriotic vision of American symbols and rights. Curiously, that formation of nativist politics, rituals, and membership boundaries emerged in the first great widening of U.S. citizenship during the first half of the nineteenth century, when the vote was extended to and participation in mass political parties encouraged for free, white men (the original U.S. model of democracy gave effective citizenship only to property-owning elite white males). Though U.S. state capacity was still very limited, this first expansion of citizenship was associated with modest taxation and submission to administrative governance. It was greatly expanded by the Civil War, which of course required huge innovations in military recruitment, taxation, and consent mechanisms in both the North and the South. In particular, the earliest citizen welfare mechanisms followed after the Civil War, specifically for veterans, and strengthened white male material and symbolic inclusion in the U.S. polity (Skocpol 1992).

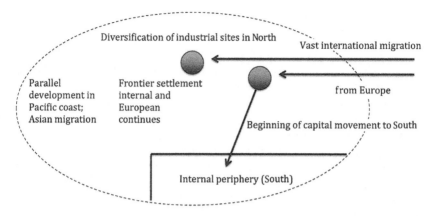

Figure 3.8 State consolidation (North defeats South in tremendous civil war); strengthened internal citizenship formation; weak external borders. Bitter conflict between citizens and immigrants by late period (1880s on).

The primary "outsiders" in all of this were nonwhites: African Americans, Native Americans, Mexican-origin people, East Asians, and so forth. White outsiders were more ambiguous, being racially included but often partly excluded politically. The Irish were caught up in a dual process of anti-Irish, anti-immigrant politics but also struggles for citizenship inclusion via electoral and administrative politics that were ultimately successful but required a very long time. Germans, who were critical to the Civil War effort and were less involved in bitter conflicts with the English and Scottish, were included as citizens rather more rapidly.

In the second half of the nineteenth century, Ireland (and to a lesser extent Germany and Scandinavia) continued as suppliers of peasant-workers, but the voracious expansion of U.S. capitalism resulted in recruitment and then self-sustaining chain migration from new fields of exploitable peasants and artisans from collapsing economies. These included southern and eastern Europe, other Mediterranean areas, and Asia (first China, then Japan, and finally the Philippines). This continued until the restrictive immigration laws of 1921 and 1924; though the legal and diplomatic restriction of Chinese and Japanese labor occurred earlier, the immigration of Filipinos and Mexicans was not restricted by these laws.

The focus of citizenship politics likewise shifted. In the case of the western United States, white Americans struggling with Big Capital (e.g., better-off workers versus railroad barons) made their claim to political membership precisely by means of racist restrictions against nonwhites. In the case of the northeastern and Midwestern United States, it was northern European (mostly British) elites who used racism against labor organization and radical political dissent, especially by Jews and Italians. Early on, this phase of anti-immigration politics was incoherent in its agenda, but by the beginning of the twentieth century a twofold development occurred. In urban, electoral politics, the post-immigrant wave (notably Irish and German) began to arrive as effective participants and members. Second, in national immigrant admissions policy, the WASP elite eugenic, anti-immigrant political movements succeeded in closing most of the European door in 1921 and 1924, when the Asian door was already mostly closed.

Just as Asian and European immigration was being closed down, a vast new population of exploitable laborers emerged from collapsing archaic rural economies of the U.S. South (if and how this was coordinated is unclear, but the coincidence in time is striking). From the late nineteenth century on, U.S. capital—in particular, the cutting-edge textile and garment industries— moved south from New England to the piedmont region of Virginia, the Carolinas, and Georgia. In the piedmont, white and African American rural workforces were plentiful, with limited competition with tidewater capitalist-plantation agriculture. Other manufacturers went to Appalachia, drawn by primary resources and extensive small producer-worker pools.

Somewhat later (1900s–1960s), highland white and lowland black southerners started to migrate north, to the cities of the east and the Midwest and to California (Gregory 2005). For example, the famous 1930s dust-bowl migrations from Texas, Oklahoma, Kansas, and Arkansas were only part of a larger and longer flow: multiracial internal migration that filled the industrial and agricultural labor markets of California's remarkable rise

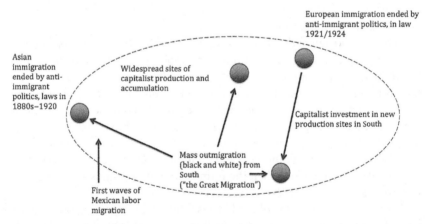

Figure 3.9 1920–1965 (some processes start earlier). Capitalist changes and migration; state formation becomes more cohesive across whole nation (inclusion of Sunbelt); vastly wealthier and larger central U.S. states; rise of U.S. militarized global imperialism. Requirements of taxation, military recruitment, and ideological loyalty result in much stronger development of citizenship politics and identity. Period of low international immigration (in most cases).

to economic primacy (and more generally the whole Pacific coast). This substituted for excluded Asian sources, while Mexicans were sporadically restricted and repatriated (e.g., Mexican-origin people were being expelled during the 1930s internal migration), though at other times they were welcomed. Likewise, migration of southern blacks and whites to northeastern and Midwestern cities and farm labor sites replaced the excluded southern and eastern European flows after 1924.

White internal migrants were initially discriminated against but over time benefited from the emerging racial-citizenship model of the United States. In the capitalizing New South, for example, extending some elements of citizenship rights and identity symbols to whites was rooted at first in recruitment of soldiers by the Confederacy and reinforced by successful elite efforts to split the multiracial radical populist movement into white racist and African American segments. This pattern of racialized citizenship was also true of places in which the political inclusion of new migrant southern whites was less important than the citizenship inclusion of previously stigmatized descendants of European immigrants. In numerous northern cities, the most exemplary being Chicago, the reconciliation of elites and state agents to Irish political power occurred precisely by drawing a new line against incoming southern African Americans and their descendants.

Clearly, the African American civil rights movement sought to expand citizenship. It is unclear how it relates to the Great Migration out of the South. Its base was in the South, and it struggled to implant itself in the new populations, settings, and issues of the migrant/post migrant African American north. The overlap in time (1940s–1960s, the late phase of the Great Migration), however, hints at some complex interactions. Meanwhile, another important citizenship formation process was occurring, perhaps with more lasting effects on citizen-immigrant relations: the rise of the so-called Sun Belt (South and West) in U.S. politics, economics, and culture.

The U.S. South and North were certainly part of one sovereign nation-state, with some degree of legislative and legal unification. However, in social structure, culture, and politics, they can be understood as two different polities only loosely confederated. Reconstruction after the Civil War briefly changed the political dynamics of the South, but Redemption (the restoration of labor control, overt racism, and political domination by alternating elite and populist white coalitions) lasted until the civil rights movement of the 1950s and 1960s (Black and Black 1987). The West and the Southwest were more integrated with the free labor Midwest and Northeast, though with an important side component of white settler colonialism over and against Native Americans and U.S. Mexicans (Limerick 1987). From the 1930s on, a complex set of processes brought the various parts of the nation closer together. These have included federal investment, military recruitment, expansion of federal taxation, administrative deepening, movement of private capital, internal migration, and political-cultural convergence. Recruitment of various populations (trust networks) across racial categories (always with more symbolic and material access for whites) as citizens—soldiers, taxpayers, administrative subjects, providers of political consent and support—has been crucial to this intensification and unification of the U.S. federal state.

Two important events then set the scenario for post-1965 immigration politics: a decline in labor supply and the integration of previously excluded groups into the citizen bargain. On one hand, capital faced the gradual exhaustion of the internal labor supply from the great northward/westward migration, on top of the previous (1924) closure of southern and eastern European immigration. Thus, the search for new labor supplies required both reopening international immigration and moving capital outward to global production sites. On the other hand, there was the deepening of the citizenship bargain, in conjunction with the expansion of military and administrative state claims on U.S. populaces, together with unification across previously massive regional divides.

From the 1920s to the 1970s, this strengthening of the U.S. national state and concomitant citizenship sentiments apparently could not be surpassed. But starting in the 1960s, its trajectory changed, with increasing economic insecurity/flexibility upon a return to globalized capitalism in production, finance, and, recently, services. The U.S. public also experienced novel risks: failure of geopolitical hegemony in protracted overseas wars (Vietnam, Iraq), terrorism within U.S. territory, and environmental disequilibria. From the 1970s on, renewed immigration intersected with intensified citizenship during a period of overall uncertainty and anxiety (Heyman 1998, 1999, 2012).

Part Two: 1965–Present

In 1965, the United States' immigration law changed in ways that allowed large-scale legal immigration from throughout the world. Given the demographics of the era, this meant mainly Asia, Latin America, the Caribbean, and Africa (later changes, such as admission of various groups of refugees, reinforced this). In the same period, unauthorized migration also expanded, for reasons explained later for the case of Mexicans. In what follows, I focus my narrative on immigration from Mexico, which certainly is a disservice to other immigrant groups but is a concession to clarity of analysis and my specific expertise (in what follows, I draw on a lifetime of fieldwork and reading; a useful reference is Massey, Durand and Malone 2002).

To understand post-1965 immigration politics, we need to step back in time to contextualize it in the longer history of immigration from Mexico. The 1848 U.S. military theft of half of Mexico's territory initiated a period concentrated on political and legal seizure of resources north of the border from local Native American and Mexican populations. Sporadically, there was labor migration of Mexican-origin populations as workers, but this was not large. However, by the 1880s, U.S. labor demand began to penetrate Mexico through the combined effects of railroads as labor recruiters and transportation linkages from one country to the other. With the exception of the Great Depression, northward Mexican labor movement has been a constant, while U.S. border and immigration policy has undergone dramatic changes. For most of the era before 1965,[3] this immigration was recruited by or later autonomously self-supplied to a fairly limited U.S. regional and sectoral markets (the West and the Southwest, farm labor, and so forth); it never supplanted the mass labor supply from Europe, Asia, or the U.S. South. Narrow employer interests were able to exempt Western Hemispheric immigration from the restrictive 1921 and 1924 immigration laws, but the numbers of legal immigrants from Latin America and the Caribbean before 1965 remained low.

In the 1930s, Mexicans and Mexican-origin people were coercively expelled in vast numbers (at least a half-million) from the United States. With the transition from depression to renewed labor demand in World War II, the United States and a somewhat reluctant Mexico developed a nonimmigrant, temporary contract labor arrangement, the Bracero Program, which lasted from 1942 to 1964. In some years, large numbers of undocumented Mexicans also came to the United States in parallel to the Braceros. Throughout this period, however, most Mexican workers were limited to specific sectors and regions, which subjected them to terrible exploitation and racism but also insulated most of the country from frontline immigrant-citizen politics with respect to this new population.

Nevertheless, during the period 1924–1965, two important changes occurred, whose strongest effects were felt after 1965. One was that the category of "illegal alien" became clearer and more rigid legally, administratively, and in terms of policing the border (Nevins 2010; Ngai 2004). The other is the Mexican-origin civil rights movement in the United States. This had its roots in the 1920s but really gained political force after 1941, with World War II military service (and subsequent veteran status) and mass industrial unionization. In other words, Mexican-origin people caused and were subjected to two contradictory processes: for some, inclusion in the modern citizenship state; for others, exclusion into unprecedented legal, social, and cultural outsiderness (Heyman 2012). While the two subpopulations (legal Mexican-origin citizens and residents and "illegal Mexican aliens") are not identical, they at the same time have extensive relationships of family, friendship, and community, helping us understand the complex and ambivalent politics of U.S. Mexicans.

This double-sided transformation was intensified after 1965. On one hand, Mexicans by 1973 (there was a lag in implementation) benefited from increased, if still flawed and insufficient, paths to legal immigration. On the other hand, the Bracero Program ended, meaning that many Mexican peasant-workers could no longer move legally as temporary money-earners, and likewise their employers had lost an advantageous labor force. Employers petitioned for some former Braceros (usually in stable, higher-productivity jobs) to be made legal immigrants, but the majority of former Braceros continued their migratory circuits, now without documents. Employers also sought out new pools of exploitable, unauthorized labor, stimulating rapid growth of migratory networks. Eventually, a binational system of supply and demand of labor became relatively self-sustaining through migration networks (Massey et al. 1990).

With this basic migratory structure set in place, important changes began. These include the widening of source regions within Mexico, greater involvement of indigenous Mexicans in international migration, the U.S.-side national expansion of migratory destinations, the diversification of employment sectors (e.g., low-skill services, construction, and some branches of manufacturing), and the gradual increase in female migration.[4] Again, it needs to be emphasized that this specific intensification of Mexican immigration took place in the context of a huge expansion and diversification of immigration from all over the world. While to immigration scholars the Mexican component is partially distinctive, in U.S. immigration-citizenship politics, undocumented Mexicans are taken as the archetypical or even the only kind of immigrant ("illegals"), an important means of negative stereotyping.

The end of the Bracero Program and the new Immigration Act of 1965 initiated these various changes, but what explains their remarkable trajectory since then? To understand this, we need to shift focus from immigrants to the capitalist economy. In an important argument, Sassen (1988) pointed out that international immigrants in the post–World War II era, and in especially recent decades, have moved in precisely the opposite direction as capital investments. For example, U.S. manufacturing capital—including the textiles and garments with which I began this history—moved to Mexico and Central America (as well as Asia) precisely at the same time that the contemporary immigration pattern took form and gained momentum. Indeed, 1965 was not only a turning point in legal and unauthorized migration; it was also the start of Mexico's maquiladora export assembly plant program on the Mexican border that has pioneered a massive spatial relocation of manufacturing across the border. Figure 3.10 synthesizes these dual movements of immigration and capital relocation.

Sassen suggests that changes in the consumption and production structure of wealthy countries (and of cities and regions within them) create new kinds of demand for peasant-worker laborers. This is seen in the shift of Mexican immigrant workers into low-wage service industries, waiting on

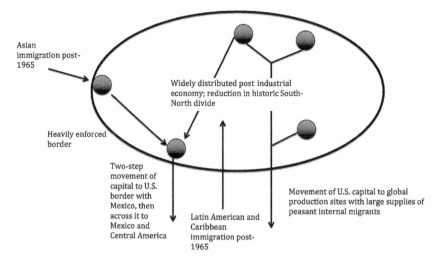

Figure 3.10 Strong state, but threatened by globalization of finance and production. Strong citizenship formation continues from 1945–1968 period but perceived as threatened. Period of widespread political conflict over new international immigration, intensification of border. Underlying anxiety about globalization and global issues (e.g., terrorism, imperial wars). Internal movement extensive but dispersed; end of socially visible internal migrant. To be migrant is now only international migrant.

prosperous U.S. consumers. Likewise, the impact of new capital (e.g., in advanced agriculture), combined with a wider set of modernizing processes in sending countries (e.g., mass consumption, communications), mobilizes potential emigrants. This stimulates not only international migration but also internal migration, as seen in the meteoric growth of Mexico's northern border cities (the main site of maquiladora production). Hence, we cannot understand Mexican migration to the United States or internal migration within Mexico without understanding the new economic configurations in the United States.

Intersecting with these economic changes have been wrenching political stresses. To summarize the preceding analysis, the twentieth century witnessed a profound widening and deepening of citizenship in Tillyian terms, including military service, tax payment, administrative obedience, and public redistribution (e.g., old-age support through social security and Medicare). Alongside this, "American" nationalism, long a component of the U.S. polity, refocused on loyalty to the U.S. military neo-imperial project. Meanwhile, important internal divisions, especially North-South ones, were transcended, and post-immigrant cleavages of the past, such as that between Protestants and Catholics, were overcome through the expansion of the categories "white" and "citizen." Nonwhites, such as African Americans and

Mexican Americans, were not as fully included in these developments, but even they struggled for and received some elements of citizenship inclusion.

This contemporary citizenship formation has intersected with two developments. One is the unprecedentedly strong distinction between legal and unauthorized ("illegal") immigrants introduced earlier. That frame has enabled a double move in recent immigration politics: disclaiming explicit racism while practicing disproportionate enforcement against Latin American, especially Mexican, immigrants for whom legal visa categories are insufficient vis-à-vis employer demand and family reunification. In a period when U.S. citizens perceive their citizenship claims as insecure, these legal practices strengthen the citizen-versus-illegitimate-outsider distinction. The other process interacting with citizenship has been the administrative consolidation of the bounded territorial nation-state, especially by means of surveillance and coercive force at the Mexican land border (Nevins 2010). Previously, the U.S. state handled immigration in an administratively weak way, through spatially fragmented seaports. Not only practically but also symbolically, the border with Mexico has come to define and represent citizen insiders. In this process, the previously blurred mix of internal and international migrants to the United States became much more clearly separated into immigrants from abroad and mobile U.S. citizens.

Recent political controversies in Arizona—a classic "Sunbelt" state—provide a telling example. These include closing the Mexican American Studies program in Tucson public schools and, through state law S.B. 1070, requiring Arizona state and local police to hold anyone they "suspected" of being out of status, if the police have lawfully stopped them. Thus, basically, local police are required by Arizona law to initiate an immigration arrest. Since its days as a territory, Arizona certainly has been racist toward Native Americans, African Americans, and Mexicans, especially in its resource-extractive economy (Sheridan 1995). This legacy exists today. But it has been reworked and reinforced in new circumstances, particularly the rise of a large service economy (retirement, tourism), as well as smaller military and electronic manufacturing sectors. The new Arizona economy involves many different labor specializations and flows, with important segments being immigrants, legal and undocumented, from Mexico and Central America. Having crossed the international boundary, they of course are "immigrants." Arizona also has been the destination of internal U.S. migration, especially of retirees, yet such people are not conceptualized as migrants; they are "citizens." While I know of no empirical study that shows that internal migrants are specifically more negative toward international immigrants, circumstantial evidence suggests that this is the case. The focal point of anti-immigration politics in Arizona is the Phoenix metropolitan area, which also is the main recipient area of retirement and service internal migration.

I do not venture here to explain the why some (not all) contemporary U.S. citizens oppose immigration broadly, and especially unauthorized immigration (for more on this, see Heyman 2012). My point here is the organizational form of the conflict itself, as citizen versus international immigrant. This intersects with anti-Latin American, especially anti-Mexican, racism. Although many people of Mexican origin are legal citizens and indeed social citizens through such institutions as mass higher education, labor unions, military service, party politics, and so on, the symbolic (but powerful) framework of anti-immigrant stereotyping that renders Mexican ancestry equal to the absolute outsider status of "illegal" (outlaw) fuses anti-immigration and anti–Latin American racism. No more evident example could be found than the rhetoric of Donald Trump about building a forty-foot wall at the Mexican border (and, preposterously, having Mexico pay for it), insinuating that a U.S.-born Mexican-origin federal judge—an unquestionable insider in the U.S.-state apparatus—actually holds traitorous Mexican prejudices, and also (to show that anti-immigrant sentiment affects not only Mexicans), proposing to bar Muslims from entering the country. Another Trumpian element, also illuminated by the analysis in this chapter, is displacement of anger over the movement of transnational manufacturing capital to Mexico and China into xenophobic hatred of Mexican and Chinese people. Fortunately, this is only one tendency in contentious politics (Tilly 2005); the opposing tendency is the deepening of non-racialized citizenship inclusion in the U.S. polity. Elements of this have been present in previous U.S. history, but the processes have become clearer as citizenship has both deepened and been rendered increasingly insecure.

Concluding Thoughts

Immigration studies, like so many other social sciences, focuses disproportionately on the "other," the poor, and the powerless. Citizenship studies, of course, directs itself to insiders within polities, though we cannot assume they are powerful and privileged. The work within immigration studies is impressive in both empirical and theoretical terms. But its disproportion with citizenship studies is striking; immigration studies is far older and more extensive than citizenship studies. Capital, the third part of this Tillyian analysis, has of course not been neglected, but the specific dynamic role of capital's search for new and expanded pools of exploitable peasant-workers is not well integrated into the study of immigrant-host relations and immigration politics. Immigration studies certainly attends to employers, specific job sectors, and overall levels of economic development, but what is largely missing (with some exceptions) is a focus on moves by capital to recruit labor as a dynamic source of change. Related to this is a failure to connect internal and international migration; typically, they are considered as different topics, often by different kinds of scholars (national anthropologists, sociologists, and historians rather than international migration specialists).

The argument I make here is that we need to go beyond the othering immigrant focus. The production over historical time of insiders and outsiders and their relations to each other and to the state emerges out of the interaction of dual processes, migration and citizenship formation. A third process, capitalist spatial fixes in the form of searching for new labor pools, dynamically disrupts previous equilibria in migration networks and citizenship politics, thus creating new conflicts and arrangements. Since the key formative features of each historical arrangement are particularly revealing, these moments of new creation are of special interest. The three processes taken together are more illuminating than any one alone and have the virtue of attending to the doings of the powerful, rich, and privileged, as well as the middle classes and the poor and oppressed.

Notes

1. "Migrant" refers to all persons moving in and out of socially bounded territories. "Immigrant" refers to that subset of migrants who move for a sustained period of time across political boundaries. However, im/migrant is an awkward term. Admitting that no one term is perfect, I generally refer to immigrants in this chapter, except for some cases of internal migrants. Likewise, I follow Tilly in using "citizen" as a social category, a relationship between state and designated members, which is looser than (though related to) strictly legal definitions.
2. Tilly (1978) is best known in migration studies for his pioneering concept of "chain migration," people moving across space through social linkages, a concept that evolved into the network migration approach. I acknowledge the importance of these phenomena, but I derive other key ideas from Tilly.
3. In the period 1900–1930, some Mexican immigrants spread out nationally, but this spreading was set back to the near-border area because of the Great Depression. The main surviving non-border state beachhead was Chicago.
4. Starting in the late 1970s, revolutionary civil wars in Central America, in which the United States was deeply involved, drove Central American refugees through Mexico to the United States. Later, this became network-organized labor migration. Central Americans are today an important part of the U.S. immigrant working class, resembling and overlapping in broad terms with the Mexican immigrant population.

References

American Social History Project, Christopher Clark, Nancy A. Hewitt, Roy Rosenzweig, Nelson Lichtenstein, Joshua Brown, and David Jaffee. 2008a. *Who Built America? Volume One: Through 1877*. Boston: Bedford/St. Martin's.

American Social History Project, Christopher Clark, Nancy A. Hewitt, Roy Rosenzweig, Nelson Lichtenstein, Joshua Brown, and David Jaffee. 2008b. *Who Built America? Volume Two: Since 1877*. Boston: Bedford/St. Martin's.

Black, Earl, and Merle Black. 1987. *Politics and Society in the South*. Cambridge, MA: Harvard University Press.
Brubaker, Rogers. 2001. *Citizenship and Nationhood in France and Germany*. Cambridge, MA: Harvard University Press.
Calavita, Kitty. 1984. *U.S. Immigration Law and the Control of Labor, 1820–1924*. London: Academic Press.
Collins, Jane L. 2003. *Threads: Gender, Labor, and Power in the Global Apparel Industry*. Chicago: University of Chicago Press.
Cowie, Jefferson. 1999. *Capital Moves: RCA's Seventy-Year Quest for Cheap Labor*. Ithaca, NY: Cornell University Press.
Dawley, Alan. 1976. *Class and Community: The Industrial Revolution in Lynn*. Cambridge, MA: Harvard University Press.
Dublin, Thomas. 1979. *Women at Work: The Transformation of Work and Community in Lowell, Massachusetts, 1826–1860*. New York: Columbia University Press.
Fassin, Didier. 2011. "Policing Borders, Producing Boundaries. The Governmentality of Immigration in Dark Times." *Annual Review of Anthropology* 40: 213–226.
Gordon, David M., Richard Edwards, and Michael Reich. 1982. *Segmented Work, Divided Workers: The Historical Transformation of Labor in the United States*. Cambridge, UK, and New York: Cambridge University Press.
Gregory, James N. 2005. *The Southern Diaspora: How the Great Migrations of Black and White Southerners Transformed America*. Chapel Hill: University of North Carolina Press.
Gutman, Herbert G. 1976. *Work, Culture, and Society in Industrializing America: Essays in American Working-Class and Social History*. New York: Knopf.
Hanagan, Michael P., and Charles Tilly. 1999. *Extending Citizenship, Reconfiguring States*. Lanham, MD: Rowman & Littlefield Publishers.
Harvey, David. 1982. *The Limits to Capital*. Chicago: University of Chicago Press.
Heyman, Josiah McC. 1998. State Effects on Labor Exploitation: The INS and Undocumented Immigrants at the Mexico-United States Border. *Critique of Anthropology* 18: 157–80.
Heyman, Josiah McC. 1999. "State Escalation of Force: A Vietnam/US-Mexico Border Analogy," In Josiah Heyman, ed., *States and Illegal Practices*. Oxford: Berg Publishers, pp. 285–314.
Heyman, Josiah McC. 2012. Constructing a "Perfect" Wall: Race, Class, and Citizenship in U.S.: Mexico Border Policing. In Pauline Gardiner Barber and Winnie Lem, eds., *Migration in the 21st Century: Political Economy and Ethnography*. New York and London: Routledge, pp. 153–74.
Higham, John. 1955. *Strangers in the Land: Patterns of American Nativism, 1860–1925*. New Brunswick, NJ: Rutgers University Press.
Krissman, Fred. 2005. Sin Coyote Ni Patrón: Why the "Migrant Network" Fails to Explain International Migration. *International Migration Review* 39: 4–44.
Limerick, Patricia Nelson. 1987. *The Legacy of Conquest: The Unbroken Past of the American West*. New York: Norton.
Massey, Douglas S., Rafael Alarcon, Jorge Durand, and Humberto González. 1990. *Return to Aztlan: The Social Process of International Migration from Western Mexico*. Berkeley: University of California Press.

Massey, Douglas S., Joaquín Arango, Graeme Hugo, Ali Kouaouci, and Adela Pellegrino. 2009. *Worlds in Motion: Understanding International Migration at the End of the Millennium.* Oxford: Clarendon Press.

Massey, Douglas S., Jorge Durand, and Nolan J. Malone. 2002. *Beyond Smoke and Mirrors: Mexican Immigration in an Era of Economic Integration.* New York: Russell Sage Foundation.

McKeown, Adam. 2008. *Melancholy Order: Asian Migration and the Globalization of Borders.* New York: Columbia University Press.

Nevins, Joseph. 2010. *Operation Gatekeeper and Beyond: The War on "Illegals" and the Remaking of the U.S.-Mexico Boundary.* New York and London: Routledge.

Ngai, Mae M. 2004. *Impossible Subjects: Illegal Aliens and the Making of Modern America.* Princeton, NJ: Princeton University Press.

Omi, Michael, and Howard Winant. 1994. *Racial Formation in the United States: From the 1960s to the 1990s.* New York and London: Routledge.

Ong, Aihwa. 1999. *Flexible Citizenship: The Cultural Logics of Transnationality.* Durham, NC: Duke University Press.

Piore, Michael J. 1979. *Birds of Passage: Migrant Labor and Industrial Societies.* Cambridge, UK, and New York: Cambridge University Press.

Sassen, Saskia. 1988. *The Mobility of Labor and Capital: A Study in International Investment and Labor Flow.* Cambridge, UK, and New York: Cambridge University Press.

Sheridan, Thomas E. 1995. *Arizona: A History.* Tucson: University of Arizona Press.

Skocpol, Theda. 1992. *Protecting Soldiers and Mothers: The Political Origins of Social Policy in the United States.* Cambridge, MA: Belknap Press of Harvard University Press.

Tilly, Charles. 1978. Migration in Modern European History. Pp. 48–72 in William McNeill and Ruth Adams, eds., *Human Migration: Patterns, Implications, Policies.* Bloomington: Indiana University Press.

Tilly, Charles. 1984. *Big Structures, Large Processes, Huge Comparisons.* New York: Russell Sage Foundation.

Tilly, Charles. 1992. *Coercion, Capital, and European States, A.D. 990–1992.* Cambridge, MA: Basil Blackwell.

Tilly, Charles. 1996. *Citizenship, Identity and Social History.* Cambridge, UK: Cambridge University Press.

Tilly, Charles. 2005. *Identities, Boundaries, and Social Ties.* Boulder, CO: Paradigm Publishers.

Wallace, Anthony F. C. 1987. *St. Clair: A Nineteenth-Century Coal Town's Experience with a Disaster-Prone Industry.* New York: Knopf.

Weber, Max. 1949. *The Methodology of the Social Sciences.* Translated and edited by Edward A. Shils and Henry A. Finch. Glencoe, IL: Free Press.

Wolf, Eric R. 1982. *Europe and the People without History.* Berkeley: University of California Press.

Zolberg, Aristide R. 2008. *A Nation by Design: Immigration Policy in the Fashioning of America.* Cambridge, MA: Harvard University Press.

4

STIGMATIZING IMMIGRANT DAY LABOR

Boundary-Making and the Built Environment in Long Island, New York

Ernesto Castañeda and Kevin R. Beck

This chapter demonstrates how the liminal space of a day labor hiring site becomes a tool for reifying notions of immigrant illegality. We argue that daily interactions between migrant day laborers and local employers reinforce the boundaries between the two groups and that the day labor hiring site plays a central role in how boundary-making processes unfold. We collected data through nonparticipant observation and interviews with migrant day laborers from Latin America working in a suburban town on Long Island, New York. Our data suggest that the day labor hiring site is a stigmatized place. We argue that this stigma shapes the process through which some employers hire temporary labor and facilitates wage theft. We introduce the concept of *flash hirings* to discuss a simultaneous need for labor and a devaluation of that laborer. The consequences of relying on day labor hiring sites to find work can include removal from the community if political and economic priorities in the local community change.

Many day laborers in the United States are men from Latin America who are unable to participate in the formal economy because they may lack local educational degrees, facility with English, or a work permit. Instead, they congregate in parking lots, street corners, and storefronts to solicit work from employers on a day-to-day basis (Valenzuela 2003; Valenzuela et al. 2005). These public hiring sites can be state sanctioned or informal, and they can be located anywhere, from busy shopping centers to curbsides in middle-class neighborhoods. Day labor typically entails irregular employment, relatively low wages, lack of regular breaks and benefits, and possibly dangerous working conditions (Cleaveland and Kelly 2008; González-López 2006, Purser 2009; Valenzuela 2001). Although there are many forms of informal and irregular work such as seasonal agricultural work, migrants from Latin America laboring in urban settings are more likely to work on construction, demolition, or landscaping. As one can attest in El Paso, Texas, or Washington, D.C., whites, blacks, Asians and Native Americans, and U.S.-born Latinos, homeless or not, may engage in day labor; yet we concentrate here on foreign-born Latino males, so we sometimes use the term *jornaleros* (day laborers in Spanish).

While many *jornaleros* access jobs through social ties, others rely on formal or semiformal open-air labor markets where employers can pick up temporary workers as needed. These places are often referred to as day labor hiring sites. These sites can be liminal spaces where the distinctions between state-sanctioned activities and illegal activities are often blurry. At the most basic level, a hiring site might be rented by the municipal government, paid for with public funds, yet the transactions occurring within the hiring site between *jornaleros* and employers are typically off the books. Many employers may lack the credentials to operate a small business but depend on day laborers to make their businesses financially viable. Most of the workers are migrants, some are legal permanent residents, others may be in the United States with temporary protected status, and others have been engaging in unauthorized circular migrations between the home and host countries for years. Despite the fact that many *jornaleros* have legal papers and the right to work, the stigma of illegality (De Genova 2004) is often ascribed to day labor work and the hiring sites where these migrants solicit jobs. As a result, the state regulates the behavior of migrant workers in order to contain perceived threats. For example, normally innocuous behaviors such as eating, resting, and sleeping are prohibited in spaces that are not sanctioned as hiring sites (Esbenshade 2000:35, 35), even if those spaces are on the curbs adjacent to a sanctioned hiring site. For people who hold negative stereotypes of immigrants, being so-called illegal implies more than an unauthorized immigration status: it suggests a propensity toward criminality (Lee and Fiske 2006). Associating abstract notions of crime and criminality with day labor hiring sites serves to mark migrants as outsiders and facilitates their exploitation in the communities where they work (Holmes 2013; Tilly 1998).

Men at informal hiring sites must attract the attention of potential employers, which may include soliciting work off the street, while simultaneously limiting their exposure to others in the community by reducing noise and limiting behavior that could be seen as disruptive (Cleaveland and Pierson 2009; Cleaveland and Kelly 2008). After observing interactions between migrant day labors and local employers in a suburban town in New York—interactions occurring both on the street and in a hiring site—we find that the day labor hiring site plays a central role in how boundary-making processes unfold. Our data suggest that the day labor hiring site is a stigmatized place in the local community. We find that this stigma shapes the process through which some employers hire temporary labor and that it facilitates wage theft. The consequences of migrants relying on the day labor hiring site as a place for finding work and therefore sustenance can be homelessness and effective removal from the community. We begin this chapter with a brief discussion of social boundaries, the embodiment of "illegality," and the right to use public space. We then present the research methodology, a description of the field site, the findings, and our conclusions.

Social Boundaries and Illegality

Lamont and Molnar (2002:168) define symbolic boundaries as "conceptual distinctions made by social actors to categorize objects, people, practices, and even time and space." Boundary work refers to the practices and "mechanisms that either facilitate or inhibit interactions with persons of foreign origin and thus serve to incorporate or exclude them" (Massey and Sanchez 2010:14). Categorical social boundaries result from a process of relational identification (Tilly 2005). In the case of migrant workers, social boundaries and categorical inequality result from the laws controlling their movements and behaviors. Exclusionary boundary-making practices include supporting residential segregation, barring migrants from a wide range of jobs, and relegating migrants to stigmatized spaces (Castañeda 2012). Boundary-making, which is often motivated by material interests, can result in exploitation and opportunity hoarding (Tilly 1998).

Immigration laws and policies have prevented many migrants from being incorporated into American society beyond their participation in the informal economy (De Genova 2004). This state-driven boundary work (Gieryn 1983) has occurred through various channels. Historically, selective immigration quotas have been used to shape who is allowed into the United States, for example, to exclude Asian migrants and hinder the incorporation of Chinese and Japanese migrants already in the country (Ngai 2004). The 1942 Bracero Program was designed to increase labor supply in the United States during World War II. This binational program gave agricultural workers from Mexico the ability to work in the United States for a few months and then return to their families in the off-season (Durand 2007). The program was unilaterally ended in 1964, but people continued migrating through their social networks and working informally. The militarization of the U.S.–Mexico border in the 1990s attempted to stem the flow of people north (Dunn 2009; Massey, Durand and Malone 2002; Nevins 2010). However, the tightening of border security since the 1990s has reduced temporary and return migration, thereby increasing immigrants' length of stay in the United States and resulting in a surplus of informal labor (Massey, Durand and Malone 2002). Migrants from Central America not only have to survive the desert in the American Southwest but also have to survive many hardships as they pass through Mexico (Menjívar 2000; Menjívar 2006).

As U.S. border security became a leading political issue, being "illegal" came to represent more than the circumvention of authorized ports of entry. As Mike Davis writes, the idea of erecting a "dam" between Mexico and the United States had the purpose of allowing the reception of cheap labor when the economy calls for it and restricting migration flows when labor markets are saturated. This became even more problematic after NAFTA increased the flow of certain goods while attempting to restrict other flows. Despite an enlarged border patrol presence, facilitating the passage of goods along the border while restricting the stream of labor and illegal drugs has proved an impossible task. As a result, migrants who attempt to enter the country without documents are conflated with prohibited items that cross international lines such as guns, untaxed money, and drugs (Chavez 2008; Nevins 2002).

Contemporary social boundaries serve to marginalize day laborers and can be observed in social categories like that of the "illegal," which is a form of "colorblind racism" (Bonilla-Silva 2006) used to justify day laborers' inhumane treatment with the assumption that they lack permission to live and work in the United States. According to Nevins (2002:148), "nominally 'colorblind' values such as fairness, individualism, and equality" are the new tropes used to fuel anti-immigrant discourse and sentiment. Anti-immigrant legislation exploits this new style of racism by evoking the idea that "illegals" undermine the integrity of the values that are widely considered to be at the core of an American identity, such as the rule of law. Consequently, migrants and *jornaleros* have become scapegoats for many social ills, including economic crises, declining job opportunities, and supposed increases in crime (Rumbaut and Ewing 2007). The "illegal" as a social category has become so closely linked with day labor work that even those workers with authorization to live and work in the United States share this stigma. Undocumented status delays assimilation, reduces commitments to the host society, and positions workers in an ambivalent situation that delays their decision to choose a permanent residence (Castañeda 2013). Their stay in the United States is contingent upon the ebbs and flows in immigration law enforcement and labor demand (Verea 2008). Thus, many *jornaleros* who have internalized the stigma against "illegals" live in a state of fear, unable to be at ease in their homes and workplaces (Núñez and Heyman 2007). In recent years, *jornaleros* have been disenfranchised by the stigma of illegality. Missing in much of the literature on illegality and racialization of migrant workers are the grounded empirical descriptions of everyday dynamics that create boundaries between locals and outsiders. This chapter helps to fill this gap in the literature.

Observations and Interviews at a Day Labor Hiring Site

Huntington Station was selected as the research site because of the community's ongoing debate over where migrant day laborers should be allowed to solicit work and whether they should be allowed to solicit work in public at all. The struggle over the town's day labor hiring site is similar to that occurring in other Long Island communities and suburban towns in the Northeast, such as Farmingville, New York and Freehold, New Jersey (Cleaveland and Pierson 2009; Cleaveland and Kelly 2008).

We conducted nonparticipant observation and semi-structured interviews between June and August 2010 at a hiring site located on Depot Road. Sessions at the field site were conducted one to three days per week, typically in the mornings, for two to three hours. We initially collected data through a survey that asked forty-three open-ended questions about the day laborers' perspectives about working in the town. Surveys were later substituted by semi-structured interviews that allowed the workers to expand on the survey questions and share their experiences with their employers and the hiring site. Most interviews were carried out on the street or inside the hiring site. Some interviews took place in a group setting with one or two individuals actively responding to questions while others listened and intervened from time to time. Discussions of the hiring site often segued into topics of worker exploitation, abuse, and discrimination. Responses were recorded in a notebook, and, soon after, comprehensive notes were typed. We also watched publicly available videos of Town Hall meetings posted on YouTube where community members expressed their views of the day labor hiring site.

In total, we conducted interviews with twenty-five day laborers, plus one journalist, a leader of a local church group, and two workers from a local nonprofit that assisted the laborers. Additionally, many conversations took place on the street and are not included in these counts. All interviews and surveys with *jornaleros* were conducted in Spanish. The workers were all men born in Mexico or Central America, ranging from eighteen to seventy years old. The time these individuals had lived in Long Island varied from a few months to fourteen years. New migrants would constantly arrive at the site, while others would leave, making it impossible to obtain a representative sample of the entire population. Furthermore, we were able to interview only workers who had not been hired on a given day, resulting in selection bias. Recurrent visits to the hiring site mitigated some of this selection bias. To protect participants, pseudonyms are used for all respondents in this study, and no identifying data were collected.

A Place of Employment and Safety

Huntington Station is a mixed-income community that hosts many immigrants, including day laborers. In the 1990s, Huntington Station's day labor hiring site was officially established on Depot Road on a vacant, quarter-acre lot. Huntington Township allocated approximately $75,000 annually to maintain this public space. The goal was for negotiations between day

Table 4.1 Demographic Overview of Huntington Station in 2000 and 2010

Ethnicity	(Percent)	
	2000	2010
Hispanic	22.7	36.7
White	60.8	47.6
Black	11.6	10.9
Asian	3.1	3.5
Median Household Income	$61,760	$72.548
Total Population	29,910	33,029

SOURCE: 2000 and 2010 US Censuses

laborers and employers to take place away from the street to avoid disrupting traffic. Table 4.1 provides some data to contextualize the area's demographic composition.

It was on Depot Road, just outside the day labor hiring site (see Figure 4.1), that workers and contractors typically engaged in curbside negotiations, much to the dismay of town authorities and local residents who disliked the resulting congestion of cars and people. Lining the northernmost section of Depot Road for five blocks were the day laborers: migrant men hailing primarily from El Salvador, Honduras, and Mexico who populated the sidewalks from early morning until noon. Most workers could be seen leaning patiently along brick walls or chain link fences or seated on a makeshift bench, a milk crate, or a large tree root. Vehicles heading north on Depot Road could not avoid exchanging long stares with these job-seeking men, who were finely tuned to the indications that a vehicle could be a potential employer or, as the workers say in Spanish, a *patron* (boss). A slight change in speed or direction, an analytical glance from a driver, or a sharp U-turn at the end of the street would send workers rushing down the sidewalks and bolting across two lanes of heavy traffic to be the first to engage an employer.

Several accommodations were provided to workers inside the hiring site: a heated trailer for shelter during the winter months, a water fountain, portable toilets, and a picnic bench. The hiring site additionally served as a hub to network with friends and other workers, exchange information about jobs and housing opportunities, discuss politics and current events, share stories about recent employment ventures, and collectively make meaning of their often-precarious living conditions. Occasionally, local nonprofits and religious groups would drop off donations of food, clothing, or flyers about sponsored English classes or sex education talks. A church group provided the laborers with one meal every morning. Ministers of various churches preached to them on-site and invited them to attend Sunday church services. The hiring

Figure 4.1 Day laborers in front of the hiring site
Photo by Kevin R. Beck

site also provided workers with a means for addressing individual needs through the Family Service League (FSL), a nonprofit organization subcontracted by the Town Board to manage the site. The FSL manager would open the gates of the hiring site every morning at 6:00 a.m. and close them again at noon. This person would often act as the day laborers spokesperson to the town. He would direct sick workers toward clinics and hospitals and arrange for the police to investigate cases of exploitation. The site served as a place for workers to connect with others, to receive services, and to find jobs.

On June 30, 2010, approximately twelve years after the day labor hiring site opened and under budgetary constraints resulting from the 2008 U.S. recession, a waning demand for day labor, and a widespread desire to clear Depot Road of job-soliciting men, town authorities permanently closed the day labor hiring site (Morris 2010a; Morris 2010b; Morris 2010c). Service groups no longer distributed food, the Family Service League stopped assisting migrants to meet their needs, and there was no longer a forum for distributing goods and services. Although the hiring site was officially closed, the day laborers continued to solicit jobs on Depot Road for several months after the closure. By 2012, the hiring site had been replaced with a mini-golf course and recreation center.

A Dangerous Place?

A resident described the day labor hiring site on Depot Road as a place that produced crime and drained the town's budget. This depiction of the day labor hiring site became common with the onset of the 2008 recession. At Town Hall meetings, individuals and organizations argued that closing the day labor hiring site would rid the community of a "social and financial problem" while balancing the town's budget. Some residents and community stakeholders publicly expressed their desire to exclude day laborers from the privileges and rights that they enjoyed as citizens.

In this section, we juxtapose the narrative of the day labor hiring site as a dangerous place with the migrant workers' understanding of the hiring site as a crucial resource. Among several complaints voiced at a Huntington Town Hall meeting on June 11, 2008, one resident spoke about his intimidating encounter with the day laborers and compared his experience at the hiring site to other experiences he had while working as a police officer in the New York Police Department: "I gotta tell ya, nine in the morning, out there at that hiring site, it's a scary place. And I did twenty-one years [working as a police officer]. I worked in the South Bronx; I worked in Queens Village; I worked in all different communities. (Uh,) out there I'm alone, (uh,) trying to assert my first amendment right, (uh) I've been intimidated, I've been invited in the back, to be, pummeled in my opinion, by the illegal immigrants" (Mitchell 2008). This resident emphasized the danger of the hiring site by comparing it to stigmatized places framed as allegedly dangerous places. Our observations of day laborers interacting with the police indicated that police officers and day laborers were accustomed to each other's presence and both sought to avoid conflict. Another speaker at the Town Hall meeting associated the day laborers with crime and overburdened public services. This woman explained, "Catering to illegals has created a magnet that has saturated our town with hidden costs, like hospitals and health, overcrowding in schools, increased drugs and crime, and out of control property taxes" (Mitchell 2008). Similarly, another woman argued that the town should not have to provide services to day laborers. This woman said, "Our town, or any other town, cannot, and should not have to absorb a large number of men, loitering, congregating, in what[ever] area. . . . Regardless of their rights, regardless of their reasons" (Mitchell 2008). Not once did we feel threatened or intimidated while conducting interviews, nor did we witness the use or sale of drugs. Where, then, do residents' feelings of insecurity originate? Ross and Jang (2000) hypothesize that in neighborhoods where there are high levels of perceived disorder, such as trash, loitering, graffiti, and vandalism, residents maintain high levels of fear and mistrust. It is possible that Huntington residents associate the ostensible disorganization of the hiring site or the large number of foreign men competing for work in public space with crime and danger. Another possibility is that residents use the term "crime" as a euphemism to label challenges to the social status quo and perceived difference (Merry 1981).

These residents spoke out about these *jornaleros* by relying heavily on the category of the "illegal immigrant" to construct narratives about how and why the hiring site posed a threat to the community. For the day laborers, however, the hiring site was primarily a place used for accessing material resources, taking breaks, and networking with co-workers. Day laborers ascribed values to the hiring site that mirrored the qualities of a home— a place that is safe and familiar. For many workers the hiring site was not primarily used for soliciting jobs. Most job solicitation took place on the sidewalks of Depot Road in front of the hiring site where employers were likely to pass by. The manner in which day laborers solicited jobs was widely considered unorganized and disorderly and was regularly used at Town Hall meetings as a justification to close the hiring site.

Fernando, a day laborer from Honduras who had been living in town for more than five years, commented on the closure of the hiring site: "I watch the news. They said that [the hiring site] was closed because [we] would not stay inside. One could sit calmly inside . . . drink a coffee, a glass of water. It was a refuge to get into the shade. Now there's nothing." Alex, a middle-aged man from Honduras, explained that as jobs became scarce and as day laborers were abundant, workers were drawn onto Depot Road to keep pace with an increasingly competitive job market. Rather than waiting for employers to enter the hiring site, day laborers would approach employers on the street to give themselves a head start over the others waiting inside the hiring site for jobs to come to them. This strategy eventually normalized street solicitation and brought all the day laborers searching for work outside the gates of the hiring site. Day laborers were aware that soliciting jobs on the street is against the law. Alex explained that the process of searching for jobs is one of patiently waiting on the street and withdrawing into the hiring site when the police decide to enforce street solicitation laws. He explained, "The truth is, when [the hiring site] was open, we sat [on the street] calmly. When the police came we went inside [the hiring site]. It was like a house."

Interviews revealed that the hiring site was also useful for escaping the cold or for getting food and drinks. For David, a twenty-nine-year-old day laborer from Honduras, the hiring site "meant happiness—a full belly." Similarly, Nero, an eighteen-year-old worker from Honduras who had been living in the United States for a year and a half, commented, "There are many people who depended on this site, more than anything for food." Esteban, a middle-aged worker from Puebla, Mexico, said, "When it snowed one could go inside for a coffee. The church used to bring us food, soda, and coffee. Now that it is closed, where are we going to go?" Esteban further explained that the Family Service League helped workers access other resources such as glasses and health care: "They bring us food, the trailer [is there] for the cold. They help if you are sick. There was a man who needed glasses, and they gave them to him for free. Many came to help. For example, one [volunteer] came to explain sexually transmitted diseases and how to use condoms." Still other workers described the loss of the hiring site as a practical setback. Marco, a fifty-five-year-old electrician from Managua, Nicaragua, asked, "¿Y ahora si quiero cagar" (And now if I want to shit?). Although half joking, Marco alluded to a serious problem. With the hiring site closed and the portable toilets gone, there were no public restrooms. Workers who continued to solicit work on the streets now faced the decision of whether to return to their homes and suspend their search for jobs or urinate on the street and risk confrontation with the police. These decisions had serious consequences not only for individuals but for all workers who solicited jobs on Deport Road. Without the hiring site, the chances of being further stigmatized by one aberrant action, such as urinating on the sidewalk, are far greater.

Although the town leaders did not envision the hiring site as a place that would shelter, feed, and clothe workers when it was originally established, these were some of the site's primary functions. Workers ascribed meanings to the hiring site that were both emotive and pragmatic such as "happiness," "refuge," and "shelter." These meanings sharply contrast conflicted with views of the hiring site as dangerous place. The result of this framing conflict was a change in the use of this space: the hiring site was closed, and day labor activities were relegated to the sidewalks of Depot Road. Closing the site had the effect of increasing the appearance and number of "idle" men loitering on the streets of the town.

Flash Hiring

The stigma surrounding Huntington's day labor hiring site, as reflected in the comments at the Town Hall meeting, shaped the interactions between employers and workers at the hiring site. This was most clear in the method that some employers used to hire workers off the curbsides of Depot Road. We noticed that there were generally two categories of employers who relied on day labor. The first were contractors who owned small businesses and hired migrant workers for landscaping, construction, demolition, masonry work, and other labor-intensive jobs. These small business owners were noticeably comfortable talking with day laborers. They would stop their vehicles inside the day labor hiring site, get out to negotiate wages with the workers face to face, try to figure out which of the workers had a good command of English, and sometimes ask workers to demonstrate their ability to use tools necessary for a particular job, such as a weed-whacker or another piece of landscaping equipment.

A different category of employers also frequently relied on day labor work. These employers did not operate businesses but sought to hire temporary labor to work in their homes or yards or on small private jobs. They drove not the large trucks that are typical of landscaping or construction companies but small cars or SUVs that were primarily personal vehicles. These employers were afraid of the hiring site and therefore picked up workers only on the streets outside it. They would only momentarily stop their cars, signal through hand gestures how many workers they needed, and when the desired number of workers entered their cars the employers would speed away, presumably to avoid being seen by the police while hiring workers off of the street. These employers did not often attempt to speak with the day laborers before hiring them. In many of these cases there was no negotiation of wages before the workers were driven away. We call this rushed hiring practice, marked by an inability to be at ease in the hiring site, a *flash hiring*. Similar to street sex workers, illegality creates a pressure to negotiate the terms of the exchange in a fast manner and develops a preoccupation with the risk of police intervention or a known passerby witnessing the hire. Men are quickly sized up by their prospective temporary employers (González-López 2006). Also, like sex workers who sell their services on the streets, day laborers' bodies were highly objectified and commodified, because workers were often hired on the basis of their physical appearance, age, muscularity, and so on.

On one morning, we observed two small luxury vehicles each quickly pick up a pair of workers and then flee as if they were being chased. The day laborers lining the streets of Depot Road laughed in chorus as the tires from one of the cars screeched as the employer attempted to make a quick getaway. When we spoke with a worker from the Family Service League about these quick curbside pickups, she described them as dangerous because it meant workers had to sprint through heavy traffic in order to get into cars. She explained that many "mom and pop" employers were afraid of being encircled by day laborers when they entered the hiring site and thus preferred to hire workers on the street. Depot Road's heavy traffic provides a degree of protection for employers who fear being surrounded by crowds of job-searching men; limiting time spent on the street secures a degree of personal space for the employer. Day laborers noted how flash hirings displayed employers' unease in and around the hiring site.

We asked the day laborers why they thought these employers were frightened of the hiring site. Alex explained, "It's difficult. When one is inside [the hiring site], the American does not like everyone touching his car. It is unorganized. Some [workers] do not have respect; it's not what employers like." Alex reaffirmed the importance of employers' personal space by recounting a recent experience: One afternoon, after several hours of unsuccessfully soliciting work on Depot Road, he decided to return home. He had just purchased lunch at a deli several blocks away from the hiring site when an employer pulled to the side of the road and asked if he was willing to work for a few hours fixing a leaking roof. Alex agreed. He went to work and was well paid. After finishing the job, Alex asked his employer why he had not gone directly to the hiring site to find a worker. The employer said he did not like being surrounded by men yanking open his car doors and trying to get inside.

Employers are not physically harmed or attacked when workers surround their cars. On the contrary, day laborers are eager to oblige employers' requests to prove they can understand English or use certain equipment. However, employers who do not regularly hire workers seek to limit their associations with migrant workers and the day labor hiring site. These employers might fear being caught hiring undocumented workers. Regardless of the motivation, these employers engage in flash hirings that accentuate the stigmatizing effects of being undocumented and the boundary work done by natives to show their difference.

Wage Theft

Day laborers are susceptible to exploitation, underpayment, and not being paid even after having completed a job. This occurs because employers understand there is little chance of being sanctioned. Most migrant day laborers speak little or no English, are often unaware of their rights, and believe the police would not assist them if they asked for help. Furthermore, day laborers are typically desperate for money and have no other means of finding employment. Therefore, many will work for employers even if they feel there is a high chance of not being paid. Recurrent wage theft has become a normalized practice. Every migrant day laborer we spoke with had been a victim of wage theft at least once during his time living and working in Huntington. We found wage theft to occur in three ways. The first was when workers were promised to be paid after completing a job but were not compensated. Other forms of wage theft occurred when they were paid less than what they were originally promised or when they were forced to work additional hours to receive the money originally promised. Even though all workers, including undocumented day laborers, are legally protected from wage theft (Meyer and Greenleaf 2011), most cases of wage theft go unreported.

Interviews with migrant workers reveal the high frequency of wage theft. Many claim to have worked full days and then to have been left by employers at the worksite without any payment. Others claim to have worked for weeks or months for the same employer and received only promises that they would be paid in the future. Alberto, a seventy-year-old day laborer from Honduras, claimed that four different bosses owed him a sum of approximately $5,000 for services he provided. This debt represented roughly one-third of Alberto's yearly earnings. He believed that he had been cheated because of his inability to speak English. Another worker, Fernando, told us about a time when he was promised he would be paid after a job was completed but received no compensation. "An old man took me to New York City to work on a ceramics project and told me, 'the next day we are going to finish the project and I'll pay you.' The next day he did not return." A worker named Guillermo described how he was driven to a port in New Jersey to remove ice from inside a large boat, and how, just when the job was about to be finished, the employer left and did not return. Guillermo was never paid. Another worker explained, "One time I worked for a week doing sheet rock and [the boss] paid me $100 . . . for four days of work! He told me, 'I'll pay you the rest tomorrow,' and he never did." As reported in other studies, these forms of wage theft were common (Valenzuela 2003).

Wage theft can also occur in the form of ultimatums that require workers to finish jobs on a fixed schedule or forfeit their pay. Cristian, a twenty-year-old day laborer who works to support his wife and three-year-old child in El Salvador, was hired to paint, affix plastic, and fumigate a building being renovated. During his first day on the job, Cristian worked several hours beyond the negotiated schedule and never received his wages. On the second day, the employer demanded that Cristian finish the project within two hours or he would not be paid. Cristian finished the project seven hours after the deadline; he was never paid, and he never reported the incident to the authorities. Mario, a seasoned electrician, took a job from a woman who was offering $240 to install the electrical wiring in a recently renovated building. The woman told Mario he would have only two days to finish or he would not be paid for his work. Mario did not finish within two days and was never paid. Carlos has worked for a plethora of bosses in the United States and has faced wage theft often. At the hiring site, he was picked up to work in a home for the mentally disabled. The woman who ran the home assigned Carlos house chores for more than twelve hours a day with a ten-minute break for lunch. Carlos worked six or seven days per week and was paid $1,500 each month. Thus, Carlos was earning between $4.64 and $5.20 per hour, far below the minimum wage. Although Carlos found the work abusive and the compensation insufficient, he did not have better job prospects elsewhere. One day, the woman offered Carlos a room in the home for $1,300 per month. Carlos felt insulted and said that accepting such a proposal would be the same as submitting to slavery. The woman was offended by Carlos's quick rejection of the offer and fired him. Carlos was not paid for the half month he worked before being fired.

Consequences of a Stigmatized Status

Homelessness

After the hiring site closed and as the economic recession diminished demand for temporary labor, day laborers were largely cut off from resources. With little access to jobs or services, many day laborers became homeless. For example, for two months Carlos had no alternative but to live in what the day laborers referred to as *La Montaña* (the mountain)—a wooded area and refuge for homeless workers. Carlos says that maintaining a rented room and not having to live among the denizens of *La Montaña* is one of his strongest motivations to find jobs and work hard. While never having committed a crime, Carlos debated whether he would be better off living in jail, a place that provides food, shelter, health care, and recreation at no cost. Carlos said that for a man of his age, fifty-seven years old, jail is surprisingly appealing. Many of the workers understood wage theft, the closure of the hiring site, and their homeless stints to be the result of their diminished status in the community.

Mario also described several brief periods when he went without work and had no choice but to camp in the woods. Since New York State does not reimburse Suffolk County for the costs of housing undocumented residents in its public shelters, places like *La Montaña* became the only feasible option for homeless laborers in Huntington. According to a 2010 article in a local newspaper, the homeless population at *La Montana* ranged from twenty-five to thirty men at a given time, and on January 5, 2010, local police officers forced homeless day laborers to leave their makeshift campsite (Brown 2010).

Experiencing Exclusion

Carlos spoke frequently and adamantly about how he felt marginalized in Huntington Station. Although quick to laud employers who treated him with honesty and respect, Carlos was appalled by the conditions that many *jornaleros* were subjected to. He told us:

> How many of us are here? We live in the darkness. I want to get out of the darkness. Racists, they don't want to see you [the migrant worker]. We are animals. We are poorly viewed. Not lunch nor water do they want to give us. They go to the hose, fill a pitcher, add a piece of ice, and say, "here is your water." We give our lives for [the employers] and they treat us like animals . . . they want to exchange gold for silver.

He pointed out the dehumanizing nature of day labor and continued by saying:

> The animals have personal veterinarians. And us, what? The Americans put us below the dogs and the cats. The dogs have their house; they are taken care of; they have vitamins; they receive injections for parasites. Why do the animals have more [than us]? They don't say, "poor man" . . . it's "poor dog." In the stables, the horses live better than us.

Carlos takes offense that pets occupy a more highly valued social status than he and his co-workers. Nero, a teenager from Honduras, does not understand

English but identified verbal abuse at work as his most significant problem. Nero says that employers' verbal insults are usually accompanied by angry body language that allows him to comprehend their comments. Nero believes that English is the key to commanding respect from his employers. He thinks that learning English is the best defense against discrimination and exploitation. He recounted an experience when, after he landed a job with a moving company, his boss insulted him, saying: "F . . . ing Hispanics, why don't you stay in your country?" Nero explained that it is important to remain calm when one is insulted by an employer. "One has to deal with the insult in fear of not finding another job." Santiago says that he's so thankful to live in the United States that he does not mind when employers insult him. He ignores these insults and carries on with his day. Alberto, one of the oldest laborers in the community, described part of the workers' duty as to "*humillarse*," or to humble oneself before Americans in appreciation for the opportunity to work in the United States, albeit illegally. The effects of "illegality" became so pervasive that workers rationalized their degraded status in the community and came to normalize certain abuse from employers.

Guillermo, a thirty-four-year-old worker from San Salvador, has legal temporary protected status (TPS), which the U.S. government grants to migrants who are unable to return to their home country because of extenuating circumstances such as a natural disaster or armed conflict. This status includes a legal work permit (Menjívar 2000). Guillermo claims that "white people look down at you" and act as though they do not want migrant laborers in their community. He reports hearing stories of blacks and whites beating up Latinos in Long Island.

Conclusion

The category of the "illegal" has been used as a justification for discriminatory and exploitive practices. Identifying people as illegal allows employers to break verbal work agreements and instills in day laborers the idea that they lack legal recourse, even though, legally, everyone has rights in the workplace, regardless of migration status. The day labor hiring site and the surrounding streets are spaces where employers are able to hire workers with a stigmatized status. As we have shown, day labor entails various types of boundary work that marginalizes workers in the host community. We find that the stigma attached to day labor work and assumed-to-be-undocumented status prevented these workers from using the space that was once a hiring site. Flash hirings highlight an appetite for cheap labor and employers' fear of being seen hiring undocumented individuals. Flash hirings and wage theft influence day laborers' internalization of their low social status.

We learned from our analysis that the hiring depot emerged as a critical site of social reproduction for these laborers. The hiring site socialized new migrants and refugees struggling to find formal jobs in day labor and served to normalize day labor among participants. The hazardous nature of day labor work became more tolerable when done along others in similar situations. The cultural norms at the site also kept this as a Hispanic, adult, male space, discouraging minors and women from engaging in this type of work—a reflection that even day laborers themselves saw their work as too risky, dangerous, and denigrating for their wives and children to perform. Informal hiring sites make day labors even more vulnerable and decrease solidarity and social support among them.

Wage theft is not the exclusive reason these day laborers become homeless. However, when work decreases, they are likely to run into financial distress. One must bear in mind that nearly all workers in this study send money to their homes in Latin America on a regular basis, no matter how desperate their own economic situation. If they did not remit these funds to their families, then they saw themselves as undermining the entire purpose of their presence in the States by failing to fulfill their responsibilities as fathers, husbands, or sons (Castañeda and Buck 2011; Zelizer and Tilly 2006). Under such tight financial constraints, wage theft can act as a tipping point leading to homelessness, alcoholism, and depression (Massey and Gelatt 2010; Sayad 2004). Authorized hiring sites created a sense of belonging and inserted some order to the hirings. This case shows how migrants in general, and day laborers in particular, do not participate in the job market as equal participants; rather, they submit to working conditions imposed not only by government officials and legislators, but also by employers and local residents.

Acknowledgments

We presented this research at the 2012 American Sociological Association, Pacific Sociological Association, and Southwestern Sociological Association meetings. We appreciate feedback from Wendy Roth, Van Tran, Hilary Silver, Maria Cristina Morales, Maura Fenelly, Antoaneta Tileva, Jasmine Ali, and Ludy Grandas, among others. We also thank five anonymous reviewers. All errors remain our own.

References

Bonilla-Silva, Eduardo. 2006. *Racism without Racists: Color-Blind Racism and the Persistence of Racial Inequality in the United States*. Lanham, MD: Rowman & Littlefield Publishers.

Brown, Joye. 2010. "Homeless No Longer Welcome in Huntington Station Woods." *Newsday*. Melville, NY.

Castañeda, Ernesto. 2012. "Places of Stigma: Ghettos, Barrios and Banlieues." Pp. 159–90 in *The Ghetto: Contemporary Global Issues and Controversies*, edited by R. Hutchison and B. D. Haynes. Boulder, CO: Westview Press.

Castañeda, Ernesto. 2013. "Living in Limbo: Transnational Households, Remittances and Development." *International Migration* 51(s1):13–35. doi: 10.1111/j.1468-2435.2012.00745.x.

Castañeda, Ernesto and Lesley Buck. 2011. "Remittances, Transnational Parenting, and the Children Left Behind: Economic and Psychological Implications." *The Latin Americanist* 55(4):85–110. doi: 10.1111/j.1557-203X.2011.01136.x.

Chavez, Leo R. 2008. *The Latino Threat: Constructing Immigrants, Citizens, and the Nation*. Stanford, CA: Stanford University Press.

Cleaveland, Carol and Laura Kelly. 2008. "Shared Social Space and Strategies to Find Work: An Exploratory Study of Mexican Day Laborers in Freehold, N.J." *Social Justice* 2008:51–65.

Cleaveland, Carol and Leo Pierson. 2009. "Parking Lots and Police: Undocumented Latinos' Tactics for Finding Day Labor Jobs." *Ethnography* 10(4):515–33. doi: 10.1177/1466138109346987.

De Genova, Nicholas. 2004. "The Legal Production of Mexican/Migrant 'Illegality.'" *Latino Studies* 2004(2):160–85.

Dunn, Timothy J. 2009. *Blockading the Border and Human Rights: The El Paso Operation That Remade Immigration Enforcement*. Austin: University of Texas Press.

Durand, Jorge. 2007. "The Bracero Program (1942–1964) a Critical Appraisal." *Migración y Desarrollo* 9:27–43.

Esbenshade, Jill. 2000. "The 'Crisis' over Day Labor." *Working USA* 3(6):27–70.

Gieryn, Thomas F. 1983. "Boundary-Work and the Demarcation of Science from Non-Science: Strains and Interests in Professional Ideologies of Scientists." *American Sociological Review* 48(1):781–95.

González-López, Gloria. 2006. "Heterosexual Fronteras: Immigrant Mexicanos, Sexual Vulnerabilities, and Survival." *Sexuality Research & Social Policy* 3(3):67–81. doi: 10.1525/srsp.2006.3.3.67.

Holmes, Seth. 2013. *Fresh Fruit, Broken Bodies: Migrant Farmworkers in the United States*. Berkeley, CA: University of California Press.

Lamont, Michèle and Virag Molnar. 2002. "The Study of Boundaries in the Social Sciences." *Annual Review of Sociology* 28:167–95.

Lee, Tiane L. and Susan T. Fiske. 2006. "Not an Outgroup, but Not yet an Ingroup: Immigrants in the Stereotype Content Model." *International Journal of Intercultural Relations* 30:751–68.

Massey, Douglas S., Jorge Durand and Nolan J. Malone. 2002. *Beyond Smoke and Mirrors: Mexican Immigration in an Era of Economic Integration*. New York: Russell Sage Foundation.

Massey, Douglas S. and Julia Gelatt. 2010. "What Happened to the Wages of Mexican Immigrants? Trends and Interpretations." *Latino Studies* 8(3):328–54.

Massey, Douglas S. and Magaly R. Sanchez. 2010. *Brokered Boundaries: Creating Immigrant Identity in Anti-American Times*. New York: Russell Sage Foundation.

Menjívar, Cecilia. 2000. *Fragmented Ties: Salvadoran Immigrant Networks in America*. Berkeley, CA: University of California Press.

Menjívar, Cecilia. 2006. "Liminal Legality: Salvadoran and Guatemalan Immigrants' Lives in the United States." *American Journal of Sociology* 111(4):999–1037.

Merry, Sally. 1981. *Urban Danger: Life in a Neighborhood of Strangers*. Philadelphia, PA: Temple University Press.

Meyer, Jacob and Robert Greenleaf. 2011. "*Enforecement of State Wage and Hour Laws: A Survey of State Regulators*." New York: National State Attorneys General Program, Columbia Law School.

Mitchell, David. 2008. "Hearing on Day Labor Loitering." Retrieved 11-June (www.youtube.com/watch?v=IOVyQN5FyE8).

Morris, Deborah S. 2010a. "Day Laborer Site Shuts Its Doors." *Newsday*.

Morris, Deborah S. 2010b. "Quiet End to Huntington Station Day Laborer Site." *Newsday*.

Morris, Deborah S. 2010c. "Huntington Town Board to Close Day Labor Hiring Site." *Newsday*.

Nevins, Joseph. 2002. *Operation Gatekeeper: The Rise of the "Illegal Alien" and the Making of the U.S.-Mexico Boundary*. New York, NY: Routledge.

Nevins, Joseph. 2010. *Operation Gatekeeper and Beyond: The War on Illegals and the Remaking of the U.S.-Mexico Boundary*. New York: Routledge.

Ngai, Mae M. 2004. *Impossible Subjects: Illegal Aliens and the Making of Modern America*. Princeton, NJ: Princeton University Press.

Núñez, Guillermina Gina and Josiah McC. Heyman. 2007. "Entrapment Processes and Immigrant Communities in a Time of Heightened Border Vigilance." *Human Organization* 66(4):354–65.

Purser, Gretchen. 2009. "The Dignity of Job Seeking Men: Boundary Work among Immigrant Day Laborers." *Journal of Contemporary Ethnography* 25:117–39.

Ross, Catherine E. and Sung J. Jang. 2000. "Neighborhood Disorder, Fear, and Mistrust: The Buffering Role of Social Ties with Neighbors." *American Journal of Community Psychology* 28(4):401–20.

Rumbaut, Rubén G. and Walter A. Ewing. 2007. *The Myth of Immigrant Criminality and the Paradox of Assimilation: Incarceration Rates among Native and Foreign-Born Men*. Washington, DC: Immigration Policy Center, American Immigration Council.

Sayad, Abdelmalek. 2004. *The Suffering of the Immigrant*. Cambridge, UK: Polity Press.

Tilly, Charles. 1998. *Durable Inequality*. Berkeley, CA: University of California Press.

Tilly, Charles. 2005. *Identities, Boundaries, and Social Ties*. Boulder, CO: Paradigm Publishers.

Valenzuela, Abel. 2001. "Day Labourers as Entrepreneurs?" *Journal of Ethnic and Migration Studies* 27(2):335–52.

Valenzuela, Abel. 2003. "Day Labor Work." *Annual Reviews* 29:307–33.

Valenzuela, Abel, Ana L. Gonzalez, Nick Theodore and Edwin Melendez. 2005. *In Pursuit of the American Dream: Day Labor in the Greater Washington D.C. Region Investigation*. Los Angeles, CA: Center for the Study of Urban Poverty, University of California, Los Angeles.

Verea, Mónica 2008. "Contradicciones Entre Las Expresiones Anti-inmigrantes y El Insaciable Apetito Por Contratar Migrantes." Pp. 389–409 in *La Migración Y Los Latinos En Estados Unidos: Visiones Y Conexiones*, edited by E. Levine. Ciudad de Mexico: Universidad Nacional Autónoma de México, Centro de Investigaciones sobre América del Norte.

Zelizer, Viviana A. and Charles Tilly. 2006. "Relations and Categories." Pp. 1–31 in *The Psychology of Learning and Motivation*, Vol. 47. Categories in Use, edited by A. Markman and B. Ross. San Diego, CA: Elsevier.

5

MIGRATION-TRUST NETWORKS

Unveiling the Social Networks of International Migration

Nadia Y. Flores-Yeffal

After applying the concept of trust networks to different types of networks in *Trust and Rule* (Tilly 2005), Charles Tilly applied the concept of trust networks to the field of international migration in his article "Trust Networks in Transnational Migration," where he states, "Trust Networks, then, consist of *ramified interpersonal connections, consisting mainly of strong ties, within which people set valued, consequential, long-term resources and enterprises at risk to the malfeasance, mistakes, or failures of others*" (Tilly 2007:7).

Tilly identified trust networks amongst the subjects in Robert Smith's (2005) book, *Mexican New York*. For example, he observed how Mexican migrants trusted other members of their social networks and sent valuable goods and money to family members at their community of origin via transnational networks. In addition, he described social and political power associated with these trust networks that went beyond personal relationships of trust and reciprocity and also functioned for the collective benefit of the members of the network. For instance, remittances were sent not just by individuals but also by larger groups of migrants who organized at the place of destination and sent relatively large sums of money back to their communities of origin for collective projects such as improving the local infrastructure. This was clear in Smith's data. Furthermore, Tilly observed that these trust networks had political manifestations as he described the extent to which the members of these flows were able to maintain such organization and cohesion in which its members were able to exert even more social, economic, and political power than the local authorities in Mexico (Tilly 2007).

Tilly argued that these trust networks "articulate with larger, longer-lasting networks of social insurance and social control, especially ties among kin and friends at both ends of the migration stream" (2007:12). From his writing, social insurance referred to the security in social exchanges and the social control of specific behavior, which could fulfill the network's specific social, political, and economic goals.

It seems that Tilly, at the time, was mostly worried about the economic and political experiences that were important for the inclusion of groups of people in democratic regimes. However, he never specifically wrote about the ways in which trust networks would have served as an aid to undocumented immigrants in particular during their migratory journey and settlement. In this chapter, I use the concept of Migration-Trust Networks (MTNs), building on Tilly's concept of trust networks, to argue that the networks provide undocumented international migrants with a safe haven that helps them overcome the risks associated with their undocumented status, entry outside official custom posts, and settlement at the place of destination.

These complex migration-trust networks are embedded in relationships of trust whose primary goal is not only to aid in economic transactions but also, and more important, to serve as a social system to overcome the more immediate dangers associated with undocumented immigration, such as the risks of death crossing the border, arrest, loss of a jobs, family separation, and deportation.

Tilly also states, "in the United States, membership in trust networks facilitates immigrants' lives in some regards, but it also tends to confine them to niches created and inhabited by other immigrants. . . . if you live in a constricted network, your contacts confine you to a limited range of opportunities" (2007:15). Indeed, Tilly's (1998) work on durable inequality contributes to the theorizing of Migration-Trust Networks. The main reason these Migration-Trust Networks experience durable inequality is their lack of legal documentation, which would allow them the possibility to detach from the MTNs and gain access to better social and economic opportunities as European immigrants were able to do in the past. In contrast to the majority of Mexican immigrants now, European immigrants at the turn of the nineteenth century were able to gain legal status relatively easy after they arrived in the United States. I will expand on this issue at the end of the chapter.

In this chapter, I summarize the main findings from my book, *Migration-Trust Networks: Social Cohesion in Mexican U.S.-Bound Emigration* (Flores-Yeffal 2013) and also present a few other studies that have helped to move the theory of Migration-Trust Networks forward and expand its functionality beyond the scope of undocumented or unauthorized migratory flows from Mexico to the United States. First, I provide a brief description of the methodology used. Then I introduce the concept of Migration-Trust Networks. Afterwards, I discuss other extensions of Migration-Trust Networks. Finally, I lay out the functionality of MTNs and explain how these MTNs are also subject to durable inequality in the United States.

Methodology and Limitations

My book on Migration-Trust Networks was the result of thirteen years (1997–2010) of quantitative analyses and ethnographic fieldwork conducted by observing and capturing the social dynamics and social networks among the members of four communities of origin in the state of Guanajuato in central Mexico. The communities studied included two rural towns, a medium-size town, and two neighborhoods in a city. I then followed some of the members of these migrant networks to different destinations in the United States. The research was transnational and longitudinal. I did this by keeping in touch with participants throughout the years by visiting them periodically and communicating with them via telephone and social media (see Flores-Yeffal 2013).

It is important to mention some particularities of the historical, geographical, and political context between Mexico and the United States. For example, 5 million Braceros came to the United States legally through the Bracero guest worker program between 1942 and 1964. This provided the opportunity for other Mexicans to have access to social networks with work experience in the United States. Finally, there is also the issue of the massive migration from Mexico to the United States and, in particular, a large undocumented migration flow during the years when the study was taking place (see Massey, Pren and Durand 2016).

U.S. Polices and Unauthorized Immigration

Strict border enforcement measures have been put in place in the recent years, and as a result the undocumented migration flow has changed from a circular pattern in which immigrants settled only in certain parts of the United States in the early 1990s to a more permanent undocumented migration settlement that has spread throughout most of the country (Flores-Yeffal 2013; Massey, Pren and Durand 2016).

In 2014 almost half (49 percent) of the 11.3 million unauthorized immigrants in the United States were from Mexico (Krogstad and Passel 2015). This estimate provides a hint of the extent of the unauthorized status that many Mexican immigrants have been experiencing since 1965, when the Bracero program was no longer in effect. This was also the year when, for the first time, the United States restricted the number of visas from Mexico and the rest of the Western Hemisphere (Flores-Yeffal 2013; Massey, Pren and Durand 2016).

Risks Associated with Unauthorized Immigration

The European migrants who arrived in the eastern United States, as discussed by Tilly (1998), Gans (1962), and many others, had an easier time obtaining legal status in the United States upon arrival after having been inspected at Ellis Island (Foner 2000; Chomsky 2007) than do today's immigrants.

Gans (1962) described how European migrants lived in segregated migrant settlements in the West End in Boston. Later, the Irish were able to leave the West End as another immigrant group arrived. Therefore, European immigrants also relied on chain migration and on fellow migrant networks for assistance with settlement and job seeking and for social support in many other ways (Gans 1962; Tilly 1990, 1998). But most Europeans who arrived at the turn of the twentieth century did not have to live in the shadows without legal documents with the continuous risk of arrest and possible deportation for years and even for entire decades as Mexican and Central American migrants do in contemporary times. I argue that the particularities of the social organization of Migration-Trust Networks from Mexico occurred as a result of migrants' lack of ability to obtain legal documentation to travel, settle, and work and live legally in the United States (Flores-Yeffal 2013).

Undocumented immigrants need a series of trustworthy sources of information and social and economic support in order to migrate without documents, find a job and get hired, and begin a life, learning to live in the shadows in the United States. For example, they need help determining where to cross the border and how to find a smuggler that he or she can trust; not traveling with a trustworthy coyote or smuggler might mean the difference between life and death. However, as argued in the book, more recently, due to increased border enforcement, more and more immigrants have to rely on organized crime to cross the border without legal documents and face higher risk and cost (Flores-Yeffal 2013). Once in the United States, they need to find a job quickly because undocumented migrants not only need money to live, they must also pay the coyote thousands of dollars and send money home. They also need to know what to say to employers so they can be hired without a social security number. They need to know how to rent an apartment without a credit history, how to enroll the children in school, where to go to the doctor, and how to find transportation without having a driver's license (Flores-Yeffal 2013).

Migrants also arrive with literarily nothing as a result of their unauthorized migration journey during which they are forced to leave everything behind. In many instances, they walk for days and carry only gallons of water in their hands. These are just a few of their challenges they confront during their unauthorized journey and settlement and during their undocumented residence in the United States.

Those helping newly arrived undocumented immigrants have to provide a lot of financial resources as well as lodging, food, clothes, transportation, and help to look for a job, so one would expect that the person providing help would be a close family member or someone with a strong tie. Why and under what circumstances do extended family, acquaintances (weak ties), and strangers help strangers in this context? How is social capital manifested? How do social networks of migration develop, function, and expand or disintegrate on the context of transnational migration?

Migration-Trust Networks

Migration-Trust Networks function at the micro as well as at the macro level. Social networks are able to develop person-to-person and within-group relations as well as relationships at a more macro level. So Migration-Trust Networks have the capacity to create new chain migration streams from new sending communities and new receiving communities as well.

At the micro level, I found that there was a series of social elements that enabled migrants to help other migrants without regard to whether the tie was weak or strong. First of all, given the dangers associated with these types of international migration movements, migrants developed a *paisanaje* sentiment, in which two migrants develop a "feeling of belonging to a common community of origin . . . it is a latent dimension of association in the home community" (Massey et al. 1987:142–43). In addition, the two *paisanos* identify with each other because of the similarities of their experiences but only when they find each other at the place of destination (Massey et al. 1987). For example, having experienced deep poverty back at home and the traumatic experience of crossing the border clandestinely, they develop a sense of mutual solidarity. A similar sentiment is the *bounded solidarity* concept proposed by Portes and Sensenbrenner (1993), as it "focuses on those situational circumstances that can lead to the emergence of principled group-oriented behavior quite apart from any early value introjections" (1324). Migrants develop a sentiment of solidarity from the similarities of their experiences back at home and/or at the place of destination, which drives them to want to support each other.

As previously identified by Tilly, the group members develop a set of behavioral expectations and means for social monitoring, which are rigorously enforced by the members of the group. The concept of enforceable trust proposed by Portes and Sensenbrenner (1993) helps to describe this behavior. It refers to a set of social expectations that migrants are expected to meet and that are enforced through social monitoring, which can result in the rejection or punishment of the network members if they do not conform to the agreed-upon values and social behaviors expected by the rest of the members of the group. In addition to the social manifestations of solidarity, cohesion, and social monitoring manifested by network members, migrants also expressed that they helped others due to religious fate and/or religious behavior (Levit 2007; Hagan 2008). The social monitoring on this Migration-Trust Networks happens in the transnational context. Therefore, social expectations for behavior and solidarity relations emerge not just at the place of origin but also at the place of destination, and the behavior of all the members is monitored simultaneously at the transnational level. Trust networks are absolutely necessary given the vulnerability of the members of the network to several types of risks associated with their lack of legal immigration status. A single mistake from one member of the group can place the entire network at jeopardy given that most of them arrive at the same community in order to be able to support each other. Therefore,

> *Migration-Trust Networks are social relationships of support, trust, and sustenance and function simultaneously between place of origin and those at destination. These ties are based on and developed from pre-existing social relationships back home. The members of the network share a collective consciousness, thinking of themselves as part of a group not as individuals. Social support, cohesion and trust are prized and expected among all the network participants. They exchange resources for the international journey, job search, and settlement at the place of destination. Network members carry social expectations for each other and encourage certain behaviors and values to new members. Any act of betrayal places everyone in the social network at risk, especially those who lack legal documentation in the host country. People who do not conform to the expectations of the MTN are usually rejected and/or punished by the other group members.*
>
> (Flores-Yeffal 2013:136–37)

In order for Migration-Trust Networks to develop, pre-migration relationships of trust among a group of people are necessary. Later on, the trust network structure allows for the MTN to have the capacity to attract and absorb new members. Social monitoring and the enforcements of values and norms, as Tilly (2007) also discussed, drive these networks. Unlike other types of clique networks described in the social networks literature, these networks have the capacity to welcome new members to these network cliques (Wasserman and Faust (1994). For example,

> *The network can consist of various types of social ties. Such as kindship, friendship, paisanaje, compadrazgo, cuatismo, coworkers, neighbors, and others. Outsiders can become members of the MTN as long as they follow the social and behavioral expectations of the network and maintain trust with each other. Examples may include migrants from other hometowns, employers, coyotes, labor recruiters, business and /or salespersons, and city officials, among many others who are able to gain the trust of the members of an MTN. These parties help provide a safe haven for themselves and the immigrants.*
>
> (Flores-Yeffal 2013:137)

Undocumented migrants risk their lives crossing through the desert or by hiring an untrustworthy smuggler or coyote. MTN members provide reliable information, such as where to go on the border, whom to ask for, what to say, and what to bring and not to bring when they cross the border in case they get arrested. Their lives are at risk. For this reason, the proper functioning of these Migration-Trust Networks serves as social insurance (Tilly 2007), and life insurance.

The types of help provided and solidarity relations expressed by the members of the MTN can be portrayed in the testimony of a respondent, who answered my question about how many people he had helped:

> "*Lots of people. I've lost count. I've helped them by lending money, paying the coyote fees, sometimes even the coyotes wait until I get my paycheck to pay them their fees.*" *As long he could help, he would. They don't have to be relatives, nor have they to be from the same hometown. They just have to know each other. He doesn't expect anything in return as he keeps having a very good relationship with the people who owe him. The most he lent was a thousand dollars and the least was one dollar.*
>
> (Flores-Yeffal 2013:84)

In addition, I also found that these Migration-Trust Networks develop from different types of social structures depending on the size of the place of origin of the migrant as discussed by Tilly in his work on internal migration in the United States (Tilly and Brown 1967):

> *On the one hand, MTNs develop more readily among rural-origin migrants (from smaller communities) because their society already shares certain commonalities, social homogeneity, cohesiveness, and relationships of trust. In addition, they share a set of social expectations in order to maintain certain values and behaviors. Prospective migrants from rural origins have also developed a collective conscience, and those who do not behave according to the community expectations are subject to rejection or punishment. On the other hand, urban-origin migrants may or may not already belong to a clique-like network or a peer group of people who expect certain social behavior and values. In some cases, migrants from urban communities may not be able to join an MTN as easily as those who migrate from rural areas. Those who lack connection to a peer group before migration may be absorbed by an MTN via the MTN effect, in which orphan migrants are absorbed into the network due to their vulnerability as undocumented migrants and their ability to project and gain trust from at least one of the members of the MTN.*
>
> (Flores-Yeffal 2013:136–37)

The MTNs develop differently depending on the size of the community of origin of the migrants. Rural-origin migrants into an established destination are automatically able to create or be welcomed into a MTN, given the already established social relations from relationships that already existed in the rural setting. On the other hand, urban-origin migrants form MTNs if they were already part of a closed group, such as a soccer team. Otherwise, they must rely on closer ties such as family members to receive the necessary support to migrate, and they will not be able to form a trust network. As a result, the family members will not become part of a MTN or be able to create a new MTN. Urban dwellers who were not part of a MTN were identified in the study when the only people they knew in the United States were family members who offered support to them and when they (the migrant and the family member) were the only ones from their place of origin who lived in that particular destination. The ties with their family members would be more likely to break up because they lacked social monitoring from other members to enforce the solidarity behaviors as happens with the members of the MTNs. When this happens, the urban migrant is most likely transformed into an orphan migrant due to the rupture of the social tie with his or her family member. When this happens, a rural-based Migration-Trust-Network would have the capability and the social structure necessary to absorb the orphan urban migrant. I call this "the MTN effect."

The MTN effect usually occurs when orphan migrants are told by their family members that they will no longer be able to provide them with any more food and lodging, so they must be on their own (even if they do not have the means to become independent). Then the orphan migrants go to their jobs, for example, and tell their coworkers about their situation. If any of these contacts already belong to a rural-based MTN, they invite the orphan migrants to become part of their MTN, producing the MTN effect. The risks and needs associated with undocumented migration are so demanding that even what are considered close ties, such as those between family members, can break if these family members are not part of a MTN. For example, Sofia, who arrived in Chicago, stated:

> *No, we don't know anyone here. We used to live in San Francisco where some of our neighborhood friends lived, but we left because my husband had problems at his job. One of his friends from the neighborhood had recommended him for the job and my husband got to work late all the time, so he got fired. Then his friends from our neighborhood back in Mexico whom had recommended him for the job stop talking to him for that reason. We then moved here to Chicago because my husband found a job on his own as he had heard of another company who needed workers over here, and so he got the phone number and contacted them*

directly. Then my husband got in trouble at his job selling drugs, and so now he is in jail. I don't want nobody to find out back at home because I feel very ashamed.

(Flores-Yeffal 2013:60)

Sofia's husband was rejected from the MTN because he did not meet the expectations for a work ethic at his job, placing in jeopardy the reputation of the entire MTN. Later on, Sofia was all by herself and had no MTN support because she was trying to hide that her husband was in jail.

The types of ties vary depending on the age of the migratory flow. Flores-Yeffal and Aysa-Lastra (2011) found from analyzing the data from the Mexican Migration Project that *paisano* (or countryman) ties tend to be the ties present during the early stages of a MTN migratory flow. When a migration chain begins, there may not be many family members available to provide support to other migrants, as not everyone has a family member abroad yet. It is not until the MTN has aged that there are more family members available to help future migrants. Indeed, the MTNs have the capacity to convert weak ties into strong ties. It is through this process that unknown *paisanos* are able to provide much of the necessary support for the migrant newcomers to migrate, settle, and live in the shadows at the place of destination.

Migration-Trust Networks have the capacity to develop collective efficacy among its members. Robert Sampson (2006) has identified the concept of collective efficacy while trying to explain "how tight-knit urban neighborhoods produce safety because of the rich supply of social networks" (150). It functions as a problem-solving social mechanism in which cohesion and shared expectations of social control are taking place. Via this collective efficacy mechanism, Migration-Trust Networks are able to provide the necessary social conditions to serve as a safe haven so that the members of the network can trust that no members will fail to behave and that they will do everything they can to provide all the necessary information and economic, social, moral, and psychological support to other members and also will behave according to the social expectations of the MTN which requires cohesion, trust, collective consciousness, very high levels of solidarity, and so on. It is under such conditions that the economic exchanges that Smith (2005) documented and that Tilly (2007) identified as trust networks were able to function to provide trustworthy economic transactions involving individual and collective remittances in the transnational context.

Furthermore, relations of reciprocity do not drive Migration-Trust Networks as one would expect. Instead, I was able to document that migrants helped future migrants and were not able to return the favors to those who had helped them in the first place. I call this "risk-pooling behavior"—*Hoy por mí, mañana por ti* (Today for myself, and tomorrow for you):

> Martin, who migrated from a medium-sized town and was interviewed in a small town in Indiana, was sharing a house with six other migrants who were neither related to him by kin nor by friendship; he met them shortly after arriving to the United States. He said: When I got here I was surprised because a guy (*un vato*) who lived in this house and who I'd never met before told me, "let's go to Wal-Mart." When we got there he told me to get a cart, and when we got to the pants section he said, "What is your size?" I said, "I don't know, 32 in Mexico, here I don't know." He looked at me closely and grabbed a pair of pants. Then he asked me, "What size underwear do you wear?" Then he asked me about socks and he also asked me if I needed a jacket; and he even got me a jacket (*Y hasta una chamarrita me compró*). That impressed me a lot and I felt very good about it. I did the same thing for others who arrived later on. I took them to Wal-Mart like they did to me when I arrived. I did not return the favor directly, but I returned it by helping others like I was once helped.
> (Flores-Yeffal 2013:67)

The reason migrants who belong to the MTNs pay their favors forward instead of paying them back is because those who provide help are usually more established migrants, so they no longer need the help, whereas the newcomers do. This is how the MTNs are able to expand and provide the necessary trust and social support and collective efficacy to future migrants—by paying the favors forward through this risk-pooling behavior practiced by the network members.

Tilly (2007) also identified that the context of reception becomes important for the functionality of the MTNs. The social, political, and economic context of reception dictates whether the MTN is going to be able to function and continue to expand at a particular migrant destination or whether it will have to be transplanted to another migrant destination. In terms of essential resources that should be available in a context of reception for the proper functionality of the MTN, I found that the availability of jobs or labor for the members of a MTN is the most important condition if the MTN is to maintain its functionality at that specific place of destination. When jobs become scarce, the MTN will have to be transplanted to another location. The transplantation of a MTN depends on at least one relationship of trust between one member of that MTN and a member of another existing MTN. This is to say, it takes only one trusted person for everyone else in that MTN to also be trusted (and so the entire MTN can be transplanted or merged into another MTN) as the social-behavioral expectations, trust, and solidarity behavior of one person are echoed in the social-behavioral expectations of the entire MTN network. For the transplantation of the network, it takes only one of the members to build a relationship of trust with the member of another MTN. This means that the trust relations embedded within these networks of migration will also help the network members be absorbed by distant Migration-Trust Networks, even those from different communities of origin and at different destinations.

I also explain in my book how these MTNs expand at the macro level as a result of collective remittances. The MTNs utilize exogenous ties (family or other trust relations with members of nearby communities) to connect their networks to other MTNs. Again, it requires only one trusting relationship between one member of the MTN and a member of another MTN to connect the members of two different communities of origin.

> *Migration-Trust Networks are embedded in extremely complex micro and macro social and economic forces that function in the transnational context. Many of these social forces just described act simultaneously. The most important factors that propagate MTNs are the relationships of trust among members, as well as the demand for cheap labor at the place of destination, which serve as magnets for the network to expand. . . . MTNs are driven mainly by relationships of social trust and support due to a series of social, behavioral, and cultural conditions. These conditions occur because of the difficulties and dangers associated with the journey from Mexico to the United States.*
>
> (Flores-Yeffal 2013:153)

Therefore, it is partly relationships of trust and sustenance, social cohesion and social solidarity, religious behavior, the *paisanaje* sentiment, bounded solidarity, and enforceable trust relations among the MTN members that enhance social monitoring and develop certain behavioral expectations among the members of the network. It is also the ability of these complex social networks to absorb new members through the transformation of weak ties into strong ties and to produce chains of risk-pooling behavior, to reproduce their ability to exchange reliable information, and to produce the collective efficacy necessary to provide a safe haven for vulnerable members of these migrant networks. All these relationships exist in the transnational context as migrants are able to monitor the social behavior of those who are abroad and at the place of origin via letters, phone calls, social media communication, and so on. This social organization is advantageous to MTN members when they send individual and collective remittances and engage in other social, economic, and political acts that benefit the interests of the entire network and/or the entire transnational community, as identified by Tilly (2007) in which he analyzed the data in the award-winning book *Mexican New York* by Robert Smith (2005).

More research needs to be done to identify the extent to which the social processes observed in the Migration-Trust Networks of migrants from Guanajuato, Mexico, apply to other migration scenarios, circumstances, or flows. For example, Tilly (1990) argued that immigrants suffer from exploitation and also tend to exploit each other. Also, research is needed to explore whether MTNs are similar or different for immigrant enterprises (i.e., Light 1980).

Since I proposed the theory of Migration-Trust Networks in 2013, Orozco (2014) analyzed the Mexican Migration Project data and found additional empirical evidence for rural and urban differences regarding the development of MNTs. In addition, at least two studies have tried to challenge and/or apply the proposed theoretical frame of Migration-Trust Networks to other types of migratory flows. For example, Raphi Rechitsky identified the applicability of the concepts of trust networks (Tilly 2007) and the Migration-Trust Networks framework proposed here to the social networks of refugees from Afghanistan, Ethiopia, Iran, and Palestine in Ukraine. He finds that refugees indeed rely on migration trust networks and concludes, "trust networks may either facilitate the onward mobility of refugees away from transit zones or facilitate settlement in these locations" (Rechitsky 2014:611).

Mario Chavez also applied the concept of Migration-Trust Networks to his M.A. thesis, titled "At the Intersection of Deferred Action for Childhood Arrivals, the Migration Trust Network and Labor." He tested "the effects of the MTN on the labor acquisition of immigrants when they are transferred from an undocumented legal status to the state of liminal legality that is DACA" (2015:43). Chavez summarizes his findings as follows:

> *In sum, migrant trust networks remain important for DACA recipients . . . though in a more indirect and macro-level way than described by Flores-Yeffal (2013). In particular, DACA recipients relied [on] the collective efficacy embedded within the community to facilitate their job search. Additionally, migrant trust networks function differently according to the DACA recipients' level of education, but to fully benefit from the advantages associated with high levels of education recipients must have access to the migrant trust network.*
>
> (2015:46)

He finds that DACA recipients in two Texas sites utilized their MTNs to find jobs by accessing the safe employment spaces that they trusted in their neighborhood in which the MTN operated. In particular, their membership in the MTN allowed them to find jobs with lower wages if they had less than a Bachelor's degree or jobs with higher wages if they had a Bachelor's degree or higher.

There have been other applications of the theorized dynamics that are manifested by Migration-Trust Networks of international migration proposed here. These applications have been in the area of refugee studies and/or forced migration and also among immigrants with temporary legal status. These migrants are vulnerable and rely heavily on other network members to continue to subsist.

Advantages and Disadvantages of Migration-Trust Networks

While the collective efficacy created by these Migration-Trust Networks may bring benefits to the network members that allow them to migrate, settle, and live in the United States and avoid arrest and deportation and family separation, it also helps them to find jobs and send individual and/or collective remittances back home to help their loved ones. Via collective remittances, the MTN modestly helps to improve the living conditions of the community back home by supporting the construction of a sewage system, or providing electricity, or building a church or a school. As Sampson (2006) may suggest, this collective efficacy helps the members of the MTN to maintain very low levels of crime in their communities and provides a safe haven in many ways. MTNs are able to produce risk-pooling behavior, very high levels of solidarity, and even are able to convert weak ties into strong ties and absorb new members and expand.

One should consider how such characteristics and high levels of trust and loyalty among network members can serve as an engine to inject important information into these networks. This is important because now I move to the application of Tilly's (1998) concept of durable inequality to the MTNs. One of the survival strategies embedded in these MTNs consists mainly of practicing self-segregation as the network members settle in daughter communities (door to door) in order to be able to exchange their relations of support and practice their solidarity and cohesive behavior. This leads to their constraining themselves to live isolated from the broader society in several ways, as Tilly (2007) expressed when he proposed the application of trust networks to migration transnational networks.

Yes, these migrants might be able to interact with a diverse group of people from other races and ethnicities, but this does not mean they are necessarily integrating themselves into a larger society. Such apparent social exchanges may suggest that these contacts exist to diversify the MTN members' network. Interestingly, according to the empirical evidence, those apparent outsiders are actually members of these MTNs.

Active nonmigrant stranger MTN participants: *A nonmigrant stranger—such as an employer, a coyote, a businessperson who serves*

> *the members of the MTN, an educator, a local authority, among others— may be welcomed as a participant of the MTN as it depends on their participation to function. For example, it needs employers who will hire undocumented immigrants. In fact, many of these employers are active recruiters themselves. As (Krissman 2005; Garcia 2005) described in their studies, the employers in many cases identify the effective functionality of the MTNs and the good work ethic of its participants and decide to utilize the MTN to recruit more workers. While the employers need the cheap labor, the members of the MTN also need jobs for prospective and/ or returning migrants. Once members of the MTN trust an employer, then the employer becomes a member of the MTN.*
>
> (Flores-Yeffal 2013:104)

Other active nonimmigrant strangers who are members of the MTN include the Asian corner store owner who cashes the checks of migrants who lack an ID and apartment managers or landlords who rent apartments to members of the MTNs without checking their credit or without asking for a social security number.

> *These apartment managers allow immigrants to have extra people living in their homes temporarily, as they begin to understand how the MTN operates. Once the migrant staying in the living room is able, he or she will then rent another apartment unit from the same landlord. The landlord and apartment managers observe the good behavior and ethics of the MTN members and come to trust that they will pay their rent on time and take care of the apartment units even if they live under more crowded conditions.*
>
> (Flores-Yeffal 2013:105)

Therefore, those who one may consider outsiders are also exchanging trust relations with the MTN network participants and are able to cooperate in some way with them. These are relationships of trust as each side benefits economically and socially.

The social structure in which these MTNs are embedded then becomes isolated in terms of housing, types of jobs the MTN members have access to, or even the types of people they can access when they shop and cash their checks. Many migrants do not learn English or sufficiently learn the laws and culture of the new country. They may also lack access to information about important resources that could potentially help them improve their health and other social and economic conditions.

European immigrant groups were able to leave their immigrant enclaves or daughter communities and move to the suburbs and later experience upward mobility after decades and, at some point, even completely assimilate into the mainstream American culture. In contrast, the undocumented immigrants today are more or less trapped living in these MTNs. Undocumented immigrants cannot even visit Mexico because of very strict border enforcement (Massey, Pren and Durand 2016). They would have to risk their lives again if they were to try to return to the United States. Even if some of the members of the MTN have legal documentation or U.S. citizenship, it takes only one undocumented person in the family for the entire family to be vulnerable to the risks associated with unauthorized status. For example, Chavez (2015) examined the case of DACA recipients and observed that even with limited legality (which is a temporary legal status), DACA recipients have to still rely on their MTNs to find jobs, but those jobs are minimum-wage jobs unless the DACA recipients have very high levels of education. Without a path for legalization, it seems that the members of Migration-Trust Networks will continue to face durable inequality for decades to come (Tilly 1998), although some studies have demonstrated that the children of Mexican Americans are able to do much better than their parents (e.g., Telles and Ortiz 2008). Future research should examine what the multigenerational consequences of this type of durable inequality might be, specifically what it means for the children of immigrants who continue to be members of these MTNs. Future research should also examine what maintaining this durable inequality among undocumented immigrants would mean for the future of the United States.

References

Chavez, Mario. J. (2015). *At the Intersection of Deferred Action for Childhood Arrivals, the Migration Trust Network and Labor*. Master's Thesis. Department of Sociology. The University of Texas at El Paso.

Chomsky, Aviva. (2007). *"They Take Our Jobs!" And 20 Other Myths about Immigration*. Boston: Beacon Press.

Flores-Yeffal, Nadia Y. (2013). *Migration-Trust Networks: Social Cohesion in Mexican U.S. Bound Emigration*. College Station, TX: Texas A&M University Press.

Flores-Yeffal, Nadia Y. and Maria Aysa-Lastra. (2011). "Place of Origin, Types of Ties, and Support Networks in Mexico-US Migration." *Rural Sociology*, 25(3):1–30.

Foner, Nancy. (2000). *From Ellis Island to JFK: New York's Two Great Waves of Immigration*. New Haven, CT: Yale University Press.

Gans, Herbert. (1962). *The Urban Villagers*. New York: The Free Press of Glencoe.

Garcia, Carlos. (2005). "Buscando Trabajo: Social Networking among Immigrants from Mexico to the United States." *Hispanic Journal of Behavioral Sciences*, 27(1):3–22.

Hagan, Jaqueline. (2008). *Migration Miracle: Faith, Hope: And Meaning on the Undocumented Journey*. Cambridge, MA: Harvard University Press.

Krogstad, Jens Manuel, and Jeffrey S. Passel. "5 Facts about Illegal Immigration in the US." Pew Research Center 19 (2015).

Levit, Peggy. (2007). *God Needs No Passport: How Immigrants Are Changing the American Religious Landscape*. New York: The New Press.

Light, Ivan. (1980). "Asian Enterprise in America: Chinese, Japanese, and Koreans in Small Business." In *Self-Help in Urban America: Patterns of Minority Business Enterprise*, edited by Scott Cummings, 33–57. New York: National University Publications, Kennikat Press.

Krissman, Fred. (2005). "Sin Coyote ni Patron: Why the 'Migrant Network' Fails to Explain International Migration." *International Migration Review*, 39(1):4–44.

Krogstad, Jens Manuel and Jeffrey S. Passel. (2015). "5 facts about illegal immigration in the U.S." The Pew Hispanic Center. November 19, 2015. Retrieved on 09–11–16 from URL: www.pewresearch.org/fact-tank/2015/11/19/5-facts-about-illegal-immigration-in-the-u-s/

Massey, Douglas S., Rafael Alarcon, Jorge Durand and Humberto Gonzalez. (1987). *Return to Aztlan: The Social Process of International Migration from Western Mexico*. Berkeley: University of California Press.

Massey, Douglas S., Karen A. Pren and Jorge Durand. (2016). "Why Border Enforcement Backfired 1." *American Journal of Sociology*, 121(5):1557–1600.

Orozco, Guillermo A. P. (2014). *Immigrant Selectivity from Rural and Urban Areas of Mexicoto the United States: The Different Roles of Migrant Networks*. Doctoral dissertation. Department of Sociology. Columbus, OH: The Ohio State University.

Portes, Alejandro and Julia Sensenbrenner. (1993). "Embeddedness and Immigration: Notes on the Social Determinants of Economic Action." *American Journal of Sociology*, 98(6):1320–50.

Rechitsky, Raphi. (2014). "Trust Networks, Human Security, The Determinants of Migration Decisions: The Case of Global Refugees in Ukraine." *Zhurnal Issledovanii Sotsialnoi Politiki: The Journal of Social Policy Studies*, 12(4):599–612.

Sampson, Robert. (2006). "Collective Efficacy Theory: Lessons Learned and Directions for Future Inquiry." In *Taking Stock: The Status of Criminological Theory, Advances in Criminological Theory*, vol. 15, edited by Francis T. Cullen, John Paul Wright, and Kristie Blevins, 149–67. Piscataway, NJ: Transaction Publishers.

Smith, Robert. (2005). *Mexican New York: Transnational Lives of New Immigrants*. Berkeley: University of California Press.

Telles, Edward M. and Vilma Ortiz. (2008). *Generations of Exclusion: Mexican-Americans, Assimilation, and Race*. New York: Russell Sage Foundation.

Tilly, Charles. (1968). "Race and Migration to the American City." In *The Metropolitan Enigma: Inquiries into the Nature and Dimensions of America's Urban Crisis*, edited by Wilson JQ, 135–157. Cambridge, MA: Harvard University Press.

Tilly, Charles. (1990). "Transplanted Networks." In *Immigration Reconsidered. History, Sociology, and Politics*, edited by Virginia Yans-McLaughlin, 79–95. New York: Oxford University Press.

Tilly, Charles. (1998). *Durable Inequality*. Berkeley: University of California Press.

Tilly, Charles. (2005). *Trust and Rule*. New York: Cambridge University Press.

Tilly, Charles. (2007). "Trust Networks in Transnational Migration." *Sociological Forum*, 22(1):3–24.

Tilly, Charles and Harold C. Brown. (1967). "On Uprooting, Kinship, and the Auspices of Migration." *International Journal of Comparative Sociology*, 8: 139–164.

Wasserman, Stanley and Faust, Katherine. (1994). *Social Network Analysis: Methods and Applications*. New York: Cambridge University Press.

6

ETHNIC WEDDINGS

Reinventing the Nation in Exile

Randa Serhan

It is Sunday evening, and the sun is slowly setting.[1] A few men in front of a home are chanting, singing, and flying a Palestinian flag. Between them, several older women dressed in *thobes,* intricately embroidered traditional Palestinian dresses, intercept the chants with their own ululations and good wishes. Facing them on the front porch is another group of younger women who clap, sway to the rhythm of the chants, and occasionally repeat the words of the older women. The groom remains the center of all this attention for about a half hour before the wedding procession moves on to the bride's home. Palestinian flags fly high in the streets as the groom's family makes its way to the bride's paternal home. Once there, the scene repeats until the bride joins her groom.

As I stand with the women, I am transported to what I imagine the West Bank to be like. My absorption is interrupted when a car drives by blasting reggaeton music or when neighbors come out in their sweats to watch in amazement and remind me that we are in New Jersey.[2] Not only is this New Jersey, but I may be the only person in the wedding who is not an American citizen. I am a Palestinian refugee born in Lebanon and raised in Kuwait, thus an outsider for this community. Most of the younger people around me were born in New Jersey or New York, have gone to public or Catholic schools locally, and are parents of the third generation of Palestinian immigrants to the United States.[3]

Is this ethnic community holding on to its pre-migration customs? Does the second generation value these customs, or is it appeasing the parents? Are these rituals an expression of "symbolic ethnicity"[4] with little effect on their daily lives? This line of questioning is suspended once we enter the wedding hall. The women congregate at the entrance in a circle, chanting about the beauty of the bride and the morals of the groom. They chant, with a single handheld drum being played by one of the women, for forty-five minutes, until all the guests are seated and the bride and groom are ready to make their entrance. All the women in the circle are dressed in *thobes* and *chitchas* (velvet caps covered with gold coins). The older and wealthier the woman, the more gold coins. Single women do not own *chitchas* since they are presented to a woman on her wedding night. Related men join in to serenade the couple before giving the stage to the wedding singer. The couple walks slowly toward the center back of the hall, where they sit on two white armchairs side by side. These chairs have bulky white patterned satin upholstery with golden armrests and legs reminiscent of Louis XIV furniture. The bride and groom are continuously beckoned to the dance floor.

The rituals are highly formalized. A family member takes control of the microphone and orchestrates the evening, but the guests essentially know what to do. Community members are inflexible about the different aspects of the weddings. At the beginning of my research in 2001, there was criticism circulating about a young woman who had moved the armchairs from the center to the corner of the hall. People were appalled, questioning who she thought she was to change tradition.

Eric Hobsbawm would explain the preoccupation with such details as part of the community's engagement in "inventing tradition." He defines "invented tradition" as the "set of practices, normally governed by overtly or tacitly accepted rules of a ritual or symbolic nature, which seek to inculcate certain values and norms of behavior by repetition, which automatically implies continuity with the past" (Hobsbawm 1983). These symbols are all the more effective when they have no practical purposes, such as the position of two armchairs at a wedding.

The specific past this community is trying to connect with and preserve is that of *falaheen* (Arabic for peasants). Community members often refer to themselves and each other as *falaheen*. In Arabic, *falaheen* is often used pejoratively, but in this community, the term is most often uttered with pride. *Falahi* (peasantry) is understood by them as a dialect, a traditional way of life, and a state of mind. When asked to elaborate, both young and old respond that these dialects, practices, and traditions are Palestinian. Farming and tending to live stock are ironically absent from these definitions of peasant lifestyle. The absence is a deliberate omission justified by the fact none of them farms in the United States. Thus, a selective celebration of the past is being reclaimed without a real nostalgia for returning to a simpler mode of livelihood and an agricultural lifestyle.

These weddings may seem like folkloric curiosities, yet they raise important theoretical questions about the social organization and politics of exile, diaspora, and emigration. How do generations born in a new country attach themselves to such self-representations? How does a distant set of conflicts become part of a community's self-representations? Hobsbawm and Ranger's "invention of tradition" helps specify these questions but does not supply the answers. In order to get beyond the fact of invention, we must draw on two other lines of analysis. One deals with ethnic nationalism. Palestinian-American self-representations belong to a much larger class of beliefs and practices that dramatize the relationship between a people. The second line deals with trust networks, the organization of significant portions of social life around sets of binding relations by means of which people carry on valued, enduring collective activities (Tilly 2005). Conceiving of Palestinian-American communities as overlapping trust networks clarifies both how they maintain their commitment to an unrealized Palestine and how they pass on that commitment from one generation to the next.

Studying wedding rituals shows the extent to which Palestinian-American collective-life pivots on the ethnic identity of particular trust networks. They are *falaheen* in the clothes they adorn and in the songs and chants selected for the weddings. The significance of the music can be gleaned from the prominence given to the wedding band (Massad 2005), which is located on a high stage overlooking the dance floor (akin to a concert). It is as visible as the bride and groom if not more so.

The wedding singer starts singing a fusion of traditional Palestinian wedding songs, Palestinian resistance songs, and recent popular Arabic songs. Regardless of the origin of these songs, they are adapted to the names of the bride and groom, their families, and the villages of their parents' origin. He sings in Arabic with a distinctly village dialect at times. The imagery in the Palestinian wedding songs is of fields, orange groves, fig trees, olive trees, valleys, hilltops, or the longing for the land. In one common *zaffa* (serenade) for the groom, the singer asks the groom's mother if she knows where her son "decorated"/prepared himself. The response given is at his maternal uncle's house, with the relevant village name included. The chorus repeatedly asks the orange, olive, and fig trees to dance for the handsome young groom. The bride's *zaffa* is more direct, requesting that she come from the groom's land of Palestine. The listeners are told that the most beautiful women come from Palestine and that they bear Palestinian children in a direct production of group identity and cohesion.

In other songs, the longing for the homeland and the bride are conflated. Time, place, and space are collapsed in these songs, and no one pays attention to the fact that the groom got dressed in a suburban home where the only visible plants are those in flowerpots or the small patches of grass. Finally, some songs are overtly political. These are performed during the men's *debcha*.[5] One of the more popular *debcha* songs is titled, "We Are Not Terrorists." The lyrics speak about political history:

> We are not terrorists
> We are the people of freedom
> Muslims and Christians, our civilization is Arab
>
> They struck us with rockets
> We struck them with rocks
> They stole the Aqsa mosque
> They stole the history
>
> And they call us terrorists
> They preoccupied us with wars
> They divided and scattered around in societies and societies
>
> The land of Palestine will maintain its Arab identity
> We want to liberate Palestine
> Palestine is Arab[6]

Another song was popularized after a summer of escalated violence in the West Bank, Gaza, and Lebanon. Titled "Hawk of the Arabs," it also speaks of strife and struggle:

> Stirring, Arab blood is stirring
> And the effort is Arab[7]
> No matter how many rockets you fire
> The proud people will not budge
>
> Scream out loud
> We are a people who are accustomed to death
> We do not want wealth or precious gems
> We want to live in freedom
>
> Blood begets blood
> You will get nothing but grief

At one wedding, this song was sung six times, and at another I attended it was sung twice but in an extended version. As I watched the men dance the *debcha* vigorously to this song, I noticed that many of the guests were mouthing the lyrics. There is a perceptible link between the politics in the West Bank and neighboring areas and the wedding songs. As a Tillyian relational understanding would predict, the more violence there is over there, the more frequently nationalist/resistance songs are sung here.

The idealization of a pastoral past is certainly not an invention of this community, for it has been an integral component of the Western model of nationalism since its inception (Anderson 1983; Calhoun 1993; Calhoun 1997; Chatterjee 1983). The peasant as the cultivator of the land is directly tied to it. Certain plants also came to represent that land. For Palestinians these are the olive tree, figs, oranges, and thyme (Said and Mohr 1986; Schulz and Hammer 2003). Even the conflation of woman with land stems from nationalist discourse whereby the nation is referred to as the motherland or the homeland (Anderson 1983; Anthias and Yuval-Davis 1995). Yet, this mythical peaceful past is rudely juxtaposed with songs about violence, the fragmentation of a people, and resistance. Reality intercepts this community's life even at the level of imagining. If one were to read it like a text, then the tale would be of a beautiful past that has been interrupted by violence and exile and that can be reclaimed through struggle.

The Western model of nation-ness comes full circle when other aspects of the wedding are taken into account: the Palestinian scarf[8] and flag, and the colors within it (black, white, red, and green). These artifacts are ever present in the wedding. The flag, scarves, *kufiya*-covered rods and cardboard swords, and flag-colored *masabih* (string of beads) are variously used by men and women while dancing. The most systemic use is during the *debcha*, when every man is handed a scarf to wear around his neck and the flag is carried at the head of the line. Weddings are another venue for national expression despite the recent history of strife, fragmentation, and exile.

Historical Background of the Migrant-Sending Communities

Reading Palestinian history, one finds that Palestinians have had little to celebrate since the turn of the past century (Khalidi 1997, 1998; Morris 2004; Sayigh 1977; Turki 1974). At a time when most former European colonies were struggling for or had achieved their independence, Palestinians were struggling to stay put. In 1948, the Zionist movement prevailed and the state of Israel was created on a large part of the land that was once Mandate Palestine (Farsoun and Zacharia 1997; Khalidi 1997; Pappé 2004; Said and Mohr 1986). To the Zionists, 1948 was the year they fought and won their independence, while for the Palestinians it was the year of the Nakba (catastrophe) (Khalidi 2006; Morris 2004; Sayigh 1977).

The word *nakba* foreshadowed the mood of Palestinians for decades to come, as 750,000 Palestinians became refugees in Lebanon, Jordan, and Syria. Most of these refugees eventually ended up in camps and received rations from the international community (Abu-Lughod 1988; Farsoun and Zacharia, 1997; Schulz and Hammer, 2003). Displacement, loss of livelihood and land, and the effort to sustain families in deplorable conditions left little room for much else (Sayigh 1978; Sirhan 1975). Considering the harsh realities of their lives in exile, it is not difficult to imagine that many refused to celebrate or sing in order to mourn their loss.[9] This mood was reinforced and prolonged by the numerous conflicts Palestinians encountered in the Arab countries where they relocated.[10] The Nakba affected even those Palestinians who remained on their land outside the newly formed Israel, because they temporarily came under Jordanian rule and Egyptian administration after the Armistice Agreement (Massad 2001; Peretz 1996). The territory under Jordanian rule was renamed the West Bank and that under Egyptian administration came to be known as Gaza. In 1967, at the end of what the world came to know as the Six-Day War and Palestinians called the Naksa (setback), Israel occupied the West Bank and Gaza (BADIL 2004).[11]

In 1965, al-Assifa, the military wing of Fateh (the Palestinian National Liberation Movement) was formed by a group of Palestinian activists who believed that armed struggle was the way to regain what Palestinians had lost (Farsoun and Zacharia, 1997). Fateh grew into a popular-based militia after the 1967 Occupation, galvanizing the Palestinians and serving as a model for additional political factions (Khalidi 2006; Sayigh 1977; Sirhan 1975). Part of the reason for this movement was to resist the resignation and hopelessness that had set in since 1948. According to Rashid Khalidi (1997), the movement signaled the reemergence of a Palestinian national identity that had been subverted by the Nakba. While the political factions reinstated pride and resistance in Palestinians, this did not translate into any occasion for collective rejoicing (Khalili 2005; Smith 1986). Palestinians in the West Bank had been organizing politically in the West Bank since the early 1960s but appeared as a concrete challenge to Israel only with the eruption of the 1987 Intifada, or uprising (Sosebee 1990; Swedenburg 1990). For the first time, the world saw Palestinian women and children taking to the streets, throwing rocks, and confronting Israeli soldiers (Gluck 1995; Hilterman 1991; Roy 1990; Strum 1992; Usher 1992). The signing of the Oslo Accords in 1993 and the establishment of the Palestinian Authority raised some hopes (Brynen 1997; Shlaim 1994). However, these hopes dwindled quickly as conditions spiraled into additional conflicts until the second Intifada broke out in 2000. Six years on, the al-Aqsa Intifada continued more brutally and costly than the previous one (Brynen 1997; Shlaim 1994).

Accordingly, Palestinians have largely presented themselves or been presented by others in terms of the Nakba (1948), the Naksa (1967), mourning, martyrdom, suicide bombers, freedom fighters, and terrorists or as a burden or as being burdened (Inbari 1996; Kimhi 2004; Peteet 1994; Sayigh 1993; Sobel 1977; Turki 1972;Turki 1976). When Palestinians do come together, it is to commemorate the Nakba, fallen heroes, and national figures and, I would add, to fund-raise for emergency aid to the destitute in the refugee camps and under occupation (BADIL 2004; Khalili 2005; Peteet 1994).

Even the wedding became a field of struggle. Post-1948 Palestinian poetry largely emerged from Israel, where censors were vigilant. In response, poets transformed the weddings between man and woman to that between man and land/Palestine (Ashrawi 1978; Elmessiri 1982; Layoun 1999; Turki 1976). Perhaps the most cited poem in this genre is Mahmoud Darwish's "Blessed Be That Which Has Not Come!" In the first stanza the poet writes:

> This is the wedding without an end,
> In a boundless courtyard,
> On an endless night
> This is the Palestinian wedding:
> Never will lover reach lover
> Except as martyr or fugitive
> (Elmessiri 1982; Layoun 1999)

It is clear from these few lines that the Palestinian wedding is used as a euphemism for the Palestinian strife. The union is desired yet unfulfilled or is impossible on this earth (Ashrawi 1978; Elmessiri 1982).

Although censorship has ebbed, artists still use the Palestinian wedding as a medium to discuss Palestinian hardships. The two most renowned and analyzed films on this topic are appropriately titled *Wedding in Galilee* and *Rana's Wedding: Jerusalem, Another Day* (Abu-Assad 2002; Khleifi 1987). *Wedding in Galilee* depicts the hardships and humiliation Palestinians in Israel endure in order to celebrate a wedding. The film starts out with the father of the bride trying to get a permit from the Israeli Defense Forces (IDF) for the festivities in their village. The encounter visibly takes its toll on the father, and the permit is granted only on the condition that the IDF soldiers be allowed to attend. Despite the agreement, it remains unclear throughout the film if the wedding will take place. In an ironic twist at the end when the couple is finally in the wedding chambers, the groom becomes impotent and the bride has to deflower herself to preserve their families' honor. The impotence, which largely stems from the presence of Israeli soldiers at the wedding, is not the groom's alone, for it signifies Palestinians' inability to resist the Israeli powers and to protect their most private relationships. The viewer is left with the message that in spite of all the resistance and struggle, the Palestinian wedding can never be consummated.

Rana's Wedding follows a young woman's search for her boyfriend, whom she wants to marry to avoid moving to Egypt. At every turn, the unpredictability and hardships of everyday Palestinian lives and love under occupation are illuminated. The film ends at an Israeli checkpoint where the couple gets married under the watchful eyes of Israeli soldiers. The couple is happy, but the viewer is left with the sense that a Palestinian union is marred by difficulties and an uncertain future.

Thus, many aspects of Palestinian life have come to be understood only in terms of disappointment and conflict. Violence and conflict are endemic in modern Palestinian history. The Palestinian community in the New York metropolitan area grew out of a cluster of villages in the West Bank that began their exile in the United States after the 1967 Israeli occupation.[12] The first generation was raised in the aftermath of the Nakba, making them acutely aware of the constraints 1948 refugees were living under. Coming from the West Bank also meant that they witnessed Fateh's armed response to the occupation of their villages. As the Naksa (1967) generation, their transition to life in the United States occurred at a time when public opinion and foreign policy were unequivocally aligned with Israel (Abraham and Abraham 1981; Hagopian 1976; Shaheen 1984; Stockton 1994; Suleiman 1994). Some American Palestinians responded by forming associations to "create understanding" about the Palestinian cause, but most of these activists were second generation or beyond.[13] In other words, these individuals were established American citizens who were 1948 Palestinian exiles or from earlier migrations not from the West Bank.

Most of the West Bank newcomers did not exhibit any overt political activity and have been described as having little connection to their new home. In 1985, Ronald Stockton found that Palestinians in Detroit felt like exiles and acted accordingly (Stockton 1985). In 1988, Louise Cainkar came to a similar conclusion on the basis of a qualitative study of Palestinian women in Chicago (Cainkar 1988). She asserted that "Palestinians feel like involuntary emigrants. . . . For although their bodies are here, their minds and spirits are in Palestine" (Cainkar 1988:18). The various Palestinian factions found in the Middle East established U.S. branches such as the General Union of Palestinian Women, the General Union of Palestinian Students, the Palestinian Front for the Liberation of Palestine, and the Democratic Front for the Liberation of Palestine. As such, their personal histories were greatly intertwined with the resistance movement, the rise of the Palestinian question on an American and world stage, and the newly appropriated symbols of Palestine (the artifacts prevalent at weddings). It would be simple enough to presume the weddings in their present form are a creation of the first generation, which was indoctrinated by the political leaders in power upon their exile, namely the Palestinian Liberation Organization (PLO).

Undoubtedly, the PLO did impact Palestinian people's imaginations and self-perceptions. It even promulgated the notion of the demographic struggle and the fertile mother who would birth the nation by bearing Palestinian sons/freedom fighters, yet it hardly intended for the manifestation of this Palestinian wedding (Abu-Duhou 2003).[14] From a purely political perspective, these weddings relegate the sought-after activism to the realm of the symbolic (similar to what the poetry had done decades ago).

Hennas

But before writing the community off as apolitical or apathetic, one needs to remember that some members were affiliated with Palestinian/PLO-affiliated associations. More important, these weddings and specifically the hennas are recent phenomena in this community. In the henna, the women would come together to sing, dance, and paint their hands with henna (herbal dye).[15] Before, this was reserved for the bride and her female relatives. It has been less than two decades since these celebrations took on a distinctly Palestinian form. The exact date hennas transformed from private affairs to large festivities is debatable, but it seems to have occurred around 1990.

Effectively, hennas are now second weddings. They take place two nights before the actual wedding in a wedding hall and are open to the entire community. According to community members, hennas are reserved for relatives; however, as a participant-observer, I found the hennas were as large as the weddings. This suggests that few nonrelatives are on the guest list. Hennas diverge from the weddings in a number of key respects; most notably, females of all ages wear traditional *thobes*. This includes the bride, except that her *thobe* is more elaborate and her veil is white. The henna itself has become symbolic remaining in the baskets used in the dance. More generally, hennas constitute the traditional celebration and in turn are entirely about Palestinian symbols, images and songs.

Weddings have always been community affairs, especially when the community had fewer resources and the women prepared the feast in their homes. The internal cohesiveness of the trust network was reinforced through contributions in kind.[16] However, the politicization of the weddings in content did not emerge until after the 1987 uprising in the West Bank.[17] The first generation recalls that period as the first time the media affected public opinion positively toward Palestinians by raising questions about the Palestinian-Israeli conflict. They were proud as Palestinians and pleased that their eldest children (the second generation) watched the conflict unfold on television. Prior to that period, weddings were celebrated on a single night and only the bride wore a white wedding dress. The rest of the guests wore whatever they chose according to personal taste or fashion. Flags, *kufiyas*, and political music were absent. As these artifacts seeped in, weddings between two Palestinians became Palestinian weddings.

In the words of a first-generation mother, "1948 Palestinians lived their lives out in sorrow; we want to enjoy and celebrate ours." Being Palestinian needed to be made more enticing for their children, as other temptations were strong in the United States. These telling statements require further unpacking. It seems she is describing a new era of Palestinian-ness for this community, perhaps one that reflects on the failure of the Palestinian Resistance Movement and on fears of losing Palestine both figuratively and literally.

A community leader offered two interrelated reasons for the embellishment of the weddings, namely the political void left by the Palestinian factions and the encroachment of religious groups in the United States. He explained that the 1983 PLO splinter in the Middle East was mirrored in the United States, leaving fragmented PLO-associations. At the same time, Muslim groups were gaining ground on university campuses by attracting individuals who would have otherwise joined political groups. His concern over organized religion falls within the model of trust network dynamics as developed by Tilly. Basically, with a trust network premised on kinship ties, organized religion, like foreign governments, is perceived as a threat to the unity of the community. In response, the community elucidated its community/national identity by dramatizing weddings. While this view might be shared by a segment of the first generation, there are undoubtedly other factors to consider. Of these, travel to the West Bank is salient. *Thobes, kufiyas,* and dancing beads are all ordered or brought back from the West Bank, as are new pendants, wristbands, and songs at the end of every summer. For instance, two young men introduced the aforementioned political songs upon returning from a trip to Ramallah, West Bank.[18]

Through some amalgamation, West Bank Palestinian-Americans transformed their weddings into celebration of Palestinian-ness. Rather than having a single day designated for rejoicing in being part of a national/ethnic group, most families average approximately ten weddings per summer along with their respective hennas. This means there are twenty events that bring a large part of the trust network together every summer, plus a few weddings sprinkled throughout the year. Furthermore, these are occasions full of the potential of finding a spouse at the wedding, since young people are raised with the understanding that the preferred "marriage pool" is to be found at these weddings.

The wedding is truly a community event attended by anyone who can walk or be carried or wheeled in. I have been to weddings that ranged in size from 600 to 1,500 guests. Despite my increasing familiarity with the community, I have felt perpetually lost because of the sheer number of children running around, the men and women coming and going, and the duration of the events, which could last anywhere from five to seven hours.

The presence of children appeared peculiar. However, as with other details of this invented tradition, any family that tries to exclude children is criticized and often ignored. A plausible explanation is found in the desire to further the internal cohesiveness of their trust network.

For the very young, weddings are an opportunity to dress up and play unsupervised. For adolescents, as noted earlier, these events offer the added incentive of seeing and being seen by potential mates. Young women must take all precautions not to appear to be doing so. They do not engage in eye contact or dance with any men outside their immediate family; male cousins are an exception if they are too young for marriage. Women never join the *debcha*, although they know the steps and dance it in a more private setting. I received a look of utter disbelief when I asked about this. The response was that it would be immodest and impractical because of the bouncing with their dresses and heels. Their gowns are part prom, part fairytale, and definitely very colorful and shiny. Dresses are designed by the women themselves, adapted from magazines and taken to a seamstress, or bought at a mall and altered. The usual alterations include some sort of sleeves, even if transparent or barely covering the shoulder for modesty. Young women spend countless hours gluing rhinestones onto their dresses. Between the bright colors and glittery rhinestones, one's eyes dazzle whichever way one looks. The final products are young women who look picturesque, romanticized, worthy of capturing in a picture frame or book as representations of an abstract ideal. Accordingly, it makes sense that sweating or energetic dancing might literally ruin this product; at the same time, it might symbolically tarnish the image of these "pure" females.

Purity is demonstrated on the dance floor through control over body movements and facial expressions. I initially wondered why the young women rarely smiled and whether perhaps they were not enjoying themselves. With time, I learned that showing too much emotion was considered immodest. Dancing too vigorously was the sign of a shameless woman begging for attention. Young women are reflexive and are acutely aware of the disparity between the performance at the weddings and their daily lives. Purity here is not used in reference to sexual purity but rather refers to an extended notion of purity that lies in the realm of the symbolic. The reflexivity of these young women often does not go beyond recognizing that they attend school and university with young men, including extended family, and thus do know and talk to young men. Purity is assessed by the visible conduct of females so that any interaction with a nonrelative male is suspicious. Questions of honor and *'ird* are important to this community but are beyond the scope of this chapter. It suffices to assert that women beyond puberty are closely monitored. When a young woman is "secretly" seeing a young man from the community, the tendency of her family is to turn a blind eye. Silence is the comfortable medium whereby families can maintain the decorum of strictness and allow young people in the community to meet without the family having to condone or condemn the relationship.

Men are expected to show respect for the women by maintaining their distance, avoiding eye contact, and stepping aside during the women's dance. Men are expected to dance the *debcha* and wear the Palestinian scarf but not the traditional male *ombaz* and *hatta* (traditional peasant attire for men consisting of black-and-white striped robe over black pants and the headscarf). Thus, their gendered role includes demonstrating solidarity with other men (men of all ages holding hands), protecting the women (making sure no one is imposing on female relatives), and having the physical capacity to partake in the *debcha*, which normally lasts around forty minutes, as measured through wedding videos.

The patriarchal overtones of these performances are undeniable and at times exaggerated for effect. Partha Chatterjee (1993) and Craig Calhoun (1993) propose that postcolonial nationalism stresses the gender divide more than Western nationalism because gender belongs to the sphere untouched by colonial rule. Women as repositories of the nation wear the traditional attire and raise Palestinian children. They also represent the virtues of the nation: purity, compassion, and passivity. Men as the protectors of the nation need to be physically strong, aggressive, and ready to defend their honor. A few scholars have pointed out how this emphasis on upholding gender roles in non-Western national movements has been used by Western and colonial nations as evidence of women's oppression (Chatterjee 1993; Calhoun 1993). Chatterjee (1993) goes to great lengths in *The Nation and Its Fragments* to demonstrate the rise of the "inner"/domestic sphere as the space where nationalism was fostered and practiced in postcolonial nations. He explains that the public sphere was already dominated by the colonial powers and that there was little that the colonized could do to change the formal national institutions. Instead, they turned inward, relying on the family and patriarchy to model their version of nationalism. He acknowledges this was largely at the expense of women's issues, yet shows that the conditions were not as static or repressive as they are portrayed in Western narratives.

Chatterjee presents the adherence to a patriarchal narrative and image as a historically specific outcome. Most other works reduce it to a cultural attribute of the people studied. Much has been written about the subjugation of non-Western women by their states or male counterparts for the sake of a national struggle (Abdo 1991; Enloe 1990; Pettus 2003). This was a central question for Palestinian women who joined the Palestinian Resistance Movement in the 1970s (Antonius 1979; Jammal 1985; Sayigh 1988). It became an unresolved question as the conflict intensified and the PLO fissured, reemerging when the Palestinian Authority assumed power and more so after Hamas came to power (Abdo 1999; Johnston 2006). Notwithstanding the importance of such a discussion, it is beyond the scope of the present chapter. What is of significance is asking the same questions of the Palestinian-American community: Where is the place of women in the community? And are women's rights being compromised in the name of the "national struggle"?

It is important to interject that the Palestinian community in the tri-state area is not a postcolonial nation but rather appropriates some elements of the postcolonial nationalism model, integrating them with aspects from the Western model. It is also located in the United States, which by default presents different obstacles and opportunities for both men and women. Louise

Cainkar found that the Palestinian Muslim West Bank women she interviewed in the 1980s were predominantly homemakers who were expected to raise Palestinian children and keep the memory of Palestine alive. Cainkar's study demonstrated how intertwined culture and politics were in the lives of first-generation post-1967 Palestinians in Chicago.[19] In many ways the second generation has continued to infuse the cultural with the political. Through the weddings, one sees that dance and posture are used to enact the ideal gender roles of the nation. It may even be suggested that the lyrics in the Palestinian songs assist or instruct in this endeavor when they describe the ideal Palestinian male and female.[20]

Beyond gender, family alliances are signaled, broken, and affirmed on the dance floor and through the monetary wedding gift (*nokout*). Older women join younger women they are "assessing" as potential mates for their sons. When a young woman dances with an older woman who has an eligible son, speculations about a possible match are sure to follow. Unfavorable intentions are signaled by moving away too quickly or refusing to dance with the person. The consequences of such action go beyond the two individuals and include entire families. Fights and arguments have broken out following such actions that can last several weeks and require community mediation to restore network links and solidarity.

Other messages are sent through the all-crucial *nokout*. Envelopes with cash or checks are dropped into a box as people leave the wedding. The dropping of the envelope is public, but the couple's families count the contents only in private. Once the *nokout* is counted, the families begin to interpret the intentions of the giver. Too large a sum can mean that the giver feels superior if the receiver cannot reciprocate or that the giver holds the receiver in high esteem. On the other hand, too small a sum indicates lack of respect and a desire to sever ties or displeasure. These assessments are weighed against the giver's financial capabilities, which are often known to others. Individual gifts may carry messages, but the *nokout* is what makes these celebrations possible. The *nokout* covers the wedding expenses and in some cases the basics of establishing a new household (e.g. furniture and appliances). The aim is to "break even" rather than "make a profit." Breaking even allows weddings to continue uninterrupted since family resources remain. It also means that couples can get married at a younger age since they do not have to worry about beginning their lives together in debt. Thus, the existence of these trust networks facilitates cultural maintenance, marriage markets, and no-interest credit that allow weddings and marriage to take place in a socially sanctioned manner.

These exchanges reaffirm the trust networks' boundaries by intensifying the webs of reliance, debt, patronage, and services offered internally (Tilly 2005). These mechanisms keep a nation/group together beyond ideology and in the absence of a state apparatus. One may wonder how it is possible to notice these messages in such congested halls. The answer is gossip or idle talk (*haki fothy*), which serves as a quintessential mechanism of control for this community. When the wedding ends, people return to their homes or pick up the phone and discuss the evening's events until the early hours of the morning. They also await the wedding videos to attain a bird's-eye view of the occasion.

Wedding videos hold multiple social meanings in the community. The first is a sort of voyeurism, whereby they can scrutinize one another in the privacy of their own living rooms. Young people appreciate this access since they can "check out who's beef" or, in other words, evaluate potential spouses. One young woman proclaimed that the videos superseded the actual weddings in importance. The truth in her words can be gauged through a delineation of the production process and consumption of these tapes. Wedding tapes take up to nine months to produce under the very watchful eyes of the couple's families. The latter inspect the raw footage from at least two cameras to decide what goes into the final edit. During the process, the unedited tapes are held onto tightly, to be viewed only by immediate family members. Once finalized, multiple copies are circulated to relatives in the tri-state area, in other states, and back in the West Bank. Thus, the audience is much wider than the wedding attendees and has access to more events than any one person could observe at the wedding. Most families get the opportunity to do their own editing, and so at least for those in this community no one family can monopolize the image projected.

A first-generation man in his sixties told me, "The wedding videos bring the community together. They make us feel like we are close together . . . like we never left each other." Later he added with pride, "We want the future generations to know what Palestine is like so they never forget." In his voice was a mixture of despair and pride. He recognized the realities of fragmentation and threat that face the community (and the Palestinian nation, since they view themselves as the prototype), yet he was proud that the community has found a way to preserve some of the history and sentiment. David Cannadine (1983), writing on the rituals of the British monarchy, argued, "in a period of change, conflict, or crisis, it [ritual] might be deliberately unaltered so as to give an impression of continuity, community and comfort, despite the overwhelming contextual evidence to the contrary." This can be taken one step further to propose that the videotapes serve to institutionalize the rituals by documenting them. People need not rely on memory and word of mouth, because they can simply watch a video and (mis)remember and relive specific reinvented traditions.

To this community, Palestine is being preserved and its history documented. To the rest of the world, this community exists only as an ethnic minority. The schism between this community's self-perception and the context it lives in is striking. After all, these are post-1965 immigrants living in urban and suburban neighborhoods with many other groups that, at least categorically, resemble them (Farley and Alba 2002; Gans 1992; Portes 1996). Yet, the community is not isolated in an enclave. It is very much part of the American system in terms of employment and residence patterns, access to education, services, and information through the mass media (Cainkar 1988; Seikaly 1999).

Conclusion

Rather than trying to define the perimeters of an enclave and the impact of its absence/presence on Palestinian-Americans, I will turn once again to my analysis, which treats the community as a trust network. Repeatedly throughout the chapter, we saw instances of perceived external and internal threats and community responses to reinforce internal cohesiveness. Thus, Tilly writes that trust networks "consist of ramified interpersonal connections, consisting of strong ties, within which people set valued, consequential, long-term resources and enterprises at risk to the malfeasance, mistakes, and failures of individual members." For example, Tilly found that Waldesians, a persecuted non-Catholic Christian group, were able to maintain their ties and identity for four centuries after their eviction from Lyon by acting as a trust network. Eventually they emerged during the Protestant Reformation and became part of the movement. In other words, Waldesians were an example of "how nonpolitical networks of trusting relations politicized themselves, connected with political networks, or gave way to politically connected networks" (Tilly 2005).

Tilly's description of ethnic groups as more appropriately trust networks is applicable to Palestinian-Americans groups that materialize in weddings. West Bank Palestinian-Americans in the tri-state area can be likened to a modern-day Waldesian network. Considering the decreasing venues for public expression of their Palestinian identity and the encroachment of organized religion coupled with incentives for letting go (personal convenience and external rewards), the seamlessness of the weddings becomes a huge feat. Weddings are more than role-playing or an appeasement of parents. While many observers may view this community as archaically conservative and/or apolitical, as a trust network its members have continued to socially reproduce and to politicize themselves and their children through weddings.

Notes

1. The findings and claims made in this study are based on field data collected between 2001 and 2006. The target population is that of Palestinians who came from the West Bank after 1967. A longer version of this chapter was previously published as Serhan Randa. "Palestinian Weddings: Inventing Palestine in New Jersey." *Journal of Palestine Studies* 37(4):21-37. Reproduced with permission.

2. The description I offer in this article is of weddings in New Jersey; however my research extended beyond New Jersey to include New York and, to a lesser extent, Philadelphia. The interactions between these locales are dense.
3. Legally and technically, Palestinian-Americans arriving after 1965 are considered "economic immigrants." They entered the United States after the passing of the Hart-Celler Act or the Immigration and Nationality Act of 1965, which removed national-origin quotas, instituted the family reunification clause, and opened the doors to skilled migrants of all nationalities. It also allowed for the admission of refugees from communist countries (LeMay, 2006). The West Bank community benefited mostly from the family reunification clause, which in the 1970s and 1980s allowed for the inclusion of a wide range of family members. It has become increasingly narrower in scope, yet families still rely on it for chain migration. They did not and do not qualify for refugee or political asylum status, which in turn has created a rift between the legal categorization and their self-perception as exiles.
4. "Symbolic ethnicity" is a term coined by Herbert Gans (1979) to describe the practices to which immigrants adhere. These are mainly ones connected to leisure activities and the private sphere and do not impinge on income generation and participation in the greater structures in society.
5. The *debcha* is a dance in which a line is formed, consisting in this community only of men, who hold hands and go around in a circle using three steps. Depending on the physical capabilities of the dancers, the steps can be taken slowly or elevated to hops and stomping (one young man described this as the stomping of the Israeli flag). Eventually the one line turns into two or three lines that correspond to generational divisions with the youngest trailing behind as they try to mimic the adults.
6. Two young men on a trip back to the West Bank several years ago heard this song and asked the wedding singer to add it to his roster of songs. The original version sung by a Lebanese singer is sung at a slower tempo and sounds melancholic, but the wedding singer's adaptation is uplifting and defiant.
7. In the original song, the word "Islamic" is used, but both wedding singers changed it to "Arab." By substituting the word "Arab" for "Islamic," they signal a commitment to their Palestinian national identity, based on regional connections rather than religious ones. Later in the discussion, a community leader reaffirms this notion by suggesting that a Muslim identity might overtake and change young people's commitment to the Palestinian nation. Another interpretation is that the community rejects Hamas's rhetoric, which places Islam ahead of an Arab identity.
8. The Palestinian scarf is a slim scarf made of *kufiya* material with the flag dangling at either end made of wool strings. It is different from the traditional *kufiya*, a large rectangular cloth with a white base and black pattern that is worn over the head by peasant men.
9. Although little was written about the actual sentiments of the refugees at the time, it can be gleaned from available texts that the primary focus was on relief and that the refugees were in a state of mourning. In interviews that I conducted in two refugee camps in the summer of 2002, I was informed that many in the first generation born in exile were discouraged from dancing, singing, or

rejoicing because of their loss. Another indication of this mood is the fact that Palestinians do not have any popular singers in the Arab mainstream, unlike their closest counterparts in Lebanon and Syria, who are well represented in this profession.
10. Al-Karameh battle in 1968, Tel-el-Zaatar refugee camp massacre in 1976, Black September massacre in Jordan in 1971, Sabra and Shatila massacre in 1982 in Beirut, the refugee camps' siege in 1988 in Lebanon, PLO's involvement in the Lebanese civil war, guerrilla attacks from Jordan, Lebanon, and Syria on Israel. These armed conflicts did not start until after the 1967 war, when the Palestinian armed resistance intensified.
11. Israel also occupied parts of Sinai and the Golan Heights.
12. A small number of men from the West Bank had already settled in the tri-state area prior to 1967, but there was no West Bank Palestinian community to speak of. Other men made their way to the United States via South America, where they had moved to as economic immigrants with the intention of saving enough funds to return to the West Bank for marriage. After 1967, these students and economic immigrants became exiles. Israeli-issued permits were required for return trips to the West Bank, and these permits were neither guaranteed nor easy to attain. A sixty-year-old community member recounted that during his first trip back from Venezuela to the West Bank after the 1967 occupation, he had realized that the rest of Palestine was gone and the Palestinians were now exiles. The relocation of entire families to the United States began in the early 1970s and continues to the present.
13. At the helm of these organizations was the Association of Arab-American University Graduates (AAUG), formed in 1967 by academics and professionals such as Ibrahim Abu-Lughod, Edward Said, Michael Sulieman, and Rashid Bashshur. See AAUG, *The First Decade: 1967–1977* (Detroit: AAUG, 1977). Opponents described AAUG as "isolationist"; conversely, its advocates described it as the first credible nonsectarian Arab-American organization. See Yossi Shain, "Arab-Americans at the Crossroads," *Journal of Palestine Studies* 25, no. 3 (1996):46-59. Within a short time span, additional organizations emerged, such as the National Association for Arab Americans (NAAA) in 1972, the Arab-American Anti-Discrimination Committee (ADC) in 1980, and the Arab-American Institute (AAI) in 1985. Although "Arab" was used in the names of these organizations, Palestinians were at the forefront of their formation. See Kathleen Christison, "The American Experience: Palestinians in the U.S.," *Journal of Palestine Studies* 18, no. 4 (1989): 18–26; Shain (1996); Michael Suleiman, *Arabs in America: Building a New Future* (Philadelphia: Temple University Press, 1999).
14. Rhoda Ann Kanaaneh, writing on Palestinian women in Israel, also found that demographics were viewed as part of the Palestinian struggle. Palestinians in this context were reacting to the demographic "war" as it was articulated by the Zionists and later the state of Israel. She also documented how, in the 1990s, the Palestinian Authority advocated challenging the imbalance of power with the Israelis through a shift in population size and distribution. See Rhoda Anne Kanaaneh, *Birthing the Nation: Strategies of Palestinian Women in Israel* (Berkeley: University of California Press, 2002).

15. Henna nights are cultural events and are not particular to Muslims or Christians. Interviewees from the Palestinian Christian community in Florida described henna nights in their community in very similar terms to those I witnessed in the Muslim community in the tri-state area. The Christian community referred to originated in Ramallah, suggesting there might be a regional influence on these practices.
16. As the community became upwardly mobile, the contributions shifted from being in kind to being monetary. People continue to do favors for one another, but most contributions to the weddings are in cash or check form.
17. The *kufiya* was seen in public spaces long before it was used at weddings.
18. I have intentionally avoided the use of the term "transnationalism" to describe this set of practices because it suggests that there was a period of time when people did not maintain contact with their place of origin. This is not to discount the contributions of transnationalism scholars who have highlighted the effects lower costs of travel, communications, and the advent of the Internet and satellite TV have had on prolonging and strengthening relations between immigrants and their countries of origin. Perhaps in terms of artifacts, this community has a transnational life; however, I am not convinced it can explain their attachment to their homeland fully. For instance, Palestinians in refugee camps in Lebanon have had no access to their place of origin for almost sixty years and yet their attachments are strong. Obviously, their presence in refugee camps has provided amply motivation/incentive to adhere to their Palestinian-ness (although one could make the inverse argument as well), but I would venture to suggest that what both Palestinian-Americans and Palestinian camp dwellers share is strong family networks. As such, I shy away from the idea of transnationalism for fear of attributing more weight to it than to other phenomena and mechanisms.
19. Cainkar's study was of both first generation post-1967 and second-generation pre-1967 Palestinian women from the Ramallah-Jerusalem area. The post-1967 second generation was too young to be included. Her conclusions can be related to two previous points. The first of these is that women are often the repositories of the nation. The second is that U.S.-based Palestinian women in the 1980s were assuming the roles once performed by refugee Palestinian women in the aftermath of the Nakba. In other words, it might be suggested that they are at a fairly early stage of political mobilization in comparison to their counterparts in the Middle East of several decades ago. One explanation for this offered by Cainkar is that the anti-Palestinian sentiment existing in the United States affected an already socially conservative immigrant group. In other words, the anti-Palestinian milieu within which these West Bank Palestinians found themselves pushed them toward additional self-containment and closure. See note 52. As a trust network based on kinship alliances formed in the West Bank prior to migration, the community enclosed itself more tightly around the mode of interaction and social structure they had become accustomed to under Jordanian rule and more forcefully under Israeli occupation. There was a reinforcement of the detachment from institutionalized politics toward family-based preservation of Palestinian-ness.

20. Interestingly, these are also the first answers given by young people I interviewed about why they wanted to marry Palestinians. Young women talked about courageous and gorgeous men, and the young men spoke of beautiful girls who bear Palestinian children.

References

Abdo, Nahla. 1999. "Gender and Politics under the Palestinian Authority." *Journal of Palestine Studies* Winter 110(28):38–51.

———. 1991. "Women of the Intifada: Gender, Class and National Liberation." *Race and Class* 32(4):19–34.

Abraham, Sameer and Nabeel Abraham. 1981. *The Arab World and Arab-Americans: Understanding a Neglected Minority.* Detroit, MI: Center for Urban Studies, Wayne State University.

Abu-Assad, Hany. 2002. *Rana's Wedding: Jerusalem, Another Day.* Seattle, WA: Arab Film Distribution.

Abu-Duhou, Jamileh. 2003. "Motherhood as 'An Act of Defiance': Palestinian Women's Reproductive Experience." *Development* 46(2):85–89.

Abu-Lughod, Janet. 1988. "Palestinians: Exiles at Home and Abroad." *Current Sociology* 36, no. 2 (1988): 61–69.

Anderson, Benedict. 1983. *Imagined Communities: Reflections on the Origin and Spread of Nationalism.* London; New York: Verso.

Anthias, Floya and Niva Yuval-Davis. 1995. "Women and the Nation-State." Pp. 312–15 in *Nationalism,* edited by John Hutchinson and Anthony Smith. A. New York: Oxford University Press.

Antonius, Soraya. 1979. "Fighting on Two Fronts: Conversations with Palestinian Women." *Journal of Palestine Studies* 8(3):26–45.

Ashrawi, Hanan Mikhail. 1978. "The Contemporary Palestinian Poetry of Occupation." *Journal of Palestine Studies* 7(3):77–101.

BADIL. 2004. "From 1948 Nakba to the 1967 Naksa". http://www.badil.org/phocadownloadpap/Badil_docs/bulletins-and-briefs/Bulletin-18.pdf. Retrieved September 18, 2006.

Brynen, Rex. 1997. "Imagining a Solution: Final Status Arrangements and Palestinian Refugees in Lebanon." *Journal of Palestine Studies* 26(2):42–58.

Cainkar, Louise. 1988. "Palestinian Women in the United States: Coping with Tradition, Change, and Alienation." PhD dissertation. Evanston, IL: Northwestern University.

Calhoun, Craig J. 1993. "Nationalism and Ethnicity." *Annual Review of Sociology* 19:211–39.

———. 1997. *Nationalism.* Minneapolis: University of Minnesota Press.

Cannadine, David. 1983. "The Context, Performance, and Meaning of Ritual: The British Monarchy and the 'Invention of Tradition', C. 1820–1977." Pp. 101–64 in *The Invention of Tradition,* edited by Eric Hobsbawm and Terence Ranger. Cambridge, UK: Cambridge University Press.

Chatterjee, Partha. 1983. *Nationalist Thought and the Colonial World: A Derivative Discourse.* Minneapolis: University of Minnesota Press.

_____. 1993. *The Nation and Its Fragments: Colonial and Postcolonial Histories.* Princeton, NJ: Princeton University Press.

Elmessiri, Abdelwahab M. 1982. *The Palestinian Wedding: A Bilingual Anthology of Contemporary Palestinian Resistance Poetry.* Washington, DC: Three Continents Press, Inc.

Enloe, Cynthia H. 1990. *Bananas, Beaches, & Bases: Making Feminist Sense of International Politics.* Berkeley: University of California.

Farley, Reynolds and Richard Alba. 2002. "The New Second-Generation in the US." *International Migration Review* 36(3):669–701.

Farsoun, Samih K. and Christina E. Zacharia. 1997. *Palestine and the Palestinians.* Boulder, CO: Westview Press.

Gans, Herbert J. 1979. "Symbolic Ethnicity: The Future of Ethnic Groups and Cultures in America." *Ethnic and Racial Studies* 2(1):1–20.

Gans, Herbert J. 1992. "Second-Generation Decline: Scenarios for the Economic and Ethnic Futures of the Post-1965 American Immigrants." *Ethnic and Racial Studies* 15(2):174–92.

Gluck, Sherna Berger. 1995. "Palestinian Women: Gender Politics and Nationalism." *Journal of Palestine Studies* 24(3):5–15.

Hagopian, Elaine Catherine. 1976. "Minority Rights in a Nation-State: The Nixon Administration's Campaign against Arab-Americans." *Journal of Palestine Studies* 5(1/2): 97–114.

Hilterman, Joost R. 1991. *Behind the Intifada.* New Jersey: Princeton Press.

Hobsbawm, Eric J. 1983. "Introduction." in *The Invention of Tradition*, edited by Eric Hobsbawm and Terence Ranger., T. New York: Cambridge University Press.

Inbari, Pinhas. 1996. *The Palestinians between Terrorism and Statehood.* Brighton, UK; Portland, OR: Sussex Academic Press.

Jammal, Laila. 1985. *Contributions by Palestinian Women to the National Struggle for Liberation.* Washington, D.C.: Middle East Public Relations.

Johnston, Alan. 2006. "Women Ponder Future under Hamas." *BBC World News.* http://news.bbc.co.uk/2/hi/middle_east/4767634.stm. Retrieved March 3, 2006.

Kaplan, Caren, Norma Alarcon and Minoo Moallem. 1999. *Between Woman and Nation: Nationalisms, Transnational Feminisms, and the State.* Durham, NC: Duke University Press.

Khalidi, Rashid. 1997. *Palestinian Identity: The Construction of Modern National Consciousness.* New York: Columbia University Press.

_____. 1998. "Fifty Years after 1948: A Universal Jubilee?" *Palestine-Israel Journal* 5(2) available at http://pij.org/details.php?id=213.

_____. 2006. *The Iron Cage: The Story of the Palestinian Struggle for Statehood.* Boston, MA: Beacon Press.

Khalili, Laleh. 2005. "Citizens of an Unborn Kingdom: Stateless Palestinian Refugees and Contentious Commemoration." Ph.D. dissertation. New York, NY: Columbia University.

Khleifi, Michel. 1987. *Wedding in Galilee.* New York, NY: Kino International Video.

Kimhi, Shaul. and Shemau Even. 2004. "Who Are the Palestinian Suicide Bombers?" *Terrorism and Political Violence* 16(4):815–40.

Layoun, Mary. 1999. "A Guest at the Wedding: Honor, Memory, and (National) Desire in Michel Khleifi's *Wedding in Galilee*." Pp. 92–110 in *Between Women and Nation:*

Nationalisms, Transnational Feminisms, and the State, edited by Caren Kaplan, Norma Alarcon and Minoo Moallem. Durham, NC: Duke University Press.

LeMay, Michael C. 2006. *Guarding the Gates: Immigration and National Security*. Santa Barbara, CA: Greenwood Publishing Group.

Massad, Joseph. 2001. *Colonial Effects: The Making of National Identity in Jordan*. New York: Columbia University Press.

———. 2005. "Liberating Songs: Palestine Put into Music." Pp. 175–201 in *Palestine, Israel, and the Politics of Popular Culture*, edited by Rebecca Stein and Ted Swedenburg. Durham, NC: Duke University Press.

Morris, Benny. 2004. *The Birth of the Palestinian Refugee Problem Revisited*. Cambridge, UK; New York: Cambridge University Press.

Pappé, Ilan. 2004. *A History of Modern Palestine: One Land, Two Peoples*. Cambridge, UK; New York: Cambridge University Press.

Peretz, Don. 1996. *The West Bank: History, Politics, Society and Economy*. Boulder, CO: Westview Press.

Peteet, Julie. 1994. "Male Gender and Rituals of Resistance in the Palestinian 'Intifada': A Cultural Politics of Violence." *American Ethnologist* 21(1):31–49.

Pettus, Ashley. 2003. *Between Sacrifice and Desire: National Identity and the Governing of Femininity in Vietnam*. New York, NY: Routledge.

Portes, Alejandro. 1996. *The New Second Generation*. New York: Russell Sage Foundation.

Roy, Sara. 1990. "From Hardship to Hunger: The Economic Impact of the Intifada on the Gaza Strip." *American-Arab Affairs* (34, Fall):109–32.

Said, Edward W. and Jean Mohr. 1986. *After the Last Sky: Palestinian Lives*. New York NY: Pantheon Books.

Sayigh, Rosemary. 1977. *Palestinians: From Peasants to Revolutionaries: A People's History*. London: Zed Press.

———. 1978. "The Struggle for Survival: The Economic Conditions of Palestinian Camp Residents in Lebanon." *Journal of Palestine Studies* 7(2):101–19.

———. 1988. "Palestinian Women: Triple Burden, Single Struggle." *Mediterranean People* 44-45:247–68.

———. 1993. *Too Many Enemies*. London: Zed Books Inc.

Schulz, Helena Lindholm and Juliane Hammer. 2003. *The Palestinian Diaspora: Formation of Identities and Politics of Homeland*. New York, NY: Routledge.

Seikaly, May. 1999. "Attachments and Identity: The Palestinian Community of Detroit." Pp. 24–39 in *Arabs in America: Building a New Future*, edited by Michael Suleiman. Philadelphia, PA: Temple University Press.

Shain, Yossi. 1996. "Arab-Americans at the Crossroads." *Journal of Palestine Studies* 25(3):46059.

Shaheen, Jack. 1984. *The TV Arab*. Bowling Green, OH: Bowling Green State University Popular Press.

Shlaim, Avi. 1994. "The Oslo Accords." *Journal of Palestine Studies* 23:24–40.

Sirhan, Bassem. 1975. "Palestinian Refugee Camp Life in Lebanon." *Journal of Palestine Studies* 4(2):91–107.

Smith, Pamela Ann. 1986. "The Palestinian Diaspora: 1948–1985." *Journal of Palestine Studies* 15(3):90–108.

Sobel, Lester A. 1977. *Palestinian Impasse: Arab Guerrillas & International Terror*. New York: Facts on File.

Sosebee, Stephen. 1990. "The Palestinian Women's Movement and the Intifada: A Historical and Current Analysis." *American-Arab Affairs* 32:81–91.
Stockton, Ronald. 1985. "The Palestinians of Dearborn." *Psychological Reports* 56 (1985): 123–29.
———. 1994. "Ethnic Archetypes and the Arab Image." in *The Development of the Arab Identity*, edited by Ernest McCarus. Ann Arbor, MI: University of Michigan Press.
Strum, Philippa. 1992. *The Women Are Marching: The Second Sex and the Palestinian Revolution*. New York, NY: Lawrence Hill Books.
Suleiman, Michael. 1994. "Arab-Americans in the Political Process." in *The Development of Arab-American Identity*, edited by Ernest McCarus. Ann Arbor, MI: University of Michigan Press.
Swedenburg, Ted. 1990. "The Palestinian Peasant as National Signifier." *Anthropological Quarterly* 63(1):18–30.
Tilly, Charles. 2005. *Trust and Rule*. Cambridge, UK: Cambridge University Press.
Turki, Fawaz. 1972. *The Disinherited; Journal of a Palestinian Exile*. New York, NY: Monthly Review Press.
———. 1974. *The Disinherited: Journal of a Palestinian Exile* New York, NY: Modern Reader.
———. 1976. "The Palestinian Estranged." *Journal of Palestine Studies* 5(1/2): 82–96.
Usher, Graham. 1992. "Palestinian Women, the Intifada and the State of Independence: An Interview with Rita Giacaman." *Race and Class* 34(3):31–43.

7

TRUST NETWORKS AND DURABLE INEQUALITY AMONG KOREAN IMMIGRANTS IN JAPAN

Hwaji Shin

While immigration is now a classic topic in sociology, only relatively recently have scholars started paying serious attention to the importance of networks to an understanding of the lives of immigrants. Charles Tilly was among those early scholars who called attention to networks among immigrants. While he started focusing on migration and their networks in his early work (Tilly and Brown 1967), he repeatedly emphasized the importance of studying these networks of migration throughout his career (Tilly 1990, 1999, 2007). Among various types of networks, Tilly was particularly interested in what he called "trust networks," which he defined as "ramified interpersonal connections, consisting mainly of strong ties, within which people set valued, consequential, long-term resources and enterprises at risk to the malfeasance, mistakes, or failures of others" (Tilly 2007:7). As such, trust networks function as "major, long-term, collective enterprises at risk of the malfeasance of others" (Tilly 2005:4).

As Tilly hoped, many scholars now pay serious attention to the function and impact of networks among immigrants. Steven Gold comprehensively identified a rich variety of case studies and poignantly summarized the utility of network-based approaches to international migration in the recent decades. He asserted that "(b)y understanding international migration as a network-based process, scholars are better able to consider both macro and micro factors and integrate them into the rich fabric of affiliations that shape migration, resettlement, and enduring ties to the country of origin" (Gold 2005:259). Gold also identified some of the unresolved challenges in studying migrant networks. One of them is the relative lack of understanding of the negative impacts of networks on immigrant lives. Earlier work focused on positive and beneficial aspects of migrant networks, such as how ethnic ties helped the migrants' economic survival. However, as Tilly suspected and as some empirical studies demonstrate, migrant networks also have negative consequences for some members, which need more scholarly exploration.

This chapter responds to the call for more research on both negative and positive aspects of migrant networks. Through a close examination of Korean immigrants' experiences in Japan, this chapter demonstrates under what circumstances immigrant trust networks have positive and/or negative effects on immigrants. The empirical case study of Japan shows how Koreans formed and relied on their own trust networks for socioeconomic survival and success but also how their trust networks inadvertently contributed to increasing socioeconomic polarization within their own community. This exploration allows us to assess the utility of Tillyian concepts such as durable inequality and trust networks, as well as to further understand the nature of the relationship between these concepts in the context of decolonialization. Such an exploration is particularly useful for an improved understanding of immigrants' lives in societies around the globe. It also helps us to consider another question that Tilly was interested in: the relationship among the trust networks, democratization, and equality. Tilly argued that the integration of trust networks into the system of rule is a key aspect of the democratization process and that increases in democracy usually bring about more equality although they do not necessarily eradicate inequality completely (Tilly 2005). This case study of Korean immigrants in Japan helps us to flesh out these mechanisms.

Historical Background

Alejandro Portes (2000) wrote, "Immigration happens not simply between random rich and poor countries. A common motivation behind the migration is usually a pursuit of a better life and opportunity, but the large influx of immigration was usually triggered by a deliberate or some non-deliberate efforts between the countries who share some historical, political or economic relationship in the past." Colonialism facilitates such a relationship and continues to produce a large influx of migrants from the colonizing to the colonized areas. Sometimes this is a result of the imperial state's deliberate act of importing cheap labor from the colonies to the metropolis, but at other times it happens regardless of the state's intention because colonialism by its nature establishes very intimate economic and political relationships between regions.

The Japanese empire was no exception to this pattern; a large migration happened between Japan and its colonies. Korean chain migration started shortly after Japan colonized the Korean peninsula in the 1910s, when the Japanese colonial policies displaced many Korean peasants, who in turn left for Japanese metropolis for jobs, and their chain migration picked up its pace in the 1930s. Many of these Koreans were engaged in low-skill manual labor and began to settle in the lower-income neighborhoods of major industrial cities such as Osaka, Fukuoka, Kyoto, and Tokyo. The increasing presence of proletarian colonial subjects in mainland Japan triggered negative sentiments toward them among the Japanese public, particularly during its economic depression, which created fierce competition among colonial laborers and Japanese. The Japanese central government repeatedly attempted to limit the number of Koreans entering the mainland but failed to reverse the course of immigration. As Japan entered Total War against the United States in the 1940s, the Japanese central government conscripted a large number of male laborers from Korea to fulfill the labor vacuum created by the military draft. As a result, by 1945 the Korean population in Japan reached into the millions (Nishinarita 1997).

The loss of the colonies at the end of World War II brought back more than 6 million Japanese settlers and soldiers to the Japanese mainland. The fragile economy of postwar Japan was ill prepared to accommodate such a large number of Japanese repatriates. Therefore, the American-led Supreme Commander for Allied Powers (henceforth SCAP) and the Japanese government prompted many former colonial subjects to move to their liberated homelands. Many conscripted colonial laborers willingly moved back. Nevertheless, approximately 600,000 colonial subjects who had long been settled in Japan (most of them Koreans but also some Taiwanese) decided not to repatriate in haste to their politically and economically unsettled homelands. Under the imperial rule of Japan, all colonial subjects were considered Japanese imperial subjects, thus Japanese citizens. While Koreans were severely discriminated against, they did enjoy some crucial civil rights as Japanese citizens such as local suffrage under Japanese imperial rule. However, the postwar Japanese government unilaterally revoked the citizenship of all colonial subjects in 1952, when it signed the San Francisco Peace Treaty that formally ended Japanese imperial and colonial rule. Consequently, all the remaining Koreans' legal status changed to that of "Alien," which entitled them to no civil rights. Since no formal sovereign state had yet been established on the Korean peninsula, the remaining Koreans became stateless and had no political entity to represent them or protect their status and rights. Thus, many Korean immigrants had to advocate for themselves and mobilize their own limited resources for survival. One such resource was their own trust network, which is the main focus of this case study and is discussed in the next section.

It is important to recognize that trust networks played a critical role not only for colonial immigrants but for the colonialists during and after colonization. As Tilly noted, the state frequently attempts to incorporate trust networks into its system of rule, and democratization occurs when trust networks are fully or partly integrated into public politics through capital or commitment (Tilly 2005). Trust networks among Japanese settlers in the colonies followed the pattern of transformation that Tilly identified. Many Japanese settlers in colonial areas developed trust networks among themselves. When they repatriated, they had very few people or assets to rely on in Japan and thus quickly formed mutual aid associations among fellow repatriates so that they could rely on their colonial trust network to find jobs, housing, spouses, and someone to look after their families while they were traveling. The postwar Japanese state also incorporated this colonial trust network among Japanese repatriates into their new state structures. While all the colonial organizational structures were dismantled under the strict gaze of the American-led SCAP, most colonial officers were reappointed to key positions in new offices of local and national government. Among such offices controlled by former colonial officers was the Alien Registration Department in the local government and the Entry-Reentry Control Department in the Ministry of Justice (Shin 2010).[1]

The direct integration of Japanese repatriates' trust networks into the postwar government offices took place as the Japanese state transitioned from a fascist imperial state to a liberal democratic nation-state. However, this integration of colonist networks also allowed the new state organizations to inherit the preexisting colonial categories of colonizer/colonized and to reproduce the preexisting exploitative, asymmetric relationship between Japanese and Koreans. Thus, Koreans were left outside the purview of formal Japanese citizenship.

This indicates that integration of trust networks into a system of rule can produce two opposing effects. On one hand, it can facilitate a democratization process and increase equality for those included inside of the boundaries of formal citizenship when it is partially or fully integrated, which was what Tilly argued. On the other hand, it also facilitates durable inequalities "that last from one social interaction to the next, with special attention to those that persist over whole careers, lifetimes, and organizational histories," especially among those who are excluded from formal citizenship (Tilly 1999:6).

This is precisely what we observed in postwar Japan with the continuation of the unequal binary relationship between Japanese and Korean residents. While Koreans in Japan were no longer colonial subjects, they were reclassified as "aliens" whose rights and life chances were very much controlled by the offices of alien registration and immigration (Shin 2010). In the following sections, I explore how these excluded colonial immigrants survived by relying on their own trust networks.

Trust Networks among Koreans

There is another tale to be told about trust networks in postwar Japan. Trust networks among Koreans in Japan played a critical role during a time in which Koreans experienced numerous structural barriers. Korean immigrants were severely marginalized during the colonial period. After the war, Korean immigrants continued to occupy the bottom strata of Japan's fragile economy, engaging in low-paid, dangerous, and exploitative occupations, which most Japanese citizens would avoid. Their newly imposed legal status as aliens legally barred them from most social benefits, bank loans, and opportunities in mainstream Japanese society. Nevertheless, Koreans in postwar Japan managed to strive economically, relying on their own trust networks developed during the colonial period.

Shortly after they migrated to Japan from the Korean peninsula, many Koreans settled in the areas where other marginalized minority groups (i.e., Burakumin)[2] resided, primarily for its cheap rent and proximity to their work places (Iwamura 1972, Sugihara 1998, Sugimoto 2000a, 2000b). It was in such ethnic enclaves that they developed their co-ethnic trust networks to mutually help one another in finding jobs and housing, meeting spouses, establishing "Kyes" (community-based rotating credit systems), and sending remittances to their families left behind in their homeland. There are multiple trust networks among Koreans; the networks commonly form around regional identity (which part of Korea participants came from) as well as which clan they belong to, which also often coincides with the regional origin.

There is a considerable amount of literature in Japan about how Koreans cooperated with their co-ethnics in order to survive during and after World War II in Japan (Iwamura 1972; Nishinarita 1997; Sugimoto 2000a, 2000b; Tonomura 2004). But what is not commonly featured in most of the previous studies is the fact that the trust networks nurtured prior to the war not only enabled Koreans to survive but allowed a few Koreans to achieve significant economic success in postwar Japan.

During the colonial period, most Koreans without any particular job skills or education tended to engage in occupations that required no prior experience. Because many Koreans at that time relied chiefly on trust networks to find their jobs, they tended to concentrate in certain sectors of industries that were either unpopular or uncultivated among the Japanese. Such sectors included but were not limited to the manufacturing industry, making products such as glass, metals, rubber, plastic products, and textiles. Such an occupational concentration gradually allowed Koreans to monopolize specific sectors of certain industries, enabling a few of them to accumulate enough capital to become entrepreneurs. This is precisely the mechanism that Tilly identified as "opportunity hoarding," which "operates when members of a categorically bounded network acquire access to a resource that is valuable, renewable, subject to monopoly, supportive of network activities, and enhanced by the network's modus operandi" (Tilly 1999:10).

One case in point is the example of Koreans in the steaming and rinsing sector in the Nishijin kimono textile manufacturing industry in Kyoto;

Koreans occupied roughly 80 percent of this sector by 2003 (Han 2010). The kimono is considered a uniquely Japanese cultural product. Few Japanese know that so many Koreans work in the Japanese kimono industry. Making kimonos involves many processes of designing, dyeing, steaming and rinsing silk, applying ink, adding texture, cutting and removing the threads, and sewing. Of all the processes, steaming and rinsing kimono textiles requires the most intense manual labor but little technical skill, knowledge, or experience, which made it easier for newly arrived laborers such as Koreans to engage in this work.

Because of the multilayered structure of this industry, the wholesalers who control design, sewing, distribution, and marketing of products are not very concerned about who is involved in the manufacturing process as long as product quality is ensured. In fact, because production of kimonos involves such a complex process of manufacturing that cannot be mass produced via machinery, the quality of the product is the most important aspect of the industry. As a result, trust in this business can be earned by the quality of work rather than one's categorical identity, such as gender, age, race, ethnicity, or nationality. Many Koreans began to occupy this particular sector of the kimono manufacturing process. Eventually, some of them started their own small-scale steaming and rinsing companies, hiring co-ethnics from their own trust networks (Han 2010).

After the war, however, many areas in the manufacturing sector, including the kimono industry, began to decline as the Japanese economic structure gradually shifted from an industrial manufacturing economy to a service-oriented one. This impacted Koreans more than the Japanese because of their heavy concentration in the manufacturing industry. However, some Korean entrepreneurs were able to weather this structural change swiftly by switching their business from the declining manufacturing industry to the booming service industry, particularly in the games and recreation sector.

One of the most common and popular businesses that Korean entrepreneurs in postwar Japan invested in was the Pachinko industry. Pachinko is a very popular mechanical game for recreation and gambling in Japan. It started in prewar Japan but halted briefly during the war period when the fascist state restricted all forms of entertainment. It reemerged in postwar Japan and became intensely popular because of its addictive nature, and many investors were attracted to the business. It did not take very long for Japanese crime syndicates (yakuza) to become heavily involved in the Pachinko business as a source of revenue. Subsequently, the Japanese government began to tighten its control over the Pachinko business by requiring very stringent restrictions on the business. Because of the state's intervention and Yakuza's involvement, the Pachinko business became socially stigmatized in Japanese society, driving many Japanese investors out of the Pachinko industry. Meanwhile, however, the popularity of Pachinko barely declined among the public. Once again, social stigma and the exit of Japanese competitors created favorable conditions for opportunity hoarding for the marginalized Koreans. While Koreans make up only 0.1 percent of the total population in Japan, approximately 70 percent of owners of Pachinko parlors were ethnic Koreans in the late 1990s (Nomura 1996; Pyon 2000; Han 2010). Over time, Pachinko became one of the most popular recreational activities in Japan, generating enormous profits for those who own Pachinko parlors.

Jaehyang Han's (2010) extensive study demonstrates how Koreans relied on trust networks to locate a new economic opportunity in nonmanufacturing industry in postwar Japan. One Korean entrepreneur in the kimono industry recalled how he shifted his business from kimono textiles to Pachinko parlors in the following way: "I felt the end of textile industry coming near. . . . So I simply gave up on my textile business and switched to another business" (Han 2010:100) [translated by the author]. He also stated that it was an invitation from his Korean friend, who had already quit his textile business and switched to a Pachinko parlor, that convinced him to switch. Another Korean Pachinko parlor owner attested to a swift business decision made by his fellow Korean entrepreneurs in the kimono industry in the following way:

> *Most of Koreans who switched their business from textile industry to Pachinko parlor ended up becoming very successful. They quickly judged that the textile industry was declining and switched to Pachinko. Not everyone switched to Pachinko parlors, but quite a few did. . . . Some switched to the construction sector while others switched to real estate. They switched to various industries, but the most ostensibly successful ones are those who switched to Pachinko parlors.*
>
> (Han 2010:100)

What enabled them to undertake a high-risk drastic business shift was their enduring co-ethnic trust networks. The experience of Han Chang-woo, an ethnic Korean who is the CEO of one of Japan's largest Pachinko parlor chains, Maruhan Group, shows the importance of trust networks for his business success and for Koreans in postwar Japan generally. Han Chan-woo is often listed as one of the richest men in Japan by *Forbes* magazine.[3] In one of his TV interviews, he recalled how he migrated to Japan to work after the war was over because his brother-in-law invited him to Japan to work with him. He publicly admitted that he had entered Japan illegally and was undocumented during the chaotic postwar period. He received advice from fellow Korean laborers in Japan and applied for permanent resident status as a colonial immigrant, despite the fact that he was a postwar undocumented migrant who technically was not qualified for this legal status. Nonetheless, he applied for and was granted permanent resident status. This allowed him to continue to work in Japan, and eventually he became a billionaire in Japan through his success in the Pachinko parlor business.

> *I call myself "boat people" because it does not sound very nice if I say I am illegal immigrant.... Even if I stayed in Korea, I couldn't study. At that time, I had my brother-in-law who was working as a bricklayer in Japan and came back to Korea shortly before the end of the war. But he immediately returned to Japan because he could not find a work in Korea. As he returned to Japan, he told me to come to Japan even if it was hard to be away from my family.... So I packed small amount of rice grains and an English dictionary and got on a small boat to sail to Japan.... [After graduating from a college], I lived and worked in one of the pachinko parlors where my brother-in-law used to work.*
>
> (TV Asahi 2005)

As his account implies, he too relied heavily on a co-ethnic trust network at a critical juncture of his life before achieving his business success in postwar Japan.

Another noteworthy piece of evidence for Korean trust networks among successful business entrepreneurs is their mercantile association, which provided the mutual and credit cooperatives for co-ethnic business peers in postwar Japan (Kashani 2011). Since many Koreans had much difficulty obtaining loans from Japanese banks, they relied heavily on their co-ethnic trust network to compensate for their lack of "trust" and "credit" in Japanese society. These mutual financial cooperatives within their co-ethnics, the existing co-ethnic cheap labor reserves, and the availability of new business opportunities in socially stigmatized sectors and industries helped a handful of ambitious Korean entrepreneurs to achieve enormous economic success in postwar Japan. Trust networks among co-ethnics were no doubt one of the most important keys to their exceptional success.

Declining Significance of Trust Networks among Koreans in Japan

A high concentration in particular occupations and geographical locations has concrete consequences for immigrant groups. Roger Waldinger noted, "Frequent interaction in a highly concentrated niche promotes a sense of group identity. Participation in the niche, one of the salient traits that group members share, helps define who they are.... The niche, in other words, identifies an us and a them" (Waldinger 1996:304). This was also the case for Koreans in Japan. As they continued to remain concentrated in specific geographical and occupational areas, they maintained their distinctive self-identification as Koreans. Even if the majority of them were born and raised in Japan, use only Japanese language and names, and could technically become naturalized Japanese citizens, many Koreans in Japan still hold onto their Korean nationality as a symbol of their distinctive ethno-national identification.

But this does not mean that their identity remains static. In the course of their decades-long residency in Japan, they developed a new form of ethno-national identity that is neither Korean nor Japanese but "Zainichi." Today, many Koreans in Japan refer to themselves and are referred to as "Zainichi," which literally means "residing in Japan" and usually suggests temporal residency. However, the majority of so-called Zainichi Koreans have no intention to return to their homeland but plan to reside in Japan permanently. The term "Zainichi Koreans" does encapsulate their unique diaspora status and self-identification in Japanese society: culturally assimilated yet not fully legally incorporated.[4]

This new category of "Zainichi" did solidify the previously divergent Korean community to a certain degree. The Korean community in Japan had been historically divided between those who supported the North Korean regime and those who associated with the South Korean regime. However, since the late 1970s, third-generation Koreans mobilized themselves beyond such a division, bringing about some key policy changes in immigration and citizenship in Japan. As previous studies suggest, the penetration of globalized notions of human rights had a strong impact on the emergence of the Zainichi Korean movement in the late twentieth century (Shin and Tsutsui 2007; Tsutsui and Shin 2008). However, undoubtedly, their tight-knit co-ethnic trust networks also contributed to the emergence of a new categorical identity among Koreans.

If we stop our observations here, then we may conclude that a categorically bounded trust network serves only positively for immigrants or other marginalized groups as a strategy to survive and eventually advance their economic status through the mechanism of "opportunity hoarding." Those successful Korean entrepreneurs in Japan indeed followed this pattern and mechanism. However, when we extend our observations further, we begin to see more complicated effects of trust networks for immigrants' experiences and identities.

Despite structural barriers that segregated Koreans from mainstream job sectors, the data suggest that the overall proportion of semiskilled and skilled Koreans increased during the 1960s and 1970s. This can be partially explained by the increase in educational attainment among Koreans in Japan. After the war, despite the lack of resources, many Koreans in Japan eagerly established their own schools to teach their children about their culture—partly because they wanted to prepare their children to go back to the homeland one day but also because they wanted to embrace their ethnic and cultural identities, which were severely suppressed under Japanese imperial rule, which imposed a cultural assimilation policy on the colonial population. However, the Japanese government, along with the American-led SCAP, considered these Korean schools, which some proletarian Koreans feverishly supported at that time, a medium of communist indoctrination. Koreans' fierce resistance to the state's order reinforced the state's perception of Koreans as a source of social instability and prompted the state to suppress their ethnic nationalism. In 1948, the Japanese government ordered all Korean parents to send their children to Japanese schools in order to control Koreans both culturally and politically.

Consequently, while Koreans were barred from mainstream economic opportunities, they could attend public educational institutions in Japan. Because public schools in Japan are very affordable and usually provide a good education, often better than that provided by expensive private schools, anyone could theoretically benefit from the relatively easy access to high-quality education regardless of nationality. Some existing research suggests that second- and third-generation Koreans, particularly males, tend to achieve a level of education comparable to that of the average Japanese, indicating the benefits of their relatively easy access to good education (Fukuoka and Kim 1997).

High educational attainment usually allows the marginalized population to exit their ethnic enclaves and seek more mainstream opportunities. This is certainly true for some but not all Koreans in Japan. Some Koreans became naturalized Japanese citizens or disguised their ethnic background and pursued job opportunities in the mainstream economy in Japan. In rare cases, a few educated and skilled Koreans also started their own businesses instead of competing for scarce opportunities in either the ethnic community or mainstream Japanese society. In addition to Han Chang-woo (CEO of Maruhan Group, mentioned earlier), Son Masayoshi, CEO of Soft Bank & Yahoo Japan, and ranked as the third richest person in Japan by *Forbes* in 2012, is also among the most prominent successful Korean entrepreneurs in Japan. However, most Koreans residing in Japan continuously rely on their co-ethnic trust networks to make their livelihood.

To support this fact, we observe a largely skewed pattern of occupation among Koreans. Compared to their Japanese counterparts with a comparable level of educational attainment, Koreans are more likely to be self-employed in relatively unstable retail and service industries. Furthermore, parallel to the emergence of these economic giants among Koreans, the polarization among them also increased between 1990 and 2005 (Kim 2011). The proportion of skilled workers among employed Koreans increased between 1990 and 2005, but during the same period unemployment rates for Koreans also increased. Although a similar trend is also present among the Japanese population as a whole, unemployment among Koreans was nearly twice that of the Japanese population, suggesting that Koreans remain more vulnerable to economic downturns (Kim 2011).

Existing studies attribute this skewed employment pattern mostly to the continuing discrimination in the private and public job sectors against Koreans in Japan (Fukuoka and Kim 1997; Nakahara 1997). But such a reason does not explain the exceptional success of some Korean entrepreneurs. Certainly individual luck and talent may explain their success to a degree. However, a closer look at how dynamics within the Korean community have shifted in the past few decades gives us a more complicated scenario.

During the first few decades after the end of the war, Koreans relied heavily on their co-ethnic trust networks. It was an essential part of their daily survival in postwar Japan, where there were extremely limited opportunities available to them. Since their homeland was divided into two political regimes shortly after liberation from Japanese colonial rule, Koreans in Japan became in practice stateless people. This was detrimental because in the post–World War II international community where one's belonging to a particular nation-state was a prerequisite for any legal protection nationally and internationally, stateless people had no state to protect them and advocate for their interests and rights. Under this circumstance, many Koreans started various co-ethnic organizations that could advocate for their interests and rights in Japan. Two particular organizations became prominent: South Korea–inclined Mindan and North Korea–affiliated Chongryon. Many Koreans obtained essential information about their legal standings and rights in Japan from these organizations. Since many Koreans became culturally assimilated and were unable to speak Korean, these organizations often became intermediaries between their homeland governments (North and South Korea) and Koreans in Japan, especially in obtaining legal records and passports. These organizations also served as the main facilitators of co-ethnic networks among Koreans in Japan through organizing various events where co-ethnics could meet other peers and keep in touch with them.

However, as more Koreans directly demanded better civic services from both the Japanese and their homeland governments, their need to rely on these co-ethnic organizations declined. Also, the more they became culturally and socially incorporated into Japanese mainstream society, the less significant it became for them to maintain ties with their co-ethnics. Furthermore, because the Japanese government strictly limited the number of incoming immigrants to its soil, the population of the Korean community did not grow over time but stagnated, unlike the populations of other ethnic migrant groups in other industrial countries. An increasing number of the younger generation of Koreans in Japan became willing to obtain Japanese citizenship and marry Japanese individuals. This also contributed to the declining significance of trust networks among them.

The declining significance of co-ethnic trust networks can also be observed among Korean entrepreneurs. Given the limited scale of the Korean community in Japan, if Koreans wish to expand their business, they inevitably need to go beyond their co-ethnic trust network, hire more Japanese employees, and expand their market beyond their ethnic enclaves. Recent research on Korean entrepreneurs confirms this pattern (Yim 2007) as the majority of successful Korean entrepreneurs chose their employees on the basis of their skills, rather than recruiting them through their co-ethnic trust network. In fact, these entrepreneurs cite their reliance on trust networks as one of the common causes of business failure among Koreans in Japan. This point was poignantly summarized in the following quote by one Korean entrepreneur in Japan:

> *A few years ago, I invested in one electric company in South Korea, but it failed. I analyzed and concluded that it was due to the fact that I did this business with my own family and relatives. Zainichi Koreans tend to easily trust their own relatives and siblings and make an investment in Korea with a hope [of success], but as in my case, it often results in failure. It is seriously problematic if you do business through an irrational co-ethnic or family bond. The era of business through such a connection is over. Today, even if we are co-ethnic, we can no longer do business unless we are rationally minded and willing to co-produce a profit together.*
>
> (Yim 2007:50–51)

As Tilly notes, unlike other types of networks, trust networks are usually small-scale, tight-knit communities that come with not only benefits but also obligations and constraints for their members:

> *Precisely because they are shielding serious long-term enterprises simultaneously from external predation and internal failures, trust networks always erect together, sharper us/them boundaries than the blurred edges of friendship and neighborhood. All such boundaries produce sharp implicit choices. On one side of the boundary lie security, solidarity, mutual aid, and restricted opportunity. On the other side beckon new opportunities, more extensive connections, and escapes from tyranny. Those who stick faithfully within trust networks generally reach new opportunities, fresh connections, and personal independence more rarely and slowly. They also suffer more acutely from shunning and expulsion when those punishments occur.*
>
> (Tilly 2007:16)

In other words, trust networks can serve as a beneficial tool of survival for the groups that are structurally barred from the system of rule or mainstream society, especially when they are able to find an economic niche and monopolize it. It was also advantageous for a handful of Koreans to achieve exceptional economic success. However, the longer they rely on this type of network, the more likely they are to miss out on greater opportunities in mainstream society. When the opportunities in mainstream society are scarce, members of trust networks continue to nurture their networks by recruiting new members. But in the case of Koreans in Japan, there was no steady flow of new members to recruit. In the meantime, successful Korean entrepreneurs rely less and less on trust networks for their business, weakening the resources available for members of their co-ethnic trust network. All these circumstances eventually led to a significant decline of co-ethnic trust networks among Koreans in Japan. The next section examines the implications of this decline in significance of trust networks on the inequality that Koreans experience in contemporary Japan.

Trust Network and Durable Inequality

Tilly argued that a declining significance of trust networks can be a sign of democratization when they are incorporated into a large group and given a say, which in turn increases equality among people in a society. A caveat needs to be inserted here. Tilly's theory of democratization hardly assumes a simple, linear causality; he was well aware of the diverse trajectories that democratization follows and the highly contingent nature of such processes. This chapter sheds some light on how such a reduction of inequality is experienced or distributed among people with different categorical identities and legal status in their everyday lives.

Successful Koreans are now indispensable to the Japanese economy and politics. Their continuous investment in the Japanese economy also exhibits these Koreans' commitment and trust in the long-term endurance of the Japanese state's ability to sustain their economic and social well-being within the country.

Japan's postwar education policy that enabled Koreans to have an opportunity to pursue higher education, in addition to structural circumstances and the categorically bounded trust network among Koreans, made opportunity hoarding possible. All of these factors contributed to reducing the overall economic deprivation that Koreans experienced. This was aided by, in the background, Japan's economic advancement and swift democratization.

Nevertheless, increasing polarization among Koreans also took place in parallel. The declining significance of trust networks did not occur evenly among Koreans in Japan. It happened faster for those who no longer needed to rely on such a network, but truly disadvantaged Koreans still need and continue to heavily rely on co-ethnic networks as an essential survival strategy. The following account by an elderly Korean woman attests to this fact.

> *To this date, my son is against [informal self-financing pools] and they say it will fail so don't do it. But it is impossible to save money and yet we cannot borrow money easily. Who can lend anyone money these days? No one lends any money to a grandma like me . . . unless you are trusted. Banks would look at your job and if your job is unstable, then they ask for a co-signer. And if you are like us, unemployed, then they will take our house away as collateral.*
>
> (Ijichi 2005:350)

However, trust networks among co-ethnics no longer have the same significance for those Koreans who became successfully incorporated into mainstream society. The more Koreans succeed as skilled professionals and entrepreneurs, the less public attention is given to the continued marginalization of some Koreans who remain socioeconomically and culturally segregated from the mainstream society and behind the shadow of successful Korean entrepreneurs.

The most infamous case to illustrate this point is the Utoro district in Kyoto, where a large number of Korean workers settled during the postwar period (Motooka and Mizuuchi 2013). Most Koreans in Utoro did not legally own their lands but settled in this district because of its proximity to factory sites; also, because the area was industrial rather than residential, few Japanese would live there. This type of settlement was common among Koreans in prewar and postwar Japan. After the war, the Japanese state began to establish clear legal demarcations of the ownership of these undeveloped regions where many Korean residents lived. After the war, the ownership of the land was transferred from Kyoto city to Nissan, which owned a factory in this region where Koreans used to work. But in the 1980s, Nissan sold the land to another private company, Nishi Nihon Shokusan, which got a court order to evict the residents of Utoro on the basis that they had been illegally residing on the land.

The legal battle between Korean residents in Utoro and the new owner of this district's land continues to this date. Due to ongoing legal battles over rights to this district, no substantial efforts to improve the infrastructure have been made. Consequently, Utoro looks much like a shantytown in developing countries, a large contrast to the rest of well-landscaped and manicured Kyoto. The condition of Utoro was well summarized by Catarina de Albuquerque, the UN Independent Expert on the issue of human rights obligations related to access to safe drinking water and sanitation, who reports annually to the General Assembly. Upon her visit to Japan in 2010, she described the following observations about Utoro in her press release:

> *I also visited the Utoro community near Kyoto, where Koreans have been living for several generations. The situation of access to water and sanitation has reportedly improved over the years, but there is room for additional progress. In a country which has achieved so much in the areas of water and sanitation, it is shocking to see that some people still have no access to water from the network. People are also not connected to the sewage network, despite the fact that the surrounding area is largely covered by sewage service. When floods occur, as happened one year ago, the lack of sewage and proper evacuation of grey water result in contamination of the environment, including with human faeces, posing serious health concerns. I am also worried that water and sanitation are extremely expensive for some people living in Utoro, who reportedly do not have a right to receive a pension.*
>
> (De Albuquerque 2010)

No offers to rescue these Korean residents of Utoro came from those successful Korean entrepreneurs who have the economic means to do so. But instead, such an offer came from a rather unexpected place: the South Korean government. Newly formed Japanese and South Korean NGOs advocating for the rights of Korean residents in Utoro lobbied South Korea, which provided financial help to buy lands from Nishinihon Shokusan to resolve the land dispute for Korean residents. This was brought largely by transnational lobbying efforts among human rights activists whose identities and solidarity are not necessarily based on categorically bounded trust networks.

Utoro's experience demonstrates how trust networks among Koreans in Japan do not necessarily protect the interests of the most disadvantaged members of their community. Nor are they effective in combating the durable inequality that some Koreans continue to experience.

Conclusion

This chapter concentrated on assessing the utility of two Tillyian concepts, trust networks and durable inequality, and aimed to further advance our understanding of the relationship between them by examining historical trajectories of Korean trust networks in postwar Japan. Koreans' experience confirmed the two opposing effects of trust networks that Tilly identified: (1) providing security, solidarity, mutual aid, and exclusive access to some opportunities, and (2) causing a restricted opportunity structure, insular connections, and isolation from the mainstream society. In other words, trust networks among co-ethnic immigrants are a double-edged sword, which could have both positive and negative impacts on their socioeconomic incorporation.

Koreans' trajectories also show us more than just the dual effects of trust networks. Tilly seemed to argue that members of trust networks, particularly those based in a particular economic niche, tend to share a similar socioeconomic fate; he explains how "niches based on trust networks help immigrants locate themselves in a new land, all right. But they also channel opportunities into a relatively narrow range. If the opportunities include access to capital, advanced education, or stardom, network members often do well. If they concentrate in low-wage labor, network members suffer the consequences" (Tilly 2007:15). The experiences of Koreans in Japan further elaborate this dynamic. Because of the very confining nature of trust networks, those exceptionally successful members are prompted to leave the network even as they trap other members who do not have enough resources to leave the confined network. This inadvertently increases polarization within a marginalized community. Rather than facilitating more equality, it facilitates inequality for those who used to share a categorically bounded trust network.

The experiences of Koreans in Japan also confirmed Tilly's argument that whether one remains within such a trust network is not just a matter of individual choice. Many Korean entrepreneurs' economic success owes much to the availability of cheap, highly skilled co-ethnic workers, at least during their take-off period. In other words, their ability to exit the co-ethnic network largely depends on their economic success or the amount of economic capital that they could accumulate, which was brought by their fellow members of the trust network. Those nonentrepreneurial Koreans without compatible economic achievement, on the other hand, had to continue to rely on their trust networks in order to survive. Such divergent trajectories emerged largely as a result of the existing structural factors such as the lack of steady flow of additional immigrants who can be recruited into their co-ethnic trust network as well as the persistent ethno-racial discrimination in both the private and the public domains. These structural factors were present in the case of Koreans in Japan and inhibited most Koreans from easily exiting their confining network in spite of their high educational attainment. Only the exceptionally successful ones can fully exit from the trust network. In short, Koreans' experiences suggest that structural elements largely influence one's ability to become independent from an ethnic trust network.

Koreans' experiences also confirm and elaborate on Tilly's prediction about the future fate of trust networks among marginalized immigrants. He argued that:

> (w)hether trust networks retain their vigor into the second and later generations depends on the extent to which members of those generations

continue to gain from membership. If the networks adapt, incorporate new connections, and facilitate members' opportunities at the migrant stream's destination, they more frequently survive and prosper. If they do not adapt, incorporate new connections, and facilitate members' opportunities at the destination, then transnational ties decline in the long run. Whether they survive or not, nevertheless, trust networks shape the lives of successive immigrant generations.

(Tilly 2007:16)

As we have seen, trust networks among Koreans in Japan declined sharply when they could not recruit new members to their groups and failed to facilitate new opportunities for their members. But when one particular type of network declines, there emerges a new type of relational effort among marginalized groups, as in the Utoro case. In this case it was not a niche-based co-ethnic network but rather a broader, transnational network among activists. In lieu of a co-ethnic trust network, this new network began to more effectively combat the persistent and aggravated durable inequality. This exploration of Koreans' experiences in postwar Japan certainly opens up an important new research opportunity to understand how truly disadvantaged and marginalized immigrants continue to strive in a society even when their original trust networks decline.

In sum, the analytical utility of Tilly's concepts of the trust network and durable inequality remain highly valuable as they allow us to conceptually navigate complex trajectories of a marginalized population's socioeconomic experience in society across time and space. However, the nature of the relationship among trust networks, democratization, and durable inequality is context-specific and thus deserves to be further explored with more diverse empirical cases than those Tilly originally considered.

Notes

1. Elsewhere, I argue that trust networks among Japanese colonial officials were transplanted from colonial Korea to mainland Japan after the end of World War II and demonstrate how this contributed to the colonial legacy of ethno-racial inequality between Japanese and Koreans in postwar Japan (Shin 2010).
2. *Burakumin* literally means "hamlet people." They are believed to be descendants of an outcast group, akin to the "untouchable" caste, in the feudal caste system in Japan. They were a historically marginalized group and are victims of ongoing socioeconomic discrimination in contemporary Japanese society.
3. He was ranked as the tenth richest in *Forbes* magazine in 2012. www.forbes.com/pictures/emlm45edkig/1-tadashi-yanai-family
4. Today, most Zainichi Koreans are legally classified as "Special Permanent Alien Residents." They can qualify for various social services such as access to the national pension program, health insurance, public education, and other local

and federal services. Yet they are without local or national suffrage rights, are restricted to only limited public-sector jobs, and are required to renew their residency every seven years and hold a re-entry permit whenever they leave Japan for more than two years.

References

De Albuquerque, Catarina. 2010. Press statement, United Nations Independent Expert on the issue of human rights obligations related to access to safe drinking water and sanitation. Retrieved from www.ohchr.org/en/NewsEvents/Pages/DisplayNews.aspx?NewsID=10233&LangID=E

Forbes Magazines. 2012. Japan's 40 richest. Retrieved from www.forbes.com/lists/2012/73/japan-billionaires-12_rank.html

Fukuoka, Yasunori and Myung-Soo Kim. 1997. *Zainichi Kankoku Seinen no Seikatsu to Ishiki*. Tokyo: Tokyo Daigaku Shuppankai.

Gold, Steven J. 2005. "Migrant Networks: A Summary and Critique of Relational Approaches to International Migration." Pp. 257–85 in *The Blackwell Companion to Social Inequalities*, edited by M. Romero and E. Margolis. Malden, MA: Blackwell.

Han, Jaehyang. 2010. *Zainichi Kigyo no Sangyou Keizaishi: Sono shakaiteki kiban to Dainamizumu*. Nagoya: Nagoya Daigaku Shuppankai.

Ijichi, Noriko. 2005. "Itonamareru Nichijo Yoriau Chikara: Katarikara no tayouna Zainichi-zo." In *Rekishi no naka no Zainichi* edited by Masaaki Ueda. Tokyo: Fujiwara Shoten.

Iwamura, Toshio. 1972. *Zainichi Chosenjin to Nihon rodosha kaikyu*. Tokyo: Azekura shobo.

Kashani, Sarah. 2011. "Success via Marginality: An Ethnographic Inquiry to Zainichi Korean Entrepreneurialism and Ethnic Economies." *Jisedai kenkyusha foram ronbunshu* 4: 189–205.

Kim, Bumsoo. 2011. "Changes in the Socio-Economic Position of Zainichi Koreans: A Historical Overview." *Social Science Japan Journal* 14(2): 233–245.

Lee, Soo-Im ed. 2012. *Zainichi Korian no Keizai Katsudo: Ijyuu Rodousha, Kigyoka no Kako Genzai Mirai*. Tokyo: Fuji Shuppan.

Motooka, Tokuya and Toshio Mizuuchi. 2013. "The Struggle for Living Space: Ethnicity, Housing, and the Politics of Urban Renewal in Japan's Squatter Areas." Pp. 148–163 in *Transforming Asian Cities: Intellectual Impasse, Asianizing Space and Emerging Translocalities* edited by Nihal Perera and Wing-Shing Tang. London: Routledge Press.

Nakahara, Ryoji. 1997. *Zainichi Kankoku Chosenjin no Shushoku sabetsu to Kokuseki Jyoko (Sosho Zainichi Korean Chosenjin no Houritsu mondai 2)*. Tokyo: Akashi Shoten.

Nishinarita, Yutaka. 1997. *Zainichi Chosenjin no Sekai to Teikoku Kokka*. Tokyo: Tokyodaigaku shuppan kai.

Nomura, Susumu. 1996. *Zaincihi Korean Sekai no Tabi*. Tokyo: Kodansha.

Portes, Alejandro. 2000. "Immigration and the Metropolis: Reflections on Urban History." *Journal of International Migration and Integration* 1(2): 152–175.

Pyon, Jin il. 2000. *Kyosha to siteno Zainichi: Keizai no me de mita mattaku atarasii siten no Zainichi ron*. Tokyo: Za Masada.

Shin, Hwaji. 2010. "Colonial Legacy of Ethno-Racial Inequality in Japan." *Theory and Society* 39: 327–342.
Shin, Hwa Ji and Kiyoteru Tsutsui. 2007. "Constructing Social Movement Actorhood: Resident Koreans' Activism in Japan since 1945." *International Journal of Comparative Sociology* 48(4):317–335.
Sugihara, Toru. 1998. *Ekkyosuru Tami: Kindai Osaka Chousenjin-shi Kenkyu*. Tokyo: Shinkansha.
Sugimoto, Hiroyuki. 2000a. "Senzen-ki Furyojyutakuchiku no Henyo katei: Furyojyutaku chiku, Hisabetsu Buraku, Zainichi Chosenjin (Jyo)." *Burakukaiho Kenkyu* 136: 39–50.
———. 2000b. "Senzen-ki Furyojyutakuchiku no Henyo katei: Furyojyutaku chiku, Hisabetsu Buraku, Zainichi Chosenjin (Jyo)." *Burakukaiho Kenkyu* 137: 78–92.
Tilly, Charles. 1968. "Race and Migration to the American City." Pp. 135–57 in *The Metropolitan Enigma* edited by James Q. Wilson. Cambridge, MA: Harvard University Press.
———. 1970 "Migration to American Cities." Pp. 171–86 in *Toward a National Urban Policy*, edited by Daniel Patrick Moynihan. New York: Harper.
———. 1990. "Transplanted Networks." Pp. 79–95 in *Immigration Reconsidered: History, Sociology, and Politics*, edited by Virginia Yans-McLaughlin. New York: Oxford University Press.
———. 1999. *Durable Inequality*. Berkeley: University of California Press.
———. 2005. *Trust and Rule*. Cambridge, UK: Cambridge University Press.
———. 2007. "Trust Networks in Transnational Migration." *Sociological Forum* 22: 3–25.
Tilly, Charles and C. Harold Brown. 1967. "On Uprooting, Kinship, and the Auspices of Migration." *International Journal of Comparative Sociology* 8: 139–164.
Tonomura, Masaru. 2004. *Zainichi Chosenjin Shakai no Rekishigakuteki Kenkyu*. Tokyo: Ryokuin Shobo.
Tsutsui, Kiyoteru and Hwa Ji Shin. 2008. "Global Norms, Local Activism, and Social Movement Outcomes: Global Human Rights and Resident Koreans in Japan." *Social Problems* 55(3):391–418.
TV Asahi. 2005. "Wide! Sukuramburu." Interviewer, Yamamoto Shinya (Film Director). May 18.
Waldinger, Roger D. 1996. *Still the Promised City? African-Americans and New Immigrants in New York, 1940–1990*. Cambridge, MA: Harvard University Press.
Yim, Young-Eon. 2007. "Zainichi Korean Kigyouka no Keieikatsudo to Network no Tenbo." *Ohara shakai mondai kenkyu zasshi* 588: 50–51.

8

ETHNIC CENTRALITIES IN BARCELONA

Foreign-Owned Businesses between "Commercial Ghettos" and Urban Revitalization

Pau Serra del Pozo

In neighborhoods where many immigrants live, there are often many small businesses owned by their compatriots or coethnics. In other cases, however, immigrant entrepreneurs locate their businesses in neighborhoods with a very high percentage of native residents. In Barcelona, the location strategies of ethnic business owners can be categorized as forms of either concentration or dispersion (Ma Mung, 1992; Kaplan, 1998). The strategies of these ethnic entrepreneurs could be of three types: (1) the orientation of products or services to immigrants or to a more general demand; (2) the concentration of their business in a neighborhood with a high proportion of immigrant population; or (3) the pursuit of the dispersion of specialized coethnic businesses over a wide metropolitan area. With the help of an abundant literature on urban ethnic businesses, I have attempted to conceptually categorize the resulting ethnic landscapes of those location strategies elsewhere (Serra, 2012). Here I intend to define the "spectral signature" of some case studies for each of the types of ethnic centralities within the Metropolitan Area of Barcelona (MAB). This chapter is an intuitive and descriptive attempt to define with basic quantitative measures the categories that I earlier explained theoretically (Serra, 2012).

In this chapter I ask: Does ethnic business concentration reinforce ethnic residential concentration? Does it contribute to urban revitalization or rather to the proliferation of "cloned businesses"? How can one avoid the proliferation of "cloned businesses" or other perceived negative effects on ethnic centralities? I avoid using the terms "segregation" and "ghetto" unless when used by other authors since the use and the meaning of such terms are controversial (Vaughan and Arbaci, 2011; Sampson, 2011; Peach, 1996; Hutchison and Haynes, 2012; Castañeda, 2012).

I use the expression "ethnic centralities" to refer to geographical concentrations of businesses owned by entrepreneurs of different geographical or cultural backgrounds from the host society. Most of the "ethnic" entrepreneurs I consider are foreign-born. Besides Barcelona, ten municipalities adjacent to the central city are included in my analysis in order to display the phenomena of ethnic centralities in this denser urban area. The case studies presented are Ciutat Vella (particularly, el Raval neighborhood), el Poble Sec, la Dreta de l'Eixample, La Rambla, La Sagrada Família, and Fort Pienc, in Barcelona; the Polígon Sud and Artigues, in Badalona; La Gavarra, in Cornellà de Llobregat; and La Torrassa, in l'Hospitalet de Llobregat (mapped in Figure 8.2).

The Geographical Distribution of Foreign Residents in the Metropolitan Area of Barcelona

In this section, I highlight the areas of concentration of foreign residents according to municipal registry data provided by the Spanish National Institute of Statistics for January 1, 2010.[1]

Figure 8.1 shows the percentage of immigrants in the total population of every census tract.

Data about Businesses in Catalonia

Neither central nor regional government records on businesses and business owners in Catalonia were available when this research was carried out. Only some municipalities had retail directories. The Barcelona Chamber of Commerce data on retail businesses were used in a publication (Parella, 2009), although it was not possible to tell the citizenship of the foreign entrepreneurs. I used the Spanish Yellow Pages online for certain limited queries. I did fieldwork in the district of Ciutat Vella (Serra, 2006) and in other neighborhoods. I also rely on other studies (Fundació Tot Raval, 2008; Moreras, 1999; Monnet, 2002; Li *et al.*, 2010).

Locational Strategies of Small Businesses Owned by Immigrants

The urban insertion of immigrant-owned businesses into Spanish cities is of particular relevance, especially where these businesses concentrate since in these cases their visibility and their differences with the businesses carried out by native entrepreneurs are often remarkable (Moreras, 1999; Parella, 2009).

Some particular foreign entrepreneurs prevail in specific retail niches: in the Barcelona area in 2011 the Pakistanis owned about 1,400 grocery stores, while in the Madrid area the Chinese owned about 3,000 grocery stores.[2] It is important to question why there is such a difference regarding the ethnicity of the grocery store owners in Madrid and in Barcelona. Charles Tilly's

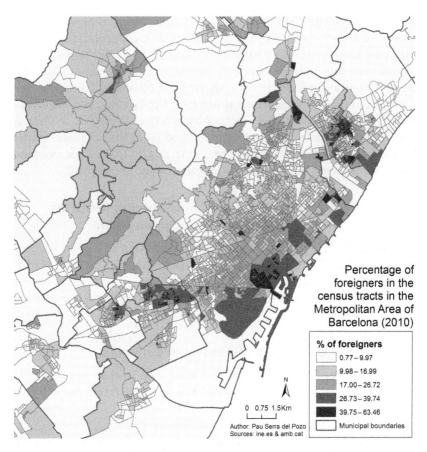

Figure 8.1 Percentage of foreigners in the census tracts in the Metropolitan Area of Barcelona (2010).

SOURCES: Instituto Nacional de Estadística and Mancomunitat de Municipis de l'Àrea Metropolitana de Barcelona. In some cases, the numbers include homeless individuals. A full-color map is available as an eResource on the book's Routledge page: www.routledge.com/9781138295414.

explanation regarding "transplanted networks" may help us understand the phenomenon. In the United States he observed job specialization of the same group of migrants according to not only their origin but also their destination. He explains that "American immigration produced remarkable specialization of work by origin, although the precise specialization varied from one locality and migrant stream to another" (Tilly, 1986). Chinese bazaar shopkeepers have leverage on cheap products manufactured in China. But why do Pakistani entrepreneurs prevail in the grocery business in Barcelona but not in Madrid, where Chinese grocers dominate? This may be a result of the concentration of Pakistani residents and entrepreneurs in Barcelona: in

2012, of all Pakistani residents in Spain (56877), 31 percent lived in Barcelona, 62 percent in Catalonia, and less than 2 percent in Madrid. In Spain, Barcelona has therefore been the preferred destination of the Pakistanis since the pioneer immigrants came in the 1970s to the Catalan capital from other European countries (Beltrán and Sáiz, 2008).

I conceive the theoretical possibility of the existence of what I call "monoethnic centralities," inspired by the "ethnic enclave" concept of Wilson and Portes (1980). In "monoethnic centralities," most or all residents and entrepreneurs of a neighborhood have the same ethnic origin. It seems as if such conditions seldom happen. In fact, Portes and Shafer (2006) restrict the true examples of the "ethnic enclave" to the Cuban enclave of "Little Havana" in Miami and to New York's "Chinatown."

Immigrant concentrations do not follow the monoethnic rationale: foreign residents of a single citizenship rarely accounted for more than 50 percent of the total number of residents in the MAB census tracts in 2012. Nor are all businesses in any neighborhood in the MAB owned by foreigners of the same citizenship or ethnic background.

Explaining Ethnic Business Centralities

I use indistinctly "entrepreneur," "merchant," "trader," and "shopkeeper" to designate the person who owns a shop or a business for selling products or services. I use the concept of "centrality" as a geographical concentration of businesses. This definition echoes somehow those of the "central place," "central business district," "concentration," and "centralization" in the economic and geography literatures (Mayhew, 1997). Businesses that concentrate spatially become a central place that is attractive to customers, no matter whether the location of the concentration is in the city center or on the periphery.

The use of "ethnic" is very common in the sociology of migration literature.[3] In Spain, "ethnic minorities" do not yet abound, and so "ethnic" is mainly associated with being an immigrant. Similarly, the expression "coethnic" is applied to someone who shares the same ethnicity as someone else; in this chapter it is also often synonymous with "compatriot." A finer consideration on the "ethnicity" of the entrepreneurs would actually stress more the specific geographical origins of these actors and on the links they keep with their kin than just on their citizenship. Most of the Chinese, Pakistani, and Indian entrepreneurs I mention in this chapter came to Barcelona's area from the provinces of Zhejiang, Punjab, and Sindh, respectively. However, they do not necessarily come straight from those origin areas: for instance, Indian Sindhis did not come originally from the current Pakistani province of Shind, but their families did and were eventually evicted from that province after the partition of India. Some Zhejiang Chinese came to Barcelona from other European locations, such as United Kingdom, the Netherlands, and France, where they owned restaurants, so as to follow their customers to their touristic destinations (Beltrán, 2000). Next, I define the types of ethnic centralities I have found, for the moment, in the MAB. I note that I have not found any monoethnic centrality.

Ethnic Centralities in the Metropolitan Area of Barcelona

The literature concerning ethnic economies is not specific on the quantitative definition of "ethnic enclaves" or other similar designations, and these concepts have rarely been "operationalized" with numerical parameters (see Serra, 2012). This is one of the goals of this text.

I summarize the MAB ethnic centralities in Tables 8.1 and 8.2. Table 8.1 includes all the cases studied, while Table 8.2 summarizes the first table. Both tables include the quantitative parameters that define the observed ethnic centralities of MAB. These parameters are ranges within which several cases of ethnic centralities fall. The ranges have been observed just once. Due to scarcity of business censuses it has not been possible so far to record more data over time for every ethnic centrality case. Thus, I reckon that the proposed classification of four types of ethnic centralities would need further observations in MAB or in other metropolitan areas to become more general.

In the coethnic specialized centralities, between 21.36 percent and 34.09 percent of all entrepreneurs present in the neighborhood are of the same heritage (specifically, Chinese or Indian are the examples demonstrated in column 1 of Table 8.1). Yet this is not an exclusive feature of these centralities, since those figures are similar in the coethnic diverse centralities (where between 22.58 percent and 26.13 percent of all entrepreneurs are coethnics) and in the multiethnic centralities (where between 25 percent and 34 percent of all businesses entrepreneurs are foreigners).

The percentage of ethnic or coethnic merchants out of the total number of entrepreneurs in an area (column 1 in both Tables 8.1 and 8.2) is not able to help us isolate or define in a precise way three of the four ethnic centralities studied. The relatively low percentages of foreign entrepreneurs exhibited in those three small-area ethnic centralities types rule out the presence of concentrated monoethnic centralities in the MAB, since none has near 100 percent of foreign-owned businesses.

What distinguishes the coethnic specialized centralities from other ethnic centralities is the predominance of a main group of foreign entrepreneurs inside a specific business sector in relation to other citizenships in a neighborhood. The data shows that between 68.75 percent and 95.77 percent of all foreign entrepreneurs in each sample consists of a single group (Chinese or Indian) of specialized entrepreneurs (column 4).

Table 8.1 Parametric analysis of all observed ethnic centralities in the Barcelona Metropolitan Area. Data from author's fieldwork or from other sources.

Ethnic centralities types	Examples of neighborhoods or areas*	Geographical boundaries of the neighborhood or area used	1) % of coethnic or ethnic entrepreneurs per total number of traders**	2) Density of coethnic or ethnic businesses per hectare***	3) % of foreign or coethnic residents per total population in 2010****	4) % of coethnic entrepreneurs more dominant among foreign traders*****	5) % of business specialization of the foreign traders, by ethnic group
Coethnic specialized centralities	Dreta de l'Eixample[1], in Barcelona (2011), a Chinese centrality specialized on textile and footwear wholesalers	Boundaries adjusted to the concentration of ethnic businesses	34.09% of all merchants are Chinese (136/399)	4.45 Chinese businesses/Ha (30.56 Ha)	3.49% of all residents are Chinese (227/6,498)	95.77% of all foreign merchants are Chinese (136/142)	75% of all Chinese businesses are textile wholesalers
	Polígon Sud[2], in Badalona (2009), a Chinese centrality specialized on textiles, footwear, and toy wholesalers		22.79% of all merchants are Chinese (80/351)	2.39 Chinese businesses/Ha (33.41 Ha)	2.38% of all residents are Chinese (41/1,723)	100% of all foreign merchants are Chinese (80/80)	100% of all the Chinese shops are wholesalers in textiles, footwear, and toys
	La Sagrada Família neighborhood[3], in Barcelona (2011), an Indian centrality specialized on souvenir shops		21.36% of all merchants are Indian (22/32)	3.54 Indian businesses/Ha (6.21 Ha)	0.44% of all residents are Indian (12/2,701)	68.75% of all foreign merchants are Indians (22/32)	100% of all Indian businesses are souvenir shops
Coethnic diverse centralities	Fort Pienc[4], in Barcelona (2011), a Chinese diverse centrality		26.13% of all merchants are Chinese (52/199)	2.28 Chinese businesses/Ha (22.83 Ha)	3.31% of all residents are Chinese (379/1,1445)	92.86% of all foreign merchants are Chinese (52/56)	28.85% of all Chinese businesses are bars and restaurants

(Continued)

Table 8.1 Continued

Ethnic centralities types	Examples of neighborhoods or areas*	Geographical boundaries of the neighborhood or area used	1) % of coethnic or ethnic entrepreneurs per total number of traders**	2) Density of coethnic or ethnic businesses per hectare***	3) % of foreign or coethnic residents per total population in 2010****	4) % of coethnic entrepreneurs more dominant among foreign traders*****	5) % of business specialization of the foreign traders, by ethnic group
	La Gavarra[5], in Cornellà de Llobregat (2011), a Chinese diverse centrality		22.58% of all merchants are Chinese (14/92)	2.25 Chinese businesses/Ha (6.21 Ha)	0.68% of all residents are Chinese (44/6,498)	73.68% of all foreign merchants are Chinese (14/19)	35.71% of all Chinese businesses are bars and restaurants
Multiethnic centralities	El Poble Sec[6], in Barcelona (2005)		25% of all merchants are foreigners (78/312)	5.69 ethnic businesses/Ha (13.7 Ha)	31.02% of all residents are foreigners (2,723/8,779)	50% of all foreign merchants are Pakistani (39/78)	29% of all ethnic businesses are bars and restaurants (ethnic group data not available)
	El Raval[7], in Barcelona (2007)	Official boundaries of the neighborhood	33.5% of all merchants are foreigners (274/817)	2.82 ethnic businesses/Ha (97.15 Ha)	47.15% of all residents are foreigners (21,929/46,506)	50,54% of all foreign merchants are Pakistani (47/93)	7.67% of all ethnic businesses are Pakistani phone call businesses (so-called Public Call Offices in Pakistan)
	La Torrassa[9], in l'Hospitalet de Llobregat (2007)		32.2% of all merchants are foreigners (123/328)	3.05 ethnic businesses/Ha (40.32 Ha)	35.19% of all residents are foreigners (8,652/24,587)	39.84% of all foreign merchants are Pakistani (49/123)	12% of all ethnic businesses are Pakistanis groceries, and another 12% are Pakistani phone call businesses

Artigues[10], in Badalona (2010)	25.52% of all merchants are foreigners (49/192)	5.38 ethnic businesses/Ha (9.1 Ha)	35% of all residents are foreigners (1,604/4,552)	Not available	30.61% of all ethnic businesses are bars and restaurants (ethnic group not available)
Metropolitan dispersion of coethnic specialized entrepreneurs					
Chinese restaurants in the MAB[11] (2011)	100% of all merchants are Chinese	0.01 ethnic businesses/Ha (22299.52 Ha)	1.05% of all residents are Chinese (27,113/2,579,024)	100% of all foreign merchants are Chinese 100% (233/233)	100% of all businesses Chinese restaurants
AMB 11 central municipalities					
Latin American Restaurants in the MAB[11] (2011)	100% of all merchants are Latin Americans	0.005 ethnic businesses/Ha (22299.52 Ha)	7.63% of all residents are Latin Americans (196,816/2579,024)	100% of all foreign merchants are Latin American (103/103)	100% of all businesses Latin American restaurants

* Data sources of every example, identified with a number inside the first parenthesis. The second parenthesis includes the year for which the data were collected or published.

(1) Fieldwork carried out by Javier Paredes and the author.
(2) BCIN (2009). The total number of wholesalers has been obtained from www.bcin.org/ (option "Companies Database").
(3) Fieldwork conducted by the author.
(4) Fieldwork carried out by Javier Paredes and author.
(5) Fieldwork conducted by the author.
(6) Zegrí et al. (2006).
(7) Fundació Tot Raval (2008); Andreu and Paricio (2007); Serra (2006), except (8).
(8) Serra (2006)
(9) Fieldwork made by students at the Universitat Internacional de Catalunya, led by the author.
(10) Li et al. (2010).
(11) www.paginasmarillas.es.

** Data inside parentheses indicate the number of ethnic businesses divided by the total number of businesses in that neighborhood or area.
*** Data inside parentheses indicate the number of hectares in that neighborhood or area.
**** Data inside parentheses indicate the number of foreign residents divided by the total number of residents in that neighborhood or area.
***** Data inside parentheses indicate the number of the most dominant foreign group of entrepreneurs divided by the total number of foreign entrepreneurs in that neighborhood or area.

Table 8.2 Summary of ethnic centralities in the Metropolitan Area of Barcelona. Data from author's fieldwork or from other sources.

Ethnic centralities types	1) % of coethnic or ethnic entrepreneurs per total number of traders	2) Density of coethnic or ethnic businesses per hectare	3) % of foreign or coethnic residents per total population in 2010	4) % of coethnic entrepreneurs more dominant among foreign traders	5) % of business specialization of the foreign traders, by ethnic group	Type of clientele*	Examples in the Barcelona Metropolitan Area**
Coethnic specialized centralities	Between 21.36% and 34.09% of all entrepreneurs are coethnics	Between 2.39 and 4.45 of coethnic businesses/Ha	Between 0.44% and 3.49% of all residents are coethnics	*Between 68.75% and 95.77% of all foreign entrepreneurs are coethnics ****	*Between 75% and 100% of all coethnic businesses are of the same type*	Specialized clientele	**Dreta de l'Eixample (Barcelona, Chinese); Polígon Sud (Badalona, Chinese), Indian souvenirs shops** in La Rambla and around the Sagrada Família (Barcelona)
Coethnic diverse centralities	Between 22.58% and 26.13% of all entrepreneurs are coethnics	Between 2.25 and 2.28 of coethnic businesses/Ha		Between 73.68% and 94.55% of all foreign entrepreneurs are coethnics	Between 28.85% and 35.71% of all coethnic businesses are of the same type		**Fort Pienc (Barcelona)** and **la Gavarra (Cornellà de Llobregat)**
Multiethnic centralities	*Between 25% and 33.5% of all entrepreneurs are foreigners*	*Between 2.82 and 5.69 of ethnic businesses/Ha*	*Between 31.02% and 47.15% of all residents are foreigners*	Between 39.84% and 50.54% of all foreign entrepreneurs are coethnics	*Between 7.67% and 30.61% of all ethnic businesses are specialized*	Multiethnic local clientele	Ciutat Vella (**Raval** and other neighborhoods) and **Poble Sec (Barcelona)**; Fondo (Santa Coloma de Gramenet); Collblanc, **La Torrassa**, Pubilla Casas and **La Florida (l'Hospitalet de Llobregat)**, La Salut, La Pau and Artigues (Badalona)
Metropolitan dispersion of coethnic specialized businesses	*100% of all entrepreneurs in a sector are coethnics*	*Between 0.005 and 0.01 of coethnic businesses/Ha*	Between 1.05% and 7.63% of all residents are coethnics	100% of all foreign entrepreneurs are coethnics	100% of all businesses are specialized	General multiethnic clientele	In the metropolitan area of Barcelona: **Chinese restaurants** and Chinese bazaars, **Latino restaurants**, Pakistani groceries

* Item without parameters.
** The examples in bold case are discussed in Table 8.1.
*** *Underlined text refers to key features that define each type of ethnic centrality.*

In the coethnic diverse centralities there is also a predominance of a particular foreign or ethnic group of entrepreneurs (predominance of between 73.68 percent and 94.55 percent). The "diversity" in these centralities is based upon the diversity of business types owned by these predominant coethnic entrepreneurs.

What distinguishes the two coethnic centralities is that between 75 percent and 100 percent of the coethnic businesses are devoted to the same business sector (they are specialized) and are owned by the dominant ethnic entrepreneurial group (Chinese or Indian in the examples). In contrast, in diverse centralities only between 28.85 percent and 35.71 percent of all coethnic businesses are of the same type.

The combination of the features in columns 4 and 5 of Tables 8.1 and 8.2 is what distinguishes the two coethnic centrality types from the multiethnic centralities, where only between 39.84 percent and 50.54 percent of all foreign entrepreneurs are of the same citizenship (column 4) and only between 7.67 percent and 30.61 percent of all ethnic businesses are specialized (column 5).

Finally, the Metropolitan dispersion of coethnic specialized businesses occurs when all entrepreneurs of a particular specialized business sector are coethnic. These entrepreneurs then look for the dispersion of their businesses, since they cater to mainstream customers. So the density of these businesses per hectare is quite low.

Once the four ethnic centralities have been distinguished in a quantitative way, I describe each one with a qualitative approach.

Coethnic Specialized Centralities

Coethnic specialized centralities of a single type of business and nationality are most abundant (columns 4 and 5 in both tables). Some examples of these centralities are small businesses of Chinese textile wholesalers in la Dreta de l'Eixample, in Barcelona (Figure 8.2); large stores of Chinese wholesalers in the Polígon Sud, in Badalona (Figures 8.2 and 8.3); and Indian-owned souvenir shops around La Sagrada Família in Barcelona (Figure 8.2), some of which were, until recently, photo-developing shops.

Another example consists of fifteen Indian-owned souvenir shops in La Rambla, Barcelona. The niche market for this type of business, focused on La Rambla and the area around La Sagrada Família, is in the hands of Indians in Barcelona. Arjan, a Sindhi entrepreneur who started a souvenir shop some decades ago in La Rambla, is originally from the Pakistani province of Sindh, though he came to Barcelona not directly from there but from London. The employees Arjan hired at the beginning of his business in La Rambla were also Sindhis. Over time, his former employees became entrepreneurs who started the rest of the fourteen Sindhi souvenirs shops that

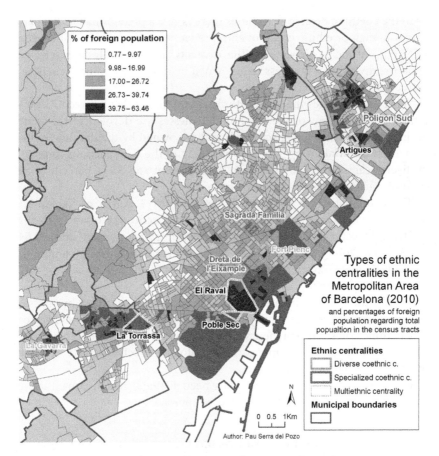

Figure 8.2 Ethnic centralities in the Metropolitan Area of Barcelona.

A full-color map is available as an eResource on the book's Routledge page: www.routledge.com/9781138295414.

were present in La Rambla by 2012. However, it is likely that this "Sindhi pattern" of La Rambla and La Sagrada Família souvenir shops refers only to entrepreneurs and not to all current employees because, during fieldwork I did in the latter neighborhood, I spoke with some Indian employees who were from other areas in India and did not consider themselves Sindhi.

Coethnic Diverse Centralities

Unlike entrepreneurs in coethnic specialized centralities, coethnic entrepreneurs in coethnic diverse centralities develop businesses of various kinds, including the numerous Chinese businesses on Massanet Street in the Fondo neighborhood of Santa Coloma de Gramenet that make up a small

"Chinatown." I prefer to restrict the use of the name "Chinatown" to a Chinese diverse centrality, a concentration of Chinese businesses of several types, not to a Chinese specialized centrality.

Another larger but less dense Chinatown is located in the neighborhood of Fort Pienc (Barcelona), adjacent to the aforementioned Chinese textile wholesalers' area in la Dreta de l'Eixample.

In Fort Pienc there are not only the typical Chinese businesses in Barcelona, such as bars, restaurants, and bazaars, but also two driving schools, a language center, hairdressers, massage parlors, acupuncture centers, medium-sized supermarkets, a business for restaurant and hospitality services, green groceries, mobile phone shops, and clothing stores. In 2012 the Chinese bank ICBC opened a branch there.

Multiethnic Centralities

Multiethnic centralities are concentrations of businesses owned by entrepreneurs from various citizenships who are engaged in numerous activities. Examples exist in el Raval and in much of the rest of the district of Ciutat Vella (Figure 8.3).

A detailed case study of the district of Ciutat Vella (Serra, 2006), which is the traditional core of the foreign immigration in Barcelona, has allowed me to show the complexity of categorizing ethnic business concentrations.

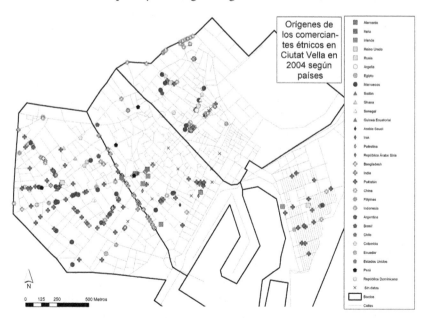

Figure 8.3 Origins of immigrant entrepreneurs in Ciutat Vella in 2004 by countries.

SOURCE: Serra (2006). A full-color map is available as an eResource on the book's Routledge page: www.routledge.com/9781138295414.

Figure 8.4 Pakistani barbershops in Sant Pau Street in el Raval in the district of Ciutat Vella (Barcelona). "Business cloning" at a very close distance is quite a common practice in multiethnic centralities.

SOURCE: Serra (2006).

In parts of the district of Ciutat Vella there are Indian-owned souvenir shops on La Rambla and Chinese textile wholesalers in la Dreta de l'Eixample. On the other hand, in el Raval, among the Pakistani convenience businesses catering to Pakistani customers or other immigrants in the neighborhood are *halal* butchers, telephone call businesses, and barbershops (Figure 8.4). These Pakistani-owned businesses and other ethnic retailers contribute to the different multiethnic centralities in Ciutat Vella, especially numbers 1, 2, and 3 in Figure 8.6. The concentration of ethnic businesses in el Raval and in Ciutat Vella (Figures 8.5 and 8.6) seems to respond largely to a significant presence of foreign residents.

In multiethnic centralities, businesses owned by foreigners are geared in a special way toward local residents, a mixture of natives and foreigners.

This orientation is found in Figure 8.6, which shows higher concentration of *locutorios* international call centers in census tracts where the presence of foreign residents is higher (except for an area marked with * in the map where homeless foreign "residents" have been registered). The correlation coefficient between these two variables, the foreign population and number of businesses by census tract, is 0.83 (the scatterplot is shown in Figure 8.7; the census tract marked with * has not intervened in the analysis).

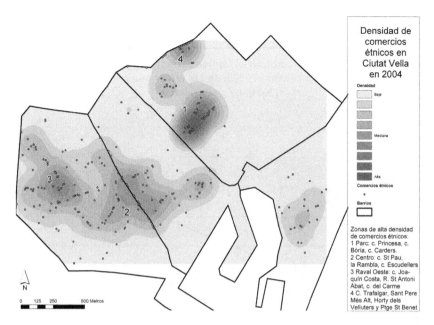

Figure 8.5 Contour zones map with the same density of businesses per hectare in the district of Ciutat Vella (Barcelona).

SOURCE: Serra (2006).

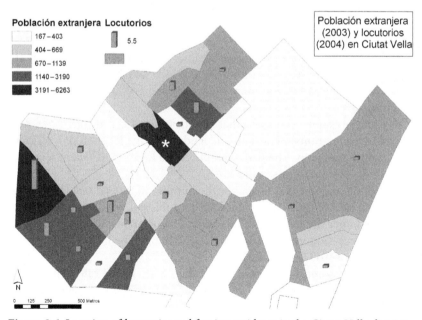

Figure 8.6 Location of *locutorios* and foreign residents in the Ciutat Vella district.

SOURCE: Serra (2006). A full-color map is available as an eResource on the book's Routledge page: www.routledge.com/9781138295414.

* Census tract with over-registration of foreign residents.

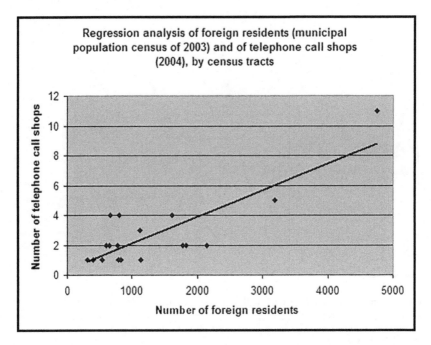

Figure 8.7 Regression analysis between number of foreign residents and number of telephone call businesses in the district of Ciutat Vella (Barcelona).

SOURCE: Serra (2006).

Multiethnic centralities serve populations of which about 30 percent are foreign immigrants. This condition seems necessary but not sufficient: in some areas of the MAB with more than 30 percent of immigrants there are few businesses.

Two more examples suggest that the location of certain activities performed by immigrants seems quite dependent on the location of a resident immigrant population. The first example is the location of federations and associations of immigrants in the MAB.[4]

The results suggest that the larger the number of foreign residents in the postcode zones[5] of the MAB (according to municipal population registry of 2010), the larger the number of migrations' associations and federations in the same zones (Figure 8.8). Indeed, the correlation coefficient between the two variables is 0.69 (Figure 8.9).

The second example consists of the location of telephone call businesses or parlors (*locutorios*, in Spanish, a shop that offers international telephone calls and Internet services and often remittances shipping, too), a business type very much addressed to foreign migrant customers and their spatial association with the location of the foreign residents in the MAB, where the correlation coefficient of 0.86 is higher than in the first example (Figures 8.10 and 8.11).

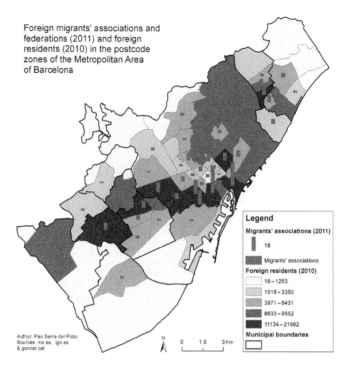

Figure 8.8 Foreign residents and immigrants' associations and federations in the postcode zones in the metropolitan area of Barcelona.

SOURCES: www.ine.es, www.ign.es, and www.gencat.cat. A full-color map is available as an eResource on the book's Routledge page: www.routledge.com/9781138295414.

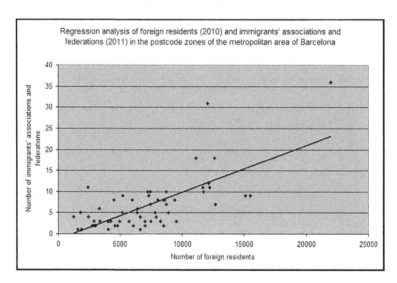

Figure 8.9 Regression with the number of foreign residents and the number of immigrants' associations and federations in the postcode areas of the Metropolitan Area of Barcelona.

SOURCES: www.ine.es, www.ign.es, and www.gencat.cat. The correlation coefficient is 0.69.

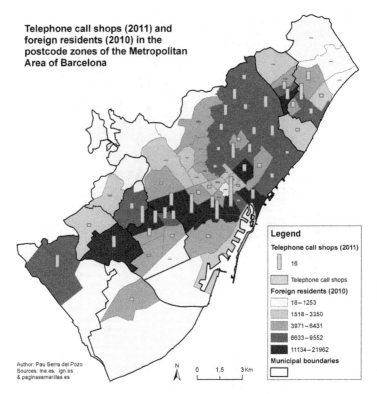

Figure 8.10 Foreign residents and telephone call businesses in the postcode zones in the Metropolitan Area of Barcelona.

SOURCES: www.ine.es, www.paginasamarillas.es, and www.ign.es. A full-color map is available as an eResource on the book's Routledge page: www.routledge.com/9781138295414.

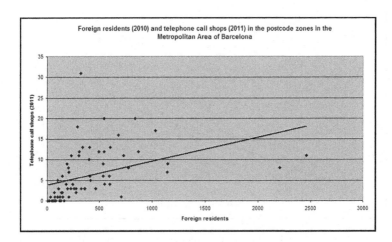

Figure 8.11 Regression between the number of foreign residents and the number of telephone call businesses in the postcode areas of the Metropolitan Area of Barcelona.

SOURCES: www.ine.es, www.paginasamarillas.es, and www.ign.es. The correlation coefficient is 0.86.

The metropolitan map of the telephone parlors is very similar to that for the immigrants' associations (Figure 8.9), not only because the former map has 420 businesses and the latter 405 associations and federations but also because of their similar geographical distribution, which is heavily dependent on the registered alien resident population.

The two results seem to support each other: first, that the location of certain activities, whether they be businesses or headquarters of migrants' associations,[6] is quite dependent on the existence of a threshold of foreign resident population; second, that these spatial correlation phenomena tend to be present in multiethnic centralities, where the percentage of foreign residents is 31 percent and 47 percent of the total population in the respective census tracts (see column 3 in Tables 8.1 and 8.2).

In short, multiethnic centralities are associated with a large multiethnic population in a neighborhood (about one-third and one-half of the total population) to which ethnic entrepreneurs have to supply products and specific services. These include *halal* butchers; cheap restaurants and bars like *kebabs* fast-food places; DVD stores; telephone call centers (often with a sign with the discreet acronym PCO, for "Public Call Offices," to attract South Asian customers); ethnic barbershops and hairdressers (with pictures of South Asians in the showcase); travel agencies; Muslim bookstores; delicatessen shops; and distributors of both foreign presses and ethnic presses published locally but published and addressed to coethnics.

Also, in multiethnic centralities, some retail and services owned by ethnic entrepreneurs do not have any ethnic orientation: a standard bar owned by a Chinese entrepreneur, a grocery store owned by a Pakistani shopkeeper who sells beer and wine, among other items, to residents and tourists from all backgrounds (although they often discreetly offer the famous South Asian *samosas*). Other ethnic businesses are rather "exotic," like the two "Medina Azahara" businesses owned by Rachid in el Raval; one, selling Moroccan craftsmanship articles, catered to the few tourists who ventured into the neighborhood, while the other one served Moroccan green tea and *shisha* or *hookah* seasoned with "exotic" chillout Arabic music and books and catered to local young people and college students (numerous in this semi-gentrified area).

Metropolitan Dispersion of Coethnic Specialized Businesses

Finally, the "metropolitan dispersion of coethnic specialized businesses" consists of the location in a large metropolitan area of businesses whose entrepreneurs are of the same ethnicity. These businesses are dispersed in a large metropolitan area and develop the same type of specialized business, such as Chinese restaurants, Pakistani green groceries, Latino restaurants, or Chinese bazaars (in Spain, bazaars are stores for the home, the equivalent of "dollar stores" in the United States).

I offer two examples of "dispersion" of ethnic businesses in the MAB. The first is Chinese restaurants and their strategy of dispersion in the MAB. These restaurant owners do not seek to concentrate these businesses in areas where there are many Chinese residents (Figure 8.12). The second example is Latino restaurant entrepreneurs who seem to have the same interest in not focusing on areas where more Latin American immigrants live (Figure 8.13).[7]

The two maps are similar, regardless of the differences in the number of restaurants and other type and the number of Chinese residents (233) and American (103). Both examples exhibit correlation coefficients between the number of businesses and the number of coethnic residents with very low positive values, emphasizing the lack of interest by the entrepreneurs in locating the ethnic restaurant businesses where more coethnics live. Indeed, Chinese

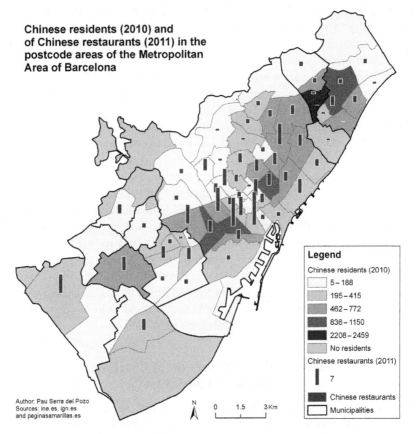

Figure 8.12 Chinese residents and Chinese restaurants in the postcode areas of the Metropolitan Area of Barcelona.

SOURCES: www.ine.es, www.paginasamarillas.es, and www.ign.es. A full-color map is available as an eResource on the book's Routledge page: www.routledge.com/9781138295414.

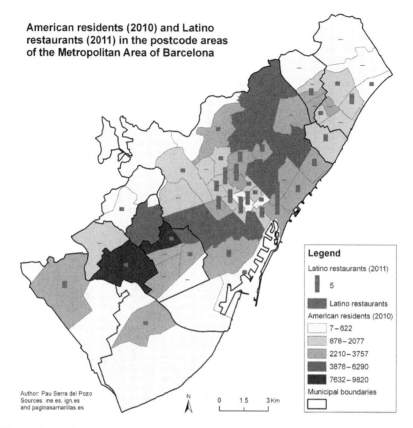

Figure 8.13 Residents from the American continent and Latino restaurants in the postcode areas of the Metropolitan Area of Barcelona.

SOURCES: www.ine.es, www.paginasamarillas.es, and www.ign.es. A full-color map is available as an eResource on the book's Routledge page: www.routledge.com/9781138295414.

and Latino restaurants are spread out in a large metropolitan area where the percentages of corresponding coethnic residents are only 1.05% and 7.63% respectively, which are similar rates to those in coethnic diverse centralities and in coethnic specialized centralities (column 4, Tables 8.1 and 8.2).

Assessment of Ethnic Centralities in the Metropolitan Area of Barcelona

I attempt to assess ethnic centralities in the MAB by answering three questions: Do foreign-owned businesses reinforce ethnic residential concentration, or do they respond to it? Do the foreign-owned businesses contribute to urban revitalization? How might the number of "cloned businesses" be reduced? Table 8.3 summarizes the answers to these questions

Table 8.3 Summary of an assessment of the ethnic centralities in the Metropolitan Area of Barcelona.

Ethnic centrality types	1) % of coethnic or ethnic entrepreneurs per total number of traders	3) % of foreign or coethnic residents per total population in 2010	Do they reinforce ethnic residential concentration?	Do they contribute to urban revitalization or rather to the proliferation of "cloned businesses"?	How to avoid the proliferation of "cloned businesses" or other perceived negative effects?
Coethnic specialized centralities	Between 21.36% and 34.09% of all entrepreneurs are coethnics.	Between 0.44% and 3.49% of all residents are coethnics.	No, they do not create a relevant "call effect" to coethnic residents.	To urban revitalization: they create new businesses and keep them in times of crisis & are competitive in nonethnic neighborhoods. Yet they may be perceived as "commercial ghettos."	Through business and neighborhood "integration" processes. Native residents press local governments for rules compliance & to stop granting licenses to some business types.
Coethnic diverse centralities	Between 22.58% and 26.13% of all entrepreneurs are coethnics.				
Multiethnic centralities	Between 25% and 34% of all entrepreneurs are foreigners.	Between 31.02% and 47.15% of all residents are foreigners.	A positive correlation or an attraction between number of foreign residents & number of businesses owned by foreign entrepreneurs (see figures 8.8 & 8.11) suggests an affirmative answer, though other factors need to be considered (such as low rents of housing, likely attracting foreign residents).	Symptoms of proliferation of "cloned businesses": ethnic orientation, saturation of repetitive businesses. Symptoms of revitalization: businesses have been opened in hundreds of commercial premises that were closed in the early 1990s crisis and keep them in times of crisis. Unplanned & undesired "ethnic gentrification" & "commercial ghettos."	Through business and neighborhood "integration" processes. Native residents press local governments for rules compliance & to stop granting licenses to some businesses types. Businesses associations & local governments for commercial revitalization. Spontaneous reorientation of "cloned" ethnic businesses toward mainstream customers is difficult (despite optimal downtown locations).
Metropolitan dispersion of coethnic specialized businesses	*100% of all entrepreneurs are coethnics.*	Between 1.05% and 7.63% of all residents are coethnics.	No, they do not create a relevant "call effect" to coethnic residents.	To urban revitalization: they create new businesses and keep them in times of crisis, are competitive in nonethnic neighborhoods. They add a certain "exotic" touch.	No perception of the proliferation of "cloned businesses," yet there may be saturation at a metropolitan scale, so dynamic ethnic entrepreneurs change businesses (from traditional Chinese restaurants to woks and bars).

for each one of the four ethnic centralities types found in the Metropolitan Area of Barcelona.

Assessment of the Specialized Centralities and of the Coethnic Diverse Centralities

Although they are quite different in certain aspects, I discuss specialized centralities and coethnic diverse centralities together since they have some common elements regarding the three questions posed:

(1) Do the foreign-owned businesses reinforce ethnic residential concentration?

In the two types of coethnic centralities, only between 0.44 percent and 3.49 percent of all residents are coethnics, so it seems coethnic centralities do not create a relevant attraction effect that pulls coethnics to move into the area.

(2) Do the foreign-owned businesses contribute to urban revitalization or to the proliferation of "cloned businesses"?

The two types of coethnic centralities tend toward urban revitalization since they create new businesses and keep them in times of crisis (as in the case of some of the traditional film photograph and souvenir shops around La Sagrada Família, replaced by souvenir shops owned by Indians). Coethnic centralities are also competitive in nonethnic neighborhoods; in other words, they do not need a high coethnic clientele. Yet in some cases they have been perceived as "commercial ghettos": in the Dreta de l'Eixample there are more than a hundred "cloned" Chinese textile wholesalers that have been blamed by a native residents' association for the withdrawal of native convenience businesses. For examples, there was a public demonstration on October 5, 2007, called by a local association of residents in the Dreta de l'Eixample neighborhood to protest against the allegedly responsibility of Chinese textile wholesaler entrepreneurs for the shutdown of traditional convenience businesses. Apparently a native butcher, in this case, was not able to pay the rising price of commercial premises rents that resulted from the increasing Chinese demand for those premises and had to shut down. The graffiti railed against the "Chinese ghetto" and in favor of native businesses in the neighborhood. The local police did not authorize the demonstration.

The urban context may respond much differently to apparently the same phenomena: in the Dreta de l'Eixample neighborhood in Barcelona, a Chinese specialized centrality was thought to be the cause of the lack of convenience stores. Another Chinese specialized centrality in the Polígon Sud in Badalona, located in the midst of a large commercial and industrial park with few residents, was not blamed the same way as were the Chinese businesses in la Dreta de l'Eixample.

(3) How might the number of "cloned businesses" be reduced?

Integration of businesses owned by foreigners into local and regional business associations and federations is seen as a way to foster the incorporation of those entrepreneurs into standard "Catalan good practices" in the trade business: rules compliance, improved quality of businesses to cater to the native general clientele, participation in events and initiatives that may foster the attractiveness of the neighborhood, and so on (Serra, 2008). Actually, the Chinese entrepreneurs in Catalonia have been integrated in a special way to form a regional federation of businesses: about four thousand Chinese businesses in Catalonia are part of an ethnic-business association, which has put itself under the aegis of the Catalan small businesses federation since 2007. How this official integration of Chinese businesses has influenced the "normalization" of those businesses is difficult to assess, although at least they have a platform and leaders to whom regional and local governments can talk, as their participation in the Chinese New Year celebration in Barcelona shows.[8]

At a neighborhood scale, it seems a non-Chinese residents' association, the Associació de Veïns per un Eixample Sostenible, pushed Barcelona's town hall to conduct inspections to check for rules compliance among Chinese textile wholesalers and to assess illegal unregulated prostitution carried out in Chinese barbershops and hair salons in la Dreta de l'Eixample and in Fort Pienc, respectively. In the Polígon Sud in Badalona a large-scale police action[9] seized thousands of fake-fashion garments in 2008 worth €24,5 million euros.[10]

To summarize, in the coethnic diverse and specialized centralities there is little coethnic residential concentration. There are very few Chinese or Indian residents in the examples of the MAB I looked at, so these centralities do not seem to attract concentrations of coethnic residents. Yet the concentration of coethnic businesses in different urban contexts, whether in a residential neighborhood or a commercial park, seems to provide an environment "of their own" where the native rules and the coethnic ways of doing business collide. While no doubt Chinese entrepreneurs have brought much business dynamism to the MAB, there is still much room for local rules compliance. On the other hand, the acceptance of the Chinese business associations into the local PIMEC federation (most important in these times of economic crisis, when investors are needed) and the approach of Catalan politicians toward the Chinese constitute welcoming signs regarding this community in Catalonia.

Assessment of the Multiethnic Centralities

(1) Do the foreign-owned businesses reinforce ethnic residential concentration?

A positive correlation between the number of foreign residents and the number of businesses owned by foreign entrepreneurs suggests an affirmative answer, though other factors need to be considered (such as low rents for housing, likely attracting foreign residents), as well as reverse causality.

(2) Do the foreign-owned businesses help with urban revitalization?

There are signs of the proliferation of "cloned businesses" since there are many businesses owned by foreigners concentrated in a small area. Repetitive businesses are located sometimes even within a few meters of distance (Castañeda, 2013; see Figure 8.4). The set of "cloned businesses" resembles an oriental bazaar, where clients look for concentrations of businesses of the same type to shop there, then it is "Allah who decides what customer is going to what shop," as a Moroccan colleague jokingly once told me. Cutthroat competition can arise when foreign entrepreneurs concentrate, but concentrations also draw a large clientele since they become a destination for particular purchases or services (see Ram *et al.*, 2004).

On the other hand, it may be said that ethnic businesses in multiethnic centralities have also cooperated to revitalize the area. New businesses owned by foreigners have been opened in hundreds of commercial premises empty since the numerous foreclosures of the early 1990s Spanish crisis. Besides, new ethnic businesses keep local premises open and active in the current times of crisis. It seems as if Barcelona's town hall has not welcomed the convenient arrival of foreign entrepreneurs from the second half of the 1990s on. Their incorporation has indeed been an unplanned surprise and perhaps an undesired one, particularly regarding the town hall's expectations to convert el Raval into a gentrified touristic area. Mass media and native traders, who are less "politically correct" than civil servants and bureaucrats and even outspoken, often use the expression "commercial ghettos"[11] in a derogatory sense.

Few seem to recognize that an "ethnic gentrification" (Loukaitou-Sideris, 2002) is going on in those multiethnic centralities, once-derelict neighborhoods. In December 2011, Barcelona's town hall along with the local associations of traders promoted two commercial routes and events for tourists, families, and kids in el Raval,[12] the so-called campaign Per Nadal vine al Raval ("In Christmas come to el Raval"). The two routes included interesting modern and historical businesses, fifty of which were selected, but carefully avoided businesses owned by foreign entrepreneurs.

I contend that, cloned or not, ethnic businesses are better than no businesses at all. Barcelona, and particularly its historical downtown, lost hundreds of retail and service businesses in the early 1990s, because of an economic crisis. Foreign entrepreneurs who came in the second half of the 1990s on did help to fill that void with their new businesses (more details in Serra, forthcoming).

(3) How might the number of "cloned businesses" be reduced?

The town hall conducted two mediation processes in two of the multiethnic centralities considered here: Poble Sec and Sant Pau Street in el Raval (Zegrí et al., 2006). The mediations were intended to revitalize the businesses there through the "integration" of the native and foreign entrepreneurs. The results were positive: some foreign entrepreneurs were incorporated into the board of the local associations of businesses. More initiatives like those ones are needed since local small-business owners often do not welcome foreign competitors (Serra, 2008). In any case, and despite the efforts of the town hall, local associations of businesses do not yet seem to have the power, the will, the language skills, or the patience to get closer to foreign entrepreneurs to talk to them or to teach them the business rules or the concern to try to attract nonimmigrant clientele through upgrading their businesses. Instead, foreign entrepreneurs are busy with their new endeavors and concerned about their families who may be far away, and they may be unconcerned about learning one of the two official languages or about making friends among their native colleagues. In this context it is unlikely that a spontaneous "reorientation" (Ram et al., 2004) of "cloned" ethnic businesses will lead to a wider demand despite the optimal historical and touristic downtown locations of Poble Sec and especially of el Raval.

Often one of the "cloned" business types in multiethnic centralities are telephone call businesses. In fact, in 2010 the Barcelona's town hall, through land use rules, decided not to grant more licenses for telephone call businesses in all of 13 land use zones of the Ciutat Vella district[13] along with other business activities, like bars and restaurants in some land use zones.

Assessment of Metropolitan Dispersion of Coethnic Specialized Businesses

(1) Do the foreign-owned businesses reinforce ethnic residential concentration?

No, they do not seem to create a relevant attraction of coethnic residents; only between 1.05 percent and 7.63 percent of all residents in the MAB, where metropolitan dispersion of coethnic specialized businesses occurs, are coethnics.

(2) Do the foreign-owned businesses cooperate with urban revitalization or contribute to the proliferation of "cloned businesses"?

Foreign-owned businesses seem to contribute to urban revitalization since they create new businesses and keep them in times of crisis. These entrepreneurs tend to be competitive in "nonethnic" neighborhoods, such as neighborhoods with a low percentage of foreign population. That "external" location outside the multiethnic centralities gives the dispersed entrepreneurs leverage from catering to a general clientele. For example, Latino and Chinese restaurants add a certain "exotic" touch to the neighborhoods where they are located and provide some sort of "unique" though cheap international experience (Ram et al., 2004). There have been signs of business cloning of Chinese restaurants, but they are dispersed throughout the metropolis.

(3) How might the number of "cloned businesses" be reduced?

Even though there is not a perception of the proliferation of "cloned businesses" among Chinese restaurants, some of the more dynamic Chinese entrepreneurs resolved to change traditional Chinese restaurants to *woks* and have taken over bars that used to be owned by Spaniards.

Conclusions

In this chapter I attempted to provide a quantitative categorization of the new urban ethnic landscapes in the Barcelona Metropolitan Area and also to offer an assessment of them. These new areas have been produced especially by the sudden appearance, more or less in the decade between 1998 and 2008, of some few thousand small businesses owned by foreign immigrants, newly arrived or transferred by previous owners.

The numeric variables that I have used to distinguish the four types of ethnic centralities found in the Metropolitan Area of Barcelona (coethnic specialized centralities, coethnic diverse centralities, multiethnic centralities, and metropolitan dispersion of coethnic specialized businesses) are (1) the percentage of coethnic or ethnic entrepreneurs per total number of traders; (2) the density of coethnic or ethnic businesses per hectare; (3) the percentage of foreign or coethnic residents per total population in 2010; (4) the percentage of coethnic entrepreneurs more dominant among foreign traders; and (5) the percentage of business specialization of the foreign traders, by ethnic group.

With the analysis of the numerical values in each one of these four ethnic centralities and with the help of data from eleven cases, I have tried to reflect the concentration and dispersion logic used by immigrant entrepreneurs as true spatial resources. This task of dissecting the ethnic centralities has relied on data coming from fieldwork since official retail and services censuses did not exist in Catalonia at the time of this writing.

Finally, I attempted to assess the ethnic centralities of the Metropolitan Area of Barcelona. First, quite visible and vibrant Chinese concentrations of businesses are much linked with both coethnic specialized and diverse centralities; their concentration makes some problems more apparent, such as the saturation of Chinese textile wholesalers in an urban residential neighborhood that does not welcome them. Other problems in other Chinese diverse or specialized centralities have been the seizure of fake commercial products or illegal prostitution run from barber and hairdresser businesses. Unfortunately, the problems seem to overpower the advantages that ethnic businesses bring in coethnic centralities. This has been a constant complaint among the mass media and among the town halls, notably, Barcelona's. Little has been said about how businesses owned by immigrants in these areas keep urban areas alive with retail and services, a sort of foreign "rescue" of the boasted Catalan model of proximity businesses.

In multiethnic centralities, which have a relevant presence of foreign residents, the presence of many low-quality "cloned" coethnic-oriented businesses owned by foreigners has given them a reputation as "commercial ghettos," especially in the popular media. Foreign-owned businesses are rarely seen as a source of urban revitalization, despite the fact that they have filled the void left by hundreds if not thousands of vacant commercial premises where there used to be Spanish-owned businesses.

Finally, metropolitan dispersion of coethnic specialized businesses compete quite successfully with businesses owned by native entrepreneurs in neighborhoods where both foreign residents and foreign entrepreneurs constitute a small minority. The presence of coethnic specialized entrepreneurs dispersed in a large metropolitan area is quite discreet and usually cause no problem.

In this chapter I tried to provide a methodological and conceptual framework to quantitatively feature and analyze the geographical distribution of foreign-owned businesses in a metropolitan context and the types of "ethnic" areas the businesses shape. Second, I attempted to assess the impact of those ethnic businesses, using not just the scholarly lenses but also summarizing the assessments given by native traders, residents, media, and local and regional government decision makers and sort of "meta" assessed them. The aim would be to continue this type of research, both "extensively" and "intensively," with the help of other colleagues by comparing the ethnic centralities of Barcelona with those of other metropolitan areas and by improving the methodological and conceptual frameworks used here. Other scholars can research whether categories of ethnic centralities similar to those found in the Metropolitan Area of Barcelona are also present elsewhere.

Acknowledgments

I am grateful to commentaries on and criticisms of an earlier version of this chapter by colleagues who attended a 2011 seminar at the MIGRINTER lab of the CNRS-Université de Poitiers (France), organized by Naïk Miret and myself.

Notes

1. In Spain there are two main sources for municipal population data: the *padrón municipal de población* (municipal population registry, kept updated) and the *censo de población* (decennial national population census). The two sources use the same territorial census tracts. The residents in Spain, whether they are Spaniards or foreigners, must register in the population registry of the municipality they inhabit. Town halls, on their part, must register in their population registries everyone who living in the corresponding municipal territory, no matter whether one is homeless.
2. *La Vanguardia* newspaper, August 16, 2011.
3. The following references mention the concept and debates on "ethnic economies" in English: Werbner (2007); Light and Gold (2000); Zhou (2004); Portes and Shafer (2006); Spanish: Checa and Arjona (2006); and, in French, Raulin (2000).
4. The data may be found at the Department of Justice of the Generalitat of Catalunya site (http://justicia.gencat.cat/ca/serveis/guia_d_entitats/).
5. For this type of analysis, I had to carry out an areal interpolation of population or data transfer from census tracts polygons to postcode or ZIP areas. I had to do it because the information of both federations and associations of migrants and of other ethnic businesses found in the Spanish Yellow Pages (www.paginas-marillas.es) that I used in the second example is provided by aggregate postcode areas. The areal interpolation can be carried out using Geographic Information Systems (GIS). I also divided those zip code polygons that include large areas that are uninhabited or sparsely populated, such as rural or industrial zones, so that I could reinforce the estimates of the number of inhabitants in urban areas at the expense of the uninhabited zip code areas.
6. Or even places of "exotic" worship or simply non-Catholic temples, which tend to be located in areas with a relevant number of immigrant residents, as I showed in my 2006 book regarding Ciutat Vella and in a text with Alfredo Smilges regarding Badalona. Nevertheless, "exotic" worship temples may have to be built or installed out of dense urban areas where there is native residents' opposition to them (Moreras, 2009).
7. Most American immigrants are from Latin America. "Latino restaurants" are grouped as such by the Spanish Yellow Pages.
8. *La Vanguardia* newspaper, 23/01/2012.
9. *El País* newspaper, 27/07/2008.
10. *La Vanguardia* newspaper, 11/02/2010.
11. http://terranoticias.terra.es/articulo/html/av21226148.htm [24–01–2012].

12. http://w110.bcn.cat/portal/site/CiutatVella/menuitem [24-01-2012]; click on the link "Campanya 'Per Nadal vine al Raval.'"
13. In the document "Pla especial d'establiments de concurrència pública, hoteleria i altres activitats del Districte de Ciutat Vella" (http://w110.bcn.cat/CiutatVella/Continguts/Documents/Fitxers/CVL_def_doc-III_NORMATIVA_md_p.pdf [3-2-2012]).

References

Andreu, Xavier and Paricio, Núria (2007). "Programa per l'assessorament, formació i inclusió en el teixit associatiu dels comerciants immigrants 2006-2007-2008". In *Comerç i Cohesió Social. Jornades Europees sobre Immigració i Comerç*. Barcelona.

BCIN, Badalona Centre Internacional de Negocis (2009). "Implantació d'empreses de capital estranger: empreses xineses a la zona del Polígon Sud de Badalona". In Badalona: Federació Empresarial de Badalona, Associació Empresarial de Montgat, Reactivació Badalona, S.A. and BCIN (Badalona Centre Internacional de Negocis).

Beltrán Antolín, Joaquín (2000). "Expansión geográfica y diversificación economica. Pautas y estrategias del asentamiento chino en Espana". In II Congreso sobre la Inmigración en España. España y las migraciones internacionales en el cambio de siglo. Madrid: Instituto Universitario de Estudios sobre Migraciones de la Universidad Pontificia Comillas/Instituto Universitario Ortega y Gasset.

Beltrán Antolín, Joaquín and Sáiz López, Amelia (2003). "Trabajadores y empresarios chinos en Cataluña". In IV Congrés Cátala de Sociología, Reus.

Beltrán, Antolín, Joaquín and Sáiz López, Amelia (2008). "La comunidad pakistaní en España". *Anuario Asia: Pacífico 2007*. Barcelona: CIDOB.

Castañeda, Ernesto. (2012). "Places of Stigma: Ghettos, Barrios and Banlieues". In Hutchison, Ray and Haynes, Bruce D., eds. *The Ghetto: Contemporary Global Issues and Controversies*. Boulder, CO: Westview Press, pp. 159-190.

Castañeda, Ernesto (2013). "Living in Limbo: Transnational Households, Remittances and Development". *International Migration*, 51, pp. 13-35.

Checa, Juan Carlos and Arjona Garrido, Ángeles (2006). "Economía étnica: teorías, conceptos y nuevos avances". *Revista internacional de sociología*, 45, pp. 117-143.

Eix Comerical Bcn De Palau a Palau and Eix Comerical Del Raval (2007). "Programa per l'assessorament, formació i inclusió en el teixit associatiu dels comerciants immigrants 2006-2007-2008". In Comerç i Cohesió Social. Jornades Europees sobre Immigració i Comerç. Conclusiones. Barcelona.

Fundació Tot Raval (2008). "Síntesi de l'estudi econòmic i comercial del Raval 2006-2007". In Barcelona.

Hutchison, Ray and Haynes, Bruce D. (2012). *The Ghetto: Contemporary Global Issues and Controversies*. Boulder, CO: Westview Press.

Kaplan, David H. (1998). "The Spatial Structure of Urban Ethnic Economies". *Urban Geography*, 19, 6, pp. 489-501.

Li, Chengcheng, Micheli, Daniela and Cervera, Montse (2010). "Relaciones comerciales y convivencia de los inmigrantes en el municipio de Badalona: de la prevención a la cohesión". In Internship report. *Máster Oficial en Gestión de la Immigración*. Barcelona: Universitat Pompeu Fabra.

Light, Ivan and Gold, Steven J. (2000). *Ethnic Economies*. San Diego, CA: Academic Press.
Loukaitou-Sideris, A. (2002). "Regeneration of Urban Commercial Strips: Ethnicity and Space in Three Los Angeles Neighborhoods". *Journal of Architectural and Planning Research*, 19, 4, pp. 335–350.
Ma Mung, Emmanuel (1992). "Dispositif économique et ressources spatiales: éléments d'une économie de diaspora". *Revue Européenne des Migrations Internationales*, 8, 3, pp. 175–193.
Mayhew, Susan (1997). *Oxford Dictionary of Geography*. Oxford, UK and New York: Oxford University Press.
Monnet, Nadja (2002). *La formación del espacio público. Una mirada etnológica sobre el Casc Antic de Barcelona*. Madrid: Los libros de la catarata.
Moreras, Jordi (1999). *Musulmanes en Barcelona. Espacios y dinámicas comunitarias*. Barcelona: CIDOB edicions.
Moreras, Jordi (2009). *Una mesquita al barri: Conflicte, espai públic i integració urbana dels oratoris musulmans a Catalunya*. Barcelona: TR[À]NSITS.
Parella, Sònia (2009). "Les empreses regentades per persones estrangeres a la ciutat de Barcelona". In En Berbel, Sara, Fernández José Antonio y and Nadal Mònica, eds. *Immigració i mercat de treball a la ciutat de Barcelona*. Barcelona: Fundació Jaume Bofill and Consell Econòmic i Social de Barcelona, pp. 153–184.
Peach, Ceri (1996). "Good Segregation, Bad Segregation". *Planning Perspectives*, 11, pp. 379–398.
Portes, Alejandro and Shafer, Steven (2006). "Revisiting the Enclave Hypothesis: Miami Twenty-Five Years Later", The Center for Migration and Development, Princeton University Working Paper Series #06–10.
Ram, Monder, Abbas, Tahir, and Jones, Trevor and Carter, Sara L. (2004). "Breaking Out of Survival Businesses: Managing Labour, Growth and Development in the South Asian Restaurant Trade". In Marlow, Susan, Patton, Dean and Ram, Monder, eds. *Managing Labour in Small Firms*. Routledge Studies in Small Business. London: Routledge, pp. 109–132.
Raulin, Anne (2000). *L'ethnique est quotidien: diasporas, marchés et cultures métropolitaines*. Paris: Connaissance des hommes, L'Harmattan.
Sampson, Robert J. (2011). "Neighborhood Effects, Causal Mechanisms and the Social Structure of the City". In Demeulenaere, Pierre, ed. *Analytical Sociology and Social Mechanisms*. Cambridge, UK: Cambridge University Press, pp. 227–249.
Serra Del Pozo, Pau (2006). *El comercio étnico en el distrito de Ciutat Vella en Barcelona*. Barcelona: Fundació La Caixa. <http://pauserra.files.wordpress.com/2008/08/pau-serra-el-comercio-etnico-en-el-distrito-de-ciutat-vella.pdf> [03–03–2011]
Serra Del Pozo, Pau (2008). "Las asociaciones de comerciantes como actores para la convivencia: el caso de Ciutat Vella (Barcelona)". In Zapata-Barrero, Ricard and Pinyol, Gemma, eds. *Los gestores del proceso de inmigración. Actores y redes de actores en España y Europa*. Barcelona: CIDOB, pp. 199–219. www.cidob.org/es/content/download/7250/72346/file/11_serra.pdf. Retrieved January 24, 2012.
Serra Del Pozo, Pau (2012). "Global Businesses 'from Below': Ethnic Entrepreneurs in Metropolitan Areas". *Urbani izziv*, 23(supplement 2) pp. S97–S106.

Serra Del Pozo, Pau (forthcoming). "The Role of Foreign-Owned Businesses in the Revitalisation of Historic Centres in three Catalan Towns". *International Journal of Entrepreneurship and Small Business*.

Tilly, Charles (1986). *Transplanted Networks*. New York: New School for Social Research.

Vaughan, Laura and Arbaci, Sonia (2011). "The Challenges of Understanding Urban Segregation". *Built Environment*, 37, 2, pp. 128–138.

Werbner, Pnina (2007). "South Asian Entrepreneurship in Britain: A Critique of the Ethnic Enclave Economy Debate". In Dana, Leo Paul, ed. *Handbook of Research on Ethnic Minority Entrepreneurship: A Co-Evolutionary View on Resource Management*. Northampton, MA: Edward Elgar Publishing, pp. 375–389.

Wilson, K. and Portes, A. (1980). "Immigrant Enclaves: An Analysis of the Labor Market Experiences of Cubans in Miami". *American Journal of Sociology*, 86, pp. 295–319.

Zegrí, Mercè, Navarro, Josep Maria and Aramburu, Míkel (2006). "El encaje de los comercios extranjeros en el tejido comercial de acogida. Análisis de una experiencia de mediación comunitaria en Barcelona". *Migraciones*, 20, pp. 233–258.

Zhou, Min (2004). "Revisiting Ethnic Entrepreneurship: Convergencies, Controversies, and Conceptual Advancements". *International Migration Review*, 38, pp. 1040–1074.

9

REMITTANCE-DRIVEN MIGRATION IN SPITE OF MICROFINANCE?

The Case of Nepalese Households

Bishal Kasu, Ernesto Castañeda, and Guangqing Chi

Many poor households in the developing world supplement their limited incomes with remittances and microfinance. Much of the literature assumes upward social mobility and economic development from increased household expenditures in nutrition, health, education, and housing driven by remittances and/or microfinance. The New Economics of Labor Migration theory states that, faced with limited access to local capital, credit, and insurance products, working-age people may emigrate to increase their household income, but what happens when people emigrate from rural communities that increasingly have access to credit through microfinance? This chapter investigates the simultaneous impact of microfinance and remittances on the livelihood of Nepalese people by using the 2003–2004 Nepal Living Standard Survey. We find that microfinance is positively associated with an increase in the proportion of household income used for health-care expenses and negatively associated with the percentage of income used for food expenses and housing improvements. Remittances are positively associated with increased expenses for children's basic education and negatively associated with higher percentages of household income going toward food expenses. The models presented control for social factors such as gender, caste, and ethnicity; education and marital status of the household head; and the number of dependents. The findings and discussion provide insights into the nexus of microfinance, remittances, and livelihoods. An interesting gendered dynamic appears in some households where women apply for microcredit, which they pay for with remittances sent by male household members.

Introduction

Remittances are the portions of wages that workers send to family members living in other countries. Microfinances are the loans given to the poor, who would otherwise have no access to formal credit. Both microfinance and remittances have been labeled as tools for development and poverty reduction by development workers. Yet there is an ongoing academic debate about the effect of each on economic development. Development workers, bankers, and businesspeople see both remittances and microfinance as avenues to bring the previously "unbanked" residents of poor areas into financial services (Bakker 2015). The academic literature on remittances is full of claims and debates about the relationship between remittances and economic development (Castañeda 2013). Microfinance is very popular in development policy circles, yet its impact has come under question recently by experimental studies. If microfinance proved to result in productive investments for poor households, it would decrease a population's need to emigrate for economic reasons.

The New Economics of Labor Migration (NELM) theories state that, faced with limited access to local capital and insurance products, working-age people may emigrate to increase their household income (Massey and Parrado 1994; Stark and Bloom 1985). NELM approaches became an alternative to dependency perspectives by linking "migration to local market failures and saw remittances as a way for households to diversify risks, accumulate capital, and overcome credit constraints" (Massey, Durand and Pren 2012). Most existing studies examine the impact of microfinance and remittances separately. Few academic papers have looked empirically at the simultaneous impacts of access to both remittances and microfinance. It is important to analyze them together and compare their effects.

An argument made by NELM proponents is that people migrate and remit because they lack access to local loans (Amuedo-Dorantes and Pozo 2011). The existence of microloans opens access to credit, but does it stop migration and remittances? This study fills the gap in the literature by simultaneously investigating the relative impact of microfinance and remittances on four consumption areas—food, health, housing, and education—using the 2003–2004 dataset of the Nepal Living Standard Survey. While many studies focus on households that have or start small businesses, we focus on a sample of all Nepalese households, including a majority of households that do not own businesses.

Microfinance

Poor people are often excluded from formal bank loans because they have no collateral to offer as security of repayment. In the 1970s, Yunus conducted an experiment, providing small loans to rural women in Bangladesh using social relations as collateral, and this experiment resulted in the birth of microfinance (Robinson 2001:506). With time, microfinance helped many of the participating women increase their income by starting microbusinesses. Decades later, microfinance is often presented as one of the most effective tools against poverty. Many others around the world have since tried to emulate these schemes. More than 100 million households in developing countries obtained microloans in 2007 (Daley-Harris 2009), and there were more than 195 million microcredit borrowers in 2011 (Banerjee 2013).

Microfinance provides financial services such as credit, savings, and insurance, and some argue that it fosters empowerment, self-advocacy, unity, and solidarity among creditors (Ledgerwood 1999; Qudrat-I Elahi and Lutfor Rahman 2006; Robinson 2001; Rogaly, Castillo and Romero Serrano 2004; Sanyal 2009). Loans are used for business and personal expenditures (Mc-Intosh, Villaran and Wydick 2011; Padia 2005; Parthasarathy 2005) such as medical treatment, education, transportation (e.g., bicycles), durable goods (e.g., televisions and radios), and house maintenance and improvement, as well as for religious purposes. Some recipients of microloans start informal businesses; buy food carts; spend money on agricultural inputs (e.g., seeds and fertilizers); purchase livestock (e.g., goats, poultry, and cows); open small businesses such as rope-making shops or flower, bangle, or grocery shops; or start co-ops and sustainable development enterprises (Gutberlet 2009).

Microfinance has been implemented via two approaches: the social service approach and the business approach (Ledgerwood 1997; Rankin 2001; Takahatake and Maharjan 2002). The social service approach focuses mainly on aiding poor people. On the other hand, the business approach places high priority on economic development, profitability, and financial sustainability. Researchers are divided over the best approach to microfinance. Hulme and Mosely (1996) argue that the social banking approach better serves the poor. But for others, such as Ledgerwood (1997), the business approach is necessary to render microfinance services effective and sustainable. Another typology differentiates nonprofit and for-profit schemas, with the latter charging high interest rates and focused on commercialization and return on investment. A more sustainable approach considers both the social well-being of the poor and banking sustainability (Takahatake and Maharjan 2002).

Some of the literature argues that access to microfinance reduces a household's vulnerability to falling further into poverty (Develtere and Huybrechts 2005). Studies looking only at microloan recipients suggest that the households participating in microfinance have an overall positive experience (Chemin 2008; Li, Gan and Hu 2011; Midgley 2008; Simanowitz and Walter 2002). Some households receiving microcredits have experienced increased income, diversified income sources, increased savings, raised asset accumulation, and spent a little more on food, education, and health care. They can better cope with food scarcity or health emergencies (Sankar 2005). However, the impact depends on the duration of their participation in a microfinance program (Islam 2011). The longer a household is involved in the program, the greater the benefits it may reap.

A higher priority has been placed on reducing the number of women in poverty on the basis that in cash-based economies in developing countries, women are often responsible for basic purchases and household budgeting (Fisher and Sriram 2002; Rogaly, Castillo and Romero Serrano 2004; Stoesz, Guzzetta and Lusk 1999). Women have proven responsible in their management of microfinance funds and pay their loans back more reliably than men (Rankin 2001). Some studies have found that loans taken out by women have a stronger effect than loans by men on alleviating poverty in the short term (Sengupta and Aubuchon 2008). The households where women have taken out loans have better health care, child nutrition, and child education (Khandker 2005, Smith 2002). A case study (Chemin 2008) found that the household impact of loans given to men are lower than those given to women, although, on average, men take out bigger loans than women do.

Though a large body of literature has documented microfinance success stories, microfinance programs are not always successfully implemented. General reasons for unsuccessful outcomes include corruption, low political commitment, lack of participation by targeted recipients, poor management, limited outreach (Bhatta 2001; Dhakal 2006; Shakya and Rankin 2008), a lack of coordination with district government agencies, low repayment rates, and the high cost of service delivery (Takahatake and Maharjan 2002). In a case study of India, it was found that although 30 percent of loans were used to start businesses, 30 percent of the funds were used to repay existing loans, 15 percent were spent on durable goods, 15 percent on nondurable goods, and 10 percent on others (Loiseau and Walsh 2015).

The goals of microfinance are often grounded in the laudable goal of ending poverty. One can find successful individual cases of microbusinesses growing with the help of microloans, as well as cases where microfinance led to women's empowerment and collective action (Sanyal 2009). Yet their overall effectiveness in reducing poverty and fostering economic development in the long run at the community level is hard to prove. Experimental studies have recently been implemented to compare groups receiving microcredits with those that are not (Adhikari and Shrestha 2013). Most findings are not encouraging. A randomized study of microfinance in Hyderabad, India, found "no impact on total nondurable consumption or on food consumption either in the short or longer run. Nor [is there] clear evidence of increased human capital investment.... In the longer run, business assets go up considerably more, but the increase in profits is no longer significant.... [W]e still see no effect on nondurable consumption, and the effect on durable consumption is also gone" (Banerjee 2013:506). A meta-study finds little evidence for poverty reduction (Banerjee 2013). Randomized evaluations in Bosnia and Herzegovina, Ethiopia, India, and Mexico did not find positive effects on the profits of borrowers' businesses (Loiseau and Walsh 2015).

Remittances

Remittances are the money or in-kind transfers that migrants send back home. Both microfinance and remittances are used to increase household income, and they both operate on the basis of social capital—that is, trust networks of existing relationships among people. Microfinance uses people's network as collateral. Similarly, remittances flow within trust networks and between migrants and their families or relatives at home (Ballard 2005; Tilly 2007).

Households use remittances for food, clothing, medicine, purchase of land, home construction and repair, marriages and religious ceremonies, education, telecommunication, savings, gifts, funding other people's migration, investment in business, health care, and repaying loans (Arguillas and Williams 2010; Deneulin 2006; Gerber and Torosyan 2013; Koc and Onan 2004; Lu and Treiman 2011; Zarate-Hoyos 2004).

A vast amount of remittances pass through informal sources—transactions conducted from person to person—and thus cannot be accounted for by government agencies or financial institutions (Hernandez Coss 2006; Ratha 2007; Seddon, Adhikari and Gurung 2002; Seddon 2004). The transactions can be made directly from person to person or indirectly through a third party. Informal channels exist for two main reasons: They are a cheap mechanism through which to send money, and formal channels may be unable to operate in remote areas (Hernandez Coss 2006).

Remittances from migrants may have a positive impact on the livelihood of their recipient households and communities in the short and medium term (Amuedo-Dorantes and Pozo 2011; Hernandez Coss 2006; Ratha 2003). The households that receive remittances spend more money on food, durable goods, health care, and housing than those that do not (Adams Jr. 2006; Airola 2007; Frank et al. 2009). They also spend more on business activities. In some regions, they buy more goods and may start and expand businesses (Arroyo Alejandre 2010; Woodruff and Zenteno 2007). The specific household impact of remittances varies by income levels. Households in both the high- and low-income brackets spend more money on education with the receipt of remittances. Furthermore, the remittances improve children's health, even in poor households (Acosta, Fajzylber and Lopez 2008).

Remittance services that show lower fees result indeed in more resources for workers' families (Ratha 2007). Yet, without a suitable environment for investment, people spend most of the money on consumption (Massey, Durand and Pren 2012) and can become expectant and dependent on remittances and may avoid engaging in labor (McDowell and Haan 1997). This, in turn, weakens the economy of the remittance-recipient community.

Next, we analyze economic activity at the household level—between individual decisions and community dynamics—and look at how poor households make a living (De Haan and Zoomers 2005).

Livelihoods of Nepalese People

Nepal is a landlocked country between China and India with a population of more than 30 million. Between 1950 and 2008, Nepal implemented ten development plans. Since the 1970s, microfinance has been central to developmental and poverty alleviation efforts in Nepal. Programs that use microfinance include the Intensive Banking Program (IBP), the Small Farmer Development Programs (SFDP), the Production Credit for Rural Women (PCRW), the Micro Credit Project for Women (MCPW), and Grameen Bank. In addition, microfinance programs have been run by savings credit organizations, cooperatives, and NGOs. In this section, we illustrate the connections among migration, remittances, and livelihood in Nepal.

Microfinance in Nepal

In 1975 the Nepal Agriculture Development Bank introduced a microfinance program, the Small Farmer Development Project, targeting poor farmers (Shrestha 2003; Uprety 2008). This regulation mandated that 3 percent of loans from commercial banks be made to rural poor people at a subsidized rate (Von Pischke, Bennett and Goldberg 1993). In the 1990s, under the Structural Adjustment Program, the major responsibilities of the microcredit program were shifted from commercial banks to rural development banks, microfinance organizations, cooperatives, financial intermediaries, and NGOs that loan to small enterprises (Rankin 2001). Even though the original targets of such programs were rural women, most of the loan borrowers were rural men. Credits since then have been extended to 4 percent of the population, or only 14 percent of those who fall under the poverty line (Thapa 2008). Thus we see that, despite strong government support, the majority of poor households do not see microfinance as useful.

Remittances to Nepal

Nepalese people have been involved in international migration for decades. They typically emigrate hoping to financially provide their households with funds for the basic health, education, and housing expenses of their households in Nepal (Massey et al. 1987). Remittances typically take the form of in-cash or in-kind support. Remittances to Nepal have increased significantly since the 1990s. The remittances migrants send home help their households handle economic difficulties and improve their living conditions. In 2004 remittances were received by 32 percent of households and accounted for 11.7 percent of Nepal's GDP (World Bank 2006). In 2012, remittances were 22 percent of its GDP, at almost 5 billion dollars (World Bank 2012). In 2014 remittances surpassed 6 billion dollars (World Bank 2015), amounting to 28.8 percent of GDP, transforming the national economy from an agricultural to a remittance economy (Wagle 2012).

Even though agriculture is the key livelihood for the majority of households in Nepal, the recent upsurge in migration shows an important diversification of household income (Upreti et al. 2012). This diversification in livelihood strategies is partly linked with a decade-long armed conflict in which people felt unsafe and were forced to leave their villages. Being away from their land, they engaged in off-farm employment. The higher wage rates may have inspired younger generations to migrate, too. Now, remittances are one of the most important sources of foreign currency for Nepal.

Domestic and international migration is a livelihood strategy, especially for the poorest people and for those who live in remote areas and in zones recovering from conflict (Hagen-Zanker and Mallett 2014; Hagen-Zanker et al. 2014). Nepalese move primarily from rural to urban areas, from the hills to the plains, from west to east, and from north to south (Gill 2003; Seddon, Adhikari and Gurung 2002). India is the favored and most accessible destination for Nepal's international migrants, but migration to the Persian Gulf countries, Malaysia, South Korea, Japan, Europe, Australia, and the United States has increased recently.

Migration in Nepal is both seasonal and long term. Seasonal migration, which starts right after the planting of the rice paddies, lasts around four months (Gill 2003). After that, migrants return for the paddy harvest. Generally, men migrate, while women stay home to take care of the chores related to farming, such as weeding, irrigating, and fertilizing (Seddon, Adhikari and Gurung 2002). Long-term migration lasts for more than four months. Certain ethnic groups in Nepal, such as the Gurung, Rai, and Limbu, tend to enlist in the military in India and the United Kingdom for several years. Other ethnic groups go to Malaysia, South Korea, and the Persian Gulf countries as laborers.

While most migration goes from rural to urban areas and from developing to developed regions, remittances go in the opposite direction. Migration for work has proven to be one of the best income sources for both the higher and the lower castes. For the lower caste, the existing caste-based inequality further entices them to migrate (McDowell and Haan 1997) to escape the stigma associated with being low caste; thus, finding employment opportunities abroad proves to be an economic and social advantage. Because of categorical inequality for these people, migration is an effective way to break the poverty cycle. However, emigration for the lower castes is limited primarily to India; the border between India and Nepal is open, there are no passport or visa requirements, and one does not need to go through a long legal process.

Higher castes prefer to migrate to countries other than India because of higher salaries. Higher-caste households have lower levels of food insecurity and higher levels of asset ownership. Such households have a higher probability of receiving loans in times of financial need because they are trusted more by financial organizations and have access to informal lending sources, such as family members, relatives, and friends with savings (Upreti et al. 2014). In addition, the higher castes have better access to information about the legal process for obtaining loans. They also have better skills and higher incomes and therefore can remit more. Thus, legal hurdles to migration reproduce inequalities born in Nepal because they open more opportunities for higher-caste individuals than for those assigned to lower castes.

Data and Methods

Data

Data are derived from the 2003–2004 Nepal Living Standard Survey (NLSS II), which was conducted by Nepal's Central Bureau of Statistics to evaluate the impact of government policies and programs on people's living standards. The first NLSS survey was conducted in 1995–1996 (NLSS I). Both NLSS surveys followed the World Bank's Living Standards Measurement Survey methodology, which has been applied in more than fifty developing countries.

The NLSS II includes both cross-sectional and panel samples. The cross-sectional sample represents the entire country and is used to identify general trends in Nepalese living standards. The panel sample consisted of a follow-up interview of 1,160 households that had already participated in the NLSS I. For the NLSS II cross-sectional sample, 3,912 households were interviewed. The NLSS II covered 326 cross-sectional primary sampling units (PSUs). From each PSU, 12 households were selected for interviews. The cross-sectional PSUs cover the entire country, which is divided into six strata (i.e., mountains, Kathmandu Valley, other urban areas in the hills, rural hills, urban Terai, and rural Terai). The NLSS II household questionnaire included questions on demographic characteristics, income, expenses, migration patterns, access to facilities, education, health, marriage history, remittances, savings, and credit information.

Response Variables

We analyze livelihood using four variables—percentage of income used for food expenses, percentage of income used for health expenses, percentage of children (between ages 5 and 18) currently attending school, and quality of housing. The quality of housing is assessed by the materials used for the roof, wall, and floor, as well as by household access to pure drinking water; this variable is measured on a scale from 1 to 4 for each of the four indicators (1 lowest, 4 highest). On average, 41 percent of income is spent on food, 2 percent is spent on health care, and an average of 72 percent of children in these households attend school (Table 9.1).

Table 9.2 shows correlations among the four response variables. The response variables are significantly but loosely correlated, and the correlations go in both directions. The relation between quality of housing and

Table 9.1 Descriptive statistics of response and explanatory variables.

	Number of cases	Mean/ percent	Standard deviation
Response variables			
% of HH food expenses	3,912	40.89	20.98
% of HH health expenses	3,912	1.58	4.40
% of children currently attending school	2,971	72.45	38.45
Housing quality	3,394	9.72	3.17
Explanatory variables			
Loan from microfinance (log)	3,912	17,240.85	67,556.32
Remittances received (log)	3,912	11,914.19	45,119.42
Socioeconomic characteristics			
Income less remittances (log)	3,910	67,990.52	3.81
HH head education			
>10th grade	277	7.10%	0.26
<10th grade	3,404	87.00%	0.26
Reference group = 10th grade	229	5.90%	0.23
Total number of HH jobs	3,912	13.13	6.85
Caste and ethnicity			
Higher caste	1,276	32.60%	0.47
Himalayan indigenous	20	0.50%	0.07
Hill indigenous	1,257	32.00%	0.47
Inner Terai indigenous	46	1.20%	0.11
Terai indigenous	280	7.20%	0.26
Madhesi	467	11.90%	0.32
Reference group = Dalit	564	14.60%	0.32
Demographic characteristics			
Gender of HH head (1 = male)	3,158	80.70%	0.39
Age of HH head	3,912	45.49	14.23
Marital status (1 = married, 0 = else)	3,345	85.50%	0.35
# Productive-age people in HH	3,912	3.12	1.64
# Dependent people in HH	3,912	2.39	1.78
Region			
Mountain	384	9.80%	0.30
Urban hill	336	8.60%	0.28
Rural hill	1,152	29.40%	0.46
Urban Terai	408	10.40%	0.31
Rural Terai	1,224	31.30%	0.46
Reference group = Kathmandu valley	406	10.50%	0.31

Table 9.2 Correlations among response variables.

	% of HH food expenses	% of HH health expenses	% of children between 5 and 18 currently attending school	Quality of house
% of HH food expenses	1			
% of HH health expenses	−0.158**	1		
% of children between 5 and 18 currently attending school	−0.257**	−0.023	1	
Quality of house	−0.214**	−0.005	0.290**	1

NOTE: ** $p \leq .01$ (two-tailed).

children's education is positive and significant, which indicates that a family that can afford a higher-quality house can also invest more in the education of its children. Expenses for food and health are negatively related with quality of housing and children's education; households with higher income levels spend a lower percentage of their income on food and health care.

Health expenses are a weaker variable than food expenses, which are significantly and negatively related to quality of housing and children's education. The inverse relationship between food expenses and health expenses is significant. It indicates that the increase in food expenses is associated with less spending on health. Investment in food may bring better food options and therefore good health and may reduce health expenses, or it could indicate that poor households—which have to spend a greater percentage of their income on food—must forgo health care.

The correlation table also suggests that households with high-quality housing and a higher percentage of children attending school spend a smaller percentage of their income on food. This is to be expected since, generally speaking, households with higher incomes need not spend such a high proportion of their total income on food and basic necessities. Indeed, a high percentage of income spent on food is a good indicator of poverty.

Explanatory Variables

The two key explanatory variables used in this chapter are the microfinance loan amount and the amount of remittances received. On average, each household takes out around 17,000 Nepalese rupees (NR), the equivalent of 228 U.S. dollars (USD), in loans from microfinance annually. The average remittance is the equivalent of between 300 and 400 USD. More than 32 percent of all Nepalese households received remittances in 2004. This study analyzes the associations of the two explanatory variables with the four response livelihood variables (percentage of income spent on food, percentage of income spent on health, percentage of children currently attending school, and quality of housing) by controlling for socioeconomic, household demographic, and geographical variables.

Socioeconomic variables include income, education, number of jobs held by all employed household members, caste, and ethnicity. The education level of the household's head was measured by two dichotomous variables—above the level of the School Leaving Certificate (SLC), or below. In Nepal, the SLC is received in tenth grade; an SLC allows students to continue their studies. Households where the head holds an SLC (i.e., at least tenth grade completed) formed the reference group. In 87 percent of the households, the head's education level is below tenth grade. The total number of jobs includes all paid jobs the household head and other members perform.

In addition, the durable categorical markers of caste and ethnicity are important social factors in Nepal. Caste and ethnicity were divided into seven categories—higher caste, Dalit, Himalayan indigenous, hill indigenous, inner Terai indigenous, Terai indigenous, and Madhesi. The higher caste and hill indigenous ethnicities are the most common in the population and in the sample; the Himalayan indigenous group is the smallest. The Dalit category was the reference group. This measure of caste and ethnicity allows us to examine the impact of microfinance and remittances on other groups compared with the Dalit, who should be targeted primarily in terms of the poverty reduction.

Demographic variables for the household include gender, age, and marital status of the head of household, as well as the number of members of productive age and dependents in the household. In the NLSS II, 81 percent of households were headed by men, and 86 percent of household heads were married. The age of household head varied from fourteen to ninety-seven years. Some households had no members of productive age or had no dependents. The highest number of household members of productive age was seventeen, and some households had as many as eighteen dependents.

Because geography is another crucial factor that affects the life of the Nepalese people, we use six geographical categories—mountain, urban hill, rural hill, urban Terai, rural Terai, and Kathmandu Valley. The Kathmandu Valley residents formed the reference group.

Methods

The associations between the four response variables (food expenses, health expenses, school attendance, and quality of housing) and two explanatory variables (microfinance and remittances) were analyzed via ordinary least squares (OLS) regression models. The OLS regression analysis investigates if there is any association between the response and explanatory variables, as well as the strength and direction of the association. The analysis can also estimate the regression coefficient of the response variable from the value of the explanatory variable. The OLS regressions allows us to control for socioeconomic, demographic, and geographic factors. Each of the four livelihood response variables was examined in four models. Model 1 included only microfinance and remittances, the two main explanatory variables. Model 2 included the socioeconomic variables in addition to the explanatory variables, Model 3 considered household demographics in addition to the previous two sets, and Model 4 included all variables, including region. The four models were applied in succession to determine the influence of these variables and the strength of relationships between explanatory variables and response variables. Moreover, there is no indication of multicollinearity.

Results

Food Expenses

Table 9.3 shows the relationships between the explanatory variables and the percentage of household income spent on food. The assumption is that the higher a household's income is, the smaller its percentage of food expenses will be, because a poor household spends a greater percentage of income on food.

Table 9.3 shows a significant but negative association between the key explanatory variables and percentage of household income spent on food. The table shows that the significance of the relationship is persistent whether or not socioeconomic, demographic, and regional factors are held constant.

The education level of the household head is significantly related to the percentage of household income used for food. The household head with an education level above the SLC spends a lower percentage of income on food than do those where the household head has an education level below SLC. All castes and ethnicities, except for the inner Terai indigenous people, spend a smaller percentage of their income on food expenses than the Dalit (reference group), which confirms that the Dalit are among the poorest. A household with a male household head spends a greater percentage of its income on food than those with a female household head. Households in all other regions spend a higher percentage of income on food than those in the Kathmandu Valley.

Health Expenses

Table 9.4 shows the associations between the percentage of income spent on health care and the same set of explanatory and control variables shown in Table 9.3. Both explanatory variables, microfinance and remittances, are positively associated with the percentage of income that goes toward health

Table 9.3 Percentage of food expenses as the response variable.

	Model 1	Model 2	Model 3	Model 4
Explanatory variables				
Loan from microfinance (log)	−0.39***	−0.22**	−0.27***	−0.32***
Remittances received (log)	−0.53***	−0.60***	−0.45***	−0.48***
Socioeconomic characteristics				
Income less remittances (log)		−1.12***	−1.01***	−1.03***
HH head education				
>10th grade		−3.89*	−3.67*	−2.68
<10th grade		9.32***	9.45***	8.85***
Reference group = 10th grade				
Total number of HH jobs		−0.55***	−0.40***	−0.59***
Caste and ethnicity				
Higher caste		−15.80***	−15.37***	−16.31***
Himalayan indigenous		−6.78	−6.72	−7.39
Hill indigenous		−7.38***	−6.51***	−7.02***
Inner Terai indigenous		−0.06	−0.07	0.23
Terai indigenous		−11.64***	−11.32***	−9.62***
Madhesi		−8.39***	−7.64***	−6.54***
Reference group = Dalit				
Demographic characteristics				
Gender of HH head (1 = male)			3.60***	3.55***
Age of HH head			−0.12***	−0.13***
Marital status (1 = married, 0 = else)			−2.19*	−1.90
# Productive-age people in HH			−1.49***	−0.95***
# Dependent people in HH			0.33	0.49*
Region				
Mountain				7.77***
Urban hill				3.55*
Rural hill				7.51***
Urban Terai				3.91**
Rural Terai				2.42
Reference group = Kathmandu valley				
R^2	0.021	0.187	0.209	0.220
Number of cases	3,912	3,912	3,912	3,912

NOTES: * $p \leq .05$
** $p \leq .01$
*** $p \leq .001$ (two-tailed).

Microfinance loans, amount of remittances received, and income less remittances are log-transformed to make normal distributions.

Table 9.4 Percentage of health expenses as the response variable.

	Model 1	Model 2	Model 3	Model 4
Explanatory variables				
Loan from microfinance (log)	0.04**	0.04**	0.05**	0.05**
Remittances received (log)	0.02	0.02	0.03	0.02
Socioeconomic characteristics				
Income less remittances (log)		0.08*	0.05	0.04
HH head education				
>10th grade		−0.21	−0.23	−0.16
<10th grade		0.42	0.37	0.34
Reference group = 10th grade				
Total number of HH jobs		−0.04***	−0.08***	−0.08***
Caste and ethnicity				
Higher caste		0.01	0.003	0.21
Himalayan indigenous		−1.09	−1.19	−0.69
Hill indigenous		−0.37	−0.48*	−0.24
Inner Terai indigenous		−0.84	−0.87	−0.88
Terai indigenous		−0.08	−0.08	−0.34
Madhesi		0.10	−0.14	−0.34
Reference group = Dalit				
Demographic characteristics				
Gender of HH head (1 = male)			0.39	0.40
Age of HH head			0.04***	0.04***
Marital status (1 = married, 0 = else)			0.37	0.33
# Productive-age people in HH			0.06	0.04
# Dependent people in HH			0.13**	0.12*
Region				
Mountain				−0.26
Urban hill				0.34
Rural hill				0.23
Urban Terai				0.50
Rural Terai				0.79*
Reference group = Kathmandu valley				
R^2	0.002	0.009	0.029	0.033
Number of cases	3,912	3,910	3,910	3,910

NOTES: * $p \leq .05$
** $p \leq .01$
*** $p \leq .001$ (two-tailed).

expenses. Microfinance shows a significant relationship, with a higher percentage of income going to health expenses in all four models.

Among socioeconomic explanatory variables, only the total number of jobs in the household has a significant inverse relationship to the proportion of income spent on health expenses. Having a household head with an education above the SLC has a negative relationship to the proportion of income spent on health. Similarly, relative to the Dalit, most of the other castes and ethnicities spend a smaller proportion of their income on health, but the effects are not statistically significant. Among all household demographic variables, age of the household head and number of dependents are positively and significantly related to a higher proportion of income spent on health expenses. All geographic regions except mountain and rural hill differ positively from the Kathmandu Valley.

Children's Education

Table 9.5 shows the associations between microfinance loans and remittances and the education of children (measured as the percentage of children ages 5 to 18 currently attending school) in the recipient households. Remittances and the percentage of children currently attending school have a significant and positive association. Microfinance loans are also positively related to children's education, but the relationship is weak.

The percentage of children currently attending school has a negative and significant relationship to the household head's education being below the SLC. All castes and ethnicities have a higher percentage than the Dalit (reference group) children currently attending school; this again substantiates the claim that the Dalit are the most disadvantaged group in Nepal. Regarding household demography, statistically significant household demographic variables are gender of household head, marital status of household head, and number of dependents in the household. If a woman heads the household, the probability of children attending school is higher. Households with a married household head are more likely to send their children to school, as are households with a higher number of dependents. All geographic regions except urban hill are significantly and negatively associated with children's education compared with Kathmandu.

Housing Quality

Table 9.6 shows the associations between housing quality and explanatory and control variables. Of the two main explanatory variables, only microfinance loans are significantly and negatively associated with the quality of housing. Households that receive a higher amount of microfinance loans have a lower quality of housing. This may indicate that poor people are more

Table 9.5 Percentage of children ages 5–18 currently attending school.

	Model 1	Model 2	Model 3	Model 4
Explanatory variables				
Loan from microfinance (log)	0.12	0.07	0.11	0.27
Remittances received (log)	0.52**	0.52**	0.36*	0.47**
Socioeconomic characteristics				
Income less remittances (log)		0.46	0.50	0.73*
HH head education				
>10th grade		−1.06	0.09	−3.18
<10th grade		−14.36***	−13.97***	−11.30***
Reference group = 10th grade				
Total number of HH jobs		−0.61***	−0.85***	−0.37*
Caste and ethnicity				
Higher caste		26.03***	26.38***	26.01***
Himalayan indigenous		21.28	23.16*	21.94
Hill indigenous		18.42***	18.80***	16.66***
Inner Terai indigenous		10.54	10.94	7.83
Terai indigenous		10.34**	10.12**	9.69**
Madhesi		1.45	0.14	0.18
Reference group = Dalit				
Demographic characteristics				
Gender of HH head (1 = male)			−6.86**	−5.94**
Age of HH head			0.09	0.10
Marital status (1 = married, 0 = else)			14.85***	14.09***
# Productive-age people in HH			0.05	−1.22*
# Dependent people in HH			1.77***	1.54**
Region				
Mountain				−23.80***
Urban hill				−6.01
Rural hill				−18.59***
Urban Terai				−8.60**
Rural Terai				−17.02***
Reference group = Kathmandu valley				
R²	0.004	0.113	0.131	0.152
Number of cases	2,971	2,971	2,971	2,971

NOTES: * $p \leq .05$
** $p \leq .01$
*** $p \leq .001$ (two-tailed).

Table 9.6 Quality of housing as the response variable.

	Model 1	Model 2	Model 3	Model 4
Explanatory variables				
Loan from microfinance (log)	−0.09***	−0.05***	−0.03**	−0.001
Amount of remittances received (log)	−0.003	.002	−0.01	0.01
Socioeconomic characteristics				
Income less remittances (log)		0.03	−0.04	−0.01
HH head education				
>10th grade		1.65***	1.58***	1.02***
<10th grade		−1.83***	−1.53***	−1.02***
Reference group = 10th grade				
Total number of HH jobs		−0.13***	−0.23***	−0.10***
Caste and ethnicity				
Higher caste		1.26***	1.34***	1.28***
Himalayan indigenous		2.53***	2.77***	2.65***
Hill indigenous		1.15***	1.15***	0.88***
Inner Terai indigenous		0.35	0.50	0.27
Terai indigenous		0.58*	0.32	0.07
Madhesi		1.50***	1.09***	0.82***
Reference group = Dalit				
Demographic characteristics				
Gender of HH head (1 = male)			0.28*	0.25*
Age of HH head			0.001	0.01
Marital status (1 = married, 0 = else)			0.69***	0.54***
# Productive age people in HH			0.51***	0.18***
# Dependent people in HH			0.14***	0.07*
Region				
Mountain				−3.67***
Urban hill				−0.78***
Rural hill				−3.58***
Urban Terai				−0.26
Rural Terai				−2.58***
Reference group = Kathmandu valley				
R^2	0.021	0.270	0.322	0.450
Number of cases	3,394	3,392	3,392	3,392

NOTES: * $p \leq .05$
** $p \leq .01$
*** $p \leq .001$ (two-tailed).

likely to use microfinance. Table 9.6 shows a very weak relationship between remittances received and the quality of housing.

Housing quality is also associated with the education of the household head, the total number of household jobs, caste and ethnicity, gender of the household head, marital status of the household head, and the number of dependents. Household heads with an education level below the SLC tend to have lower-quality housing. Households with more jobs also tend to have poorer housing quality. High caste groups, as well as the hill and Terai indigenous ethnic groups, have housing quality higher than do the Dalit. Male-headed households and married household heads have higher-housing quality as well. The more productive-age members and dependents a household has, the better its housing quality. It is likely that household income increases as the number of family members increases. All geographic regions have lower-quality housing than Kathmandu.

Among all explanatory variables, the total number of jobs in the household is the only variable that is significantly and negatively associated with all four livelihood variables. Household livelihoods are also impacted by the gender, marital status, and education level of the household head; caste and ethnicity; and the number of dependents in the household. These variables are significantly associated with food, education, and housing. The age of household head, number of people of productive age in the house, and geographic regions are also significantly related to some of the livelihood variables, especially food and housing.

Discussion

The state has tried hard to make microfinance available in Nepal. Yet, as in many other countries, only a few poor households take advantage of microfinance programs (Banerjee 2013), especially when people realize that it will be difficult to repay the debt. Thus, the existence of widespread microfinance services in Nepal, while providing access to emergency cash, does not remove the allure to emigrate to earn income in a stronger foreign currency. Migration and remittances keep growing. The 2003–2004 Nepal Living Standard Survey showed that 32 percent of households received remittances; this amount increased to 55.8 percent in the NLSS 2010–2011 survey (Paudel 2012). According to the NLSS 2010–2011 survey, 79 percent of remittances are used for consumption, and 7 percent are used to repay loans (Paudel 2012).

Our findings show a very weak relationship between remittances received and the quality of housing. This is understandable because people of various socioeconomic statuses, castes, and ethnicities emigrate. Households that receive more microfinance loans, however, tend to have a lower quality of housing. This is to be expected because microfinance targets the poor.

In Nepal, the men tend to migrate and remit, and women stay home and participate in microfinance programs available to them; this often happens in the same household (Maharjan, Bauer and Knerr 2012). In households with fathers working abroad, mothers are most often the ones in charge of the monthly budgeting for expenses on education, food, health care, and emergencies. Short-term microfinance loans can be requested by a wife and repaid when remittances from the husband abroad arrive. In this sense, migration makes microfinance feasible and repayment possible by those who are not business owners. Thus, households access microfinance and remittances in a gendered way and combine the income from both sources to meet growing demands and expectations at the short, mid, and long term.

Development workers frame microfinance as a tool for poverty reduction, but simply lending money to the poor may not be enough. As Damian von Stauffenberg, founder of MicroRate argues,

> *[What differentiates real microfinance from consumer credits is] the merchant banking aspect. As a microfinance institution, you have to know the business of your client. Now if you do not know the business of your client, now if you do not watch what the money is used for, then chances are a large part is going to be used for consumption, and if you borrow to consume, you are not the richer at the end of it. You are poorer because you have to pay the loan and high interest at the end. . . . You have to detect . . . those that will become productive with that loan.*
>
> (PovertyCure 2013)

According to Loiseau and Walsh, "if entrepreneurs' returns on their investments are higher than the cost of the loans, credit may lead to increases in household income. With additional income, borrowers and their families can increase spending on food, health care, housing, education, their businesses, leisure, or any number of other goods and services" (Loiseau and Walsh 2015). However, Mexican MFI Compartamos Banco, for example, charges interest rates from 69 percent to 125 percent APRs (Compartamos Banco 2015; Rosenberg, Adrian Gonzalez and Narain 2009; Waterfield 2008), which renders the loans prohibitive to many of the people the loan is intended to help.

Most inhabitants of developing countries are not and cannot be entrepreneurs. According to Banerjee, if

> *We look at what businesses the poor go into, the lack of diversification is striking. Among urban borrowers, a small number of occupations dominate, such as selling fruits and vegetables on the streets, running a small grocery store, selling prepared food, and tailoring. In rural areas, it is again non-specialized retail, plus livestock rearing and growing some*

> cash crops. Given that everyone else is in the exact same business in the same neighborhood, the possibility of earning very large profits is obviously limited.
>
> (Banerjee 2013)

Therefore, when people open businesses in poor and migrant-sending areas, they tend to engage in similar businesses and practice "business cloning" (Castañeda 2013), which does not support generalized economic development (Arroyo Alejandre 2010). Furthermore, Bylander and Hamilton (2015) find that households with higher use of credit are more likely to emigrate. Public funds have been channeled into microfinance in the name of alleviating poverty, yet, as some have argued recently, providing direct money transfers would be a more effective practice and not necessarily costlier (Blattman and Niehaus 2014).

Conclusion

This study explores the impact of microfinance and remittances on the percentage of household income spent on food and health care in Nepal. Microfinance is significantly associated with food, health, and housing but not with education. Microfinance loans are negatively associated with the percentage of income spent on food and quality of housing, while they are positively associated with the percentage of total income that goes toward health expenses. This indicates that if microfinance loans increase in the household, the percentage of the household income spent on food decreases. Households that take out a higher amount of loans from microfinance tend to have housing of poor quality. The positive relationship between microfinance and a higher proportion of household income being spent on health care suggests that people might take out more microloans if someone in their household faces health problems. This can happen because microcredit is faster to obtain than migrating, getting a job, and remitting.

The size of remittances is significantly associated with the percentage of income spent on food and education. It has a negative association with the percentage of household income spent on food; remittances bring additional money to a household, and an increase in a household's overall funds reduces the proportion of income that must go toward food expenses. However, remittances have a positive association with the number of minors enrolled in school. This significant association suggests that improvement in the financial situation of a household has a positive impact on the education of its children, at least at the basic level. Another explanation could be reverse causation, where households facing or forecasting increases in expenditures in education will make plans to migrate in order to afford them.

As no significant relationships could be established between microfinance and education, and among remittances, health-care expenditure, and housing quality, further investigation is deserved. Studying the use of microfinance and remittances simultaneously could help answer this question. Additional qualitative research should be conducted to confirm that (1) microfinance is useful in trying to meet a health-care emergency and most successful when supplemented by remittances to pay back the debt, and that (2) remittances and microfinance often are not sufficient to lift households and communities out of poverty.

Because access to credit has not been shown conclusively to discourage migration, this chapter offers a critique of some of the basic assumptions of New Economics of Labor Migration theories. While NELM has become hegemonic (Abreu 2012), researchers should look more carefully at household financial decisions, development contexts, and structural limitations to escaping poverty. Yet, as NELM theories propose, migration and remittances diversify income sources, reduce exposure to financial shocks, and serve as insurance (Amuedo-Dorantes and Pozo 2011). Given the 2015 earthquakes in Nepal, having workers abroad who can send remittances to households in Nepal to rebuild houses, stores, and temples gains increased importance, and microfinance could pay for small reconstruction projects in the short term. However, the earthquake also underscores the difficulty of being physically apart from family members in time of need (NPR 2015). The emigration of many healthy men of working age slows rescue and reconstruction efforts, yet the earthquake will probably result in more people leaving Nepal to find employment abroad (Zhong 2015).

International migration can help reduce poverty, but, to provide more benefits for the migrant households, the costs and risks associated with international migration must be reduced (Hagen-Zanker and Mallett 2014). The associated costs and risks of international migration can be reduced through regulations, work permits, and laws that prevent exploitation that actively manage migration and refugee flows, which would be beneficial for all. The creation of financial tools for the poor—including access to microcredit and lower fees for remittances—helps household economies, but it is hardly enough to compensate for either the vulnerability of workers in an undocumented status in migrant-receiving societies or endemic poverty in migrant-sending communities. The findings of this chapter indicate that, contrary to some of the assumptions of the New Economics Labor Migration theory, in most cases, neither remittances nor microfinance—alone or combined—are enough for households in the developing world to escape poverty.

References

Abreu, Alexandre. 2012. "The New Economics of Labor Migration: Beware of Neoclassicals Bearing Gifts." *Forum for Social Economics* 41(1):46–67. doi: 10.1007/s12143-010-9077-2.

Acosta, Pablo, Pablo Fajnzylber and Humberto Lopez. 2008. "Remittances and Household Behavior: Evidence for Latin America." Pp. 133–69 in *Remittances and Development: Lesson from Latin America*, edited by P. Fajnzylber and H. Lopez. Washington, DC: The World Bank.

Adams Jr., Richard H. 2006. "International Remittances and the Household: Analysis and Review of Global Evidence." *Journal of African Economies* 15(2):396–425.

Adhikari, Dipak Bahadur and Jayanti Shrestha. 2013. "Economic Impact of Microfinance in Nepal: A Case Study of the Manamaiju Village Development Committee, Kathmandu." *Economic Journal of Development Issues* 15:36–49.

Airola, Jim. 2007. "The Use of Remittance Income in Mexico." *International Migration Review* 41(4):850–59. doi: 10.1111/j.1747-7379.2007.00111.x.

Amuedo-Dorantes, Catalina and Susan Pozo. 2011. "Remittances and Income Smoothing." *The American Economic Review* 101(3):582–87.

Arguillas, Marie Joy B. and Lindy Williams. 2010. "The Impact of Parents' Overseas Employment on Educational Outcomes of Filipino Children." *International Migration Review* 44(2):300–19. doi: 10.1111/j.1747-7379.2010.00807.x.

Arroyo Alejandre, Jesús. 2010. "Migración México-Estados Unidos, Remesas Y Desarrollo Regional: Trinomio Permanente." Pp. 227–70 in *Los Grandes Problemas De México: Migraciones Internacionales*, edited by F. Alba, M. Á. Castillo and G. Verduzco. Ciudad de Mexico: Colegio de Mexico.

Bakker, Matt. 2015. *Migrating into Financial Markets: How Remittances Became a Development Tool*. Oakland, CA: University of California Press.

Ballard, Roger. 2005. "Remittances and Economic Development in India and Pakistan." Pp. 103–18 in *Remittances: Development Impact and Future Prospects*, edited by S. M. Maimbo and D. Ratha. Washington, DC: The World Bank.

Banerjee, Abhijit Vinayak. 2013. "Microcredit under the Microscope: What Have We Learned in the Past Two Decades, and What Do We Need to Know?" *Annual Review of Economics* 5(1):487–519. doi: 10.1146/annurev-economics-082912-110220.

Bhatta, Gambhir. 2001. "'Small Is Indeed Beautiful but': The Context of Microcredit Strategies in Nepal." *Policy Studies Journal* 29(2):283–95. doi: 10.1111/j.1541-0072.2001.tb02092.x.

Blattman, Christopher and Paul Niehaus. 2014. "Show Them the Money: Why Giving Cash Helps Alleviate Poverty." *Foreign Affairs* 93(3).

Bylander, Maryann and Erin R. Hamilton. 2015. "Loans and Leaving: Migration and the Expansion of Microcredit in Cambodia." *Population Research and Policy Review* 34(5):687–708.

Castañeda, Ernesto. 2013. "Living in Limbo: Transnational Households, Remittances and Development." *International Migration* 51(s1):13–35. doi: 10.1111/j.1468-2435.2012.00745.x.

Chemin, Matthieu. 2008. "The Benefits and Costs of Microfinance: Evidence from Bangladesh." *The Journal of Development Studies* 44(4):463–84. doi: 10.1080/00220380701846735.

Compartamos Banco. 2015. "Cat, Apr & Comissions". Compartamos Banco. Retrieved July 1, 2015 (https://www.compartamosbanco.com/).

Daley-Harris, Sam. 2009. "State of the Microcredit Summit Campaign Report 2009." Washington, DC: The Microcredit Summit Campaign.

De Haan, Leo and Annelies Zoomers. 2005. "Exploring the Frontier of Livelihoods Research." *Development and Change* 36(1):27–47. doi: 10.1111/j.0012-155X.2005.00401.x.

Deneulin, Severine. 2006. "Individual Well-Being, Migration Remittances and the Common Good." *The European Journal of Development Research* 18(1):45–58.

Develtere, Patrick and An Huybrechts. 2005. "The Impact of Microcredit on the Poor in Bangladesh." *Alternatives: Global, Local, Political* 30(2):165–89.

Dhakal, Tek Nath. 2006. *Ngos in Livelihoods Developments: Nepalese Experience*. New Delhi, India: Adroit Publishers.

Fisher, Thomas and M.S. Sriram. 2002. *Beyond Micro–Credit: Putting Development Back into Micro–Finance*. New Delhi, India: Vistaar Publications.

Frank, Reanne, Oswaldo Palma-Coca, Juan Rauda-Esquivel, Gustavo Olaiz-Fernández, Claudia Díaz-Olavarrieta and Dolores Acevedo-García. 2009. "The Relationship between Remittances and Health Care Provision in Mexico." *American Journal of Public Health* 99(7):1227–31. doi: 10.2105/ajph.2008.144980.

Gerber, Theodore P and Karine Torosyan. 2013. "Remittances in the Republic of Georgia: Correlates, Economic Impact, and Social Capital Formation." *Demography* 50(4):1279–301. doi: 10.1007/s13524-013-0195-3.

Gill, Gerard. 2003. "Seasonal Labour Migration in Rural Nepal: A Preliminary Overview." *Working Paper 218*. London, UK: Overseas Development Institute.

Gutberlet, Jutta. 2009. "Micro–Credit and Recycling Co–Ops: Grassroots Initiatives to Alleviate Poverty." *Development in Practice* 19(6):737–51.

Hagen-Zanker, Jessica and Richard Mallett. 2014. "Gambling on a Better Future: Is International Labor Migration Worth It?" London, UK: Secure Livelihoods Research Consortium.

Hagen-Zanker, Jessica, Richard Mallett, Anita Ghimire, Qasim Ali Shah, Bishnu Upreti and Haider Abbas. 2014. "Migration from the Margins: Mobility, Vulnerability and Inevitability in Mid–Western Nepal and North–Western Pakistan." London: Secure Livelihoods Research Consortium.

Hernandez Coss, Raul 2006. "The Impact of Remittances: Observations in Remitting and Receiving Countries." Paper presented at "The G24 XXIII Technical Group Meeting." Intergovernmental Group of Twenty-Four, Singapore.

Hulme, David and Pul Mosely. 1996. *Finance against Poverty Vols. 1 and 2*. London: Routledge.

Islam, Asadul. 2011. "Medium- and Long-Term Participation in Microcredit: An Evaluation Using a New Panel Dataset from Bangladesh." *American Journal of Agricultural Economics* 93(3):847–66. doi: 10.1093/ajae/aar012.

Khandker, Shahidur R. 2005. "Microfinance and Poverty: Evidence Using Panel Data from Bangladesh." *The World Bank Economic Review* 19(2):263–86. doi: 10.1093/wber/lhi008.

Koc, Ismet and Isil Onan. 2004. "International Migrants' Remittances and Welfare Status of the Left-Behind Families in Turkey." *International Migration Review* 38(1):78–112. doi: 10.1111/j.1747-7379.2004.tb00189.x.

Ledgerwood, Joanna. 1997. "Critical Issues in Nepal's Micro Finance Circumstances." Development Project Service Centre, Nepal; Micro Finance International, Canada.

Ledgerwood, Joanna. 1999. "Sustainable Banking with the Poor: Microfinance Handbook: An Institutional and Financial Perspective." Washington, DC: The World Bank.

Li, Xia, Christopher Gan and Baiding Hu. 2011. "The Welfare Impact of Microcredit on Rural Households in China." *The Journal of Socio-Economics* 40(4):404–11. doi: http://dx.doi.org/10.1016/j.socec.2011.04.012.

Loiseau, Justin and Claire Walsh. 2015. "Where Credit Is Due." *J-PAL and IPA Policy Bulletin*. Cambridge, MA: Abdul Latif Jameel Poverty Action Lab and Innovations for Poverty Action.

Lu, Yao and Donald J. Treiman. 2011. "Migration, Remittances and Educational Stratification among Blacks in Apartheid and Post-Apartheid South Africa." *Social Forces* 89(4):1119–43. doi: 10.1093/sf/89.4.1119.

Maharjan, Amina, Siegfried Bauer and Beatrice Knerr. 2012. "Do Rural Women Who Stay Behind Benefit from Male Out-Migration? A Case Study in the Hills of Nepal." *Gender, Technology and Development* 16(1):95–123. doi: 10.1177/097185241101600105.

Massey, Douglas S. and Emilio Parrado. 1994. "Migradollars: The Remittances and Savings of Mexican Migrants to the USA." *Population Research and Policy Review* 13(1):3–30.

Massey, Douglas S., Rafael Alarcon, Jorge Durand and Humberto González. 1987. *Return to Aztlan: The Social Process of International Migration from Western Mexico*. Berkeley, CA: University of California Press.

Massey, Douglas S., Jorge Durand and Karen A. Pren. 2012. "Migradollars in Latin America: A Comparative Analysis." Pp. 243–64 in *Migration and Remittances from Mexico: Trends, Impacts, and New Challenges*, edited by A. Cuecuecha and C. Pederzini. Lanham, MD: Lexington Books.

McDowell, Christopher and Arjan de Haan. 1997. "Migration and Sustainable Livelihoods: A Critical Review of the Literature." Sussex, UK: Institute of Development Studies, University of Sussex.

McIntosh, Craig, Gonzalo Villaran and Bruce Wydick. 2011. "Microfinance and Home Improvement: Using Retrospective Panel Data to Measure Program Effects on Fundamental Events." *World Development* 39(6):922–37. doi: http://dx.doi.org/10.1016/j.worlddev.2011.03.001.

Midgley, James. 2008. "Microenterprise, Global Poverty and Social Development." *International Social Work* 51(4):467–79.

NPR. 2015. "Persian Gulf System Prohibits Nepali Migrant Workers from Returning Home", May 04, 2015. Washington DC: National Public Radio. Retrieved July 7, 2017 (www.npr.org/2015/05/04/404236526/persian-gulf-system-prohibits-nepali-migrant-workers-from-returning-home).

Padia, Veena. 2005. "Social Mobilization and Micro–Credit for Women's Empowerment: A Study of the Dhan Foundation." Pp. 161–99 in *Micro–Credit, Poverty and Empowerment: Linking the Triad*, edited by N. Burra, J. Deshmukh-Ranadive and R. K. Murthy. Thousand Oaks: SAGE Publications and UNDP.

Parthasarathy, Soma Kishore. 2005. "Awareness, Access, Agency: Experiences of Swayam Shikshan Prayog in Microfinance and Women's Empowerment." Pp. 200–44 in *Micro–Credit, Poverty and Empowerment: Linking the Triad*, edited by N. Burra, J. Deshmukh-Ranadive and R. K. Murthy. Thousand Oaks: SAGE Publications and UNDP.

Paudel, Nawaraj Sharma. 2012. "Migration Trend and Remittance Inflow the Experience of Nepal." M.Phil., Economics, Tribhuvan University, Kritipur, Kathmandu, Nepal.
PovertyCure. 2013. "Microfinance 101." PovertyCure. Retrieved (www.youtube.com/watch?v=_LK4XMF2u8Y&feature=player_detailpage).
Qudrat-I Elahi, Khandakar and M. Lutfor Rahman. 2006. "Micro-Credit and Micro-Finance: Functional and Conceptual Differences." *Development in Practice* 16(5):476–83. doi: 10.1080/09614520600792481.
Rankin, Katharine N. 2001. "Governing Development: Neoliberalism, Microcredit, and Rational Economic Woman." *Economy and Society* 30(1):18–37. doi: 10.1080/03085140020019070.
Ratha, Dilip. 2003. "Workers' Remittances: An Important and Stable Source of External Development Finance." *Global Development Finance*. Washington, DC: The World Bank.
Ratha, Dilip. 2007. "Leveraging Remittances for Development." Washington, DC: The World Bank.
Robinson, Marguerite S. 2001. *The Microfinance Revolution: Sustainable Finance for the Poor*. Washington, DC: World Bank Publications.
Rogaly, Ben, Alfonso Castillo and Martha Romero Serrano. 2004. "Building Assets to Reduce Vulnerability: Microfinance Provision by a Rural Working People's Union in Mexico." *Development in Practice* 14(3):381–95.
Rosenberg, Richard, Adrian Gonzalez and Sushma Narain. 2009. "The New Moneylenders: Are the Poor Being Exploited by High Microcredit Interest Rates?" *CGAP Occasional Paper 15*. Washington, DC: Consultative Group to Assist the Poor.
Sankar, Kalpana. 2005. "Social Mobilization and Microfinance for Women's Empowerment: Lessons from the Asa Trust." Pp. 286–321 in *Micro–Credit, Poverty and Empowerment: Linking the Triad*, edited by Neera Burra, Joy Deshmukh-Ranadive and Ranjani K. Murthy. Thousand Oaks, CA: SAGE Publications and UNDP.
Sanyal, Paromita. 2009. "From Credit to Collective Action: The Role of Microfinance in Promoting Women's Social Capital and Normative Influence." *American Sociological Review* 74(4):529–50. doi: 10.1177/000312240907400402.
Seddon, David. 2004. "South Asian Remittances: Implications for Development." *Contemporary South Asia* 13(4):403–20.
Seddon, David, Jagannath Adhikari and Ganesh Gurung. 2002. "Foreign Labor Migration and the Remittance Economy of Nepal." *Critical Asian Studies* 34(1):19–40.
Sengupta, Rajdeep and Craig P. Aubuchon. 2008. "The Microfinance Revolution: An Overview." *Federal Reserve Bank of St. Louis Review* 90(1):9–30.
Shakya, Yogendra B. and Katharine N. Rankin. 2008. "The Politics of Subversion in Development Practice: An Exploration of Microfinance in Nepal and Vietnam." *The Journal of Development Studies* 44(8):1214–35. doi: 10.1080/00220380802242461.
Shrestha, Shankar Man. 2003. "Microfinance in Nepal: Experiences of Rmdc as an Apex Microfinance Organization." Paper presented at the International Seminar "Attacking Poverty with Microcredit" Palli Karma–Sahayak Foundation, Dhaka, Bangladesh.
Simanowitz, Anton and Alice Walter. 2002. "Ensuring Impact: Reaching the Poorest While Building Financially Self–Sufficient Institution, and Showing Improvement in the Lives of the Poorest Women and Their Families." Pp. 1–73 in *Pathways out of Poverty: Innovations in Microfinance for the Poorest Families*, edited by S. Daley–Harris. Bloomfield, CT: Kumarian Press.

Smith, Stephen C. 2002. "Village Banking and Maternal and Child Health: Evidence from Ecuador and Honduras." *World Development* 30(4):707–23. http://dx.doi.org/10.1016/S0305-750X(01)00128-0.

Stark, Oded and David E. Bloom. 1985. "The New Economics of Labor Migration." *American Economic Review* 75:173–8.

Stoesz, David, Carles Guzzetta and Mark W. Lusk. 1999. *International Development*. Boston, MA: Allyn and Bacon.

Takahatake, Takashi and Keshav L. Maharjan. 2002. "An Examination of the Socio-Economic Implications of Microfinance Programs: An Alternative Approach in Nepal." *Nepalese Studies* 29(1):97–127.

Thapa, Ganesh B. 2008. "The State of Microfinance: Breadth and Depth." Paper presented at the Microfinance Summit, February 14–16, Kathmandu, Nepal (www.microfinancegateway.org/library/state-microfinance-depth-breadth).

Tilly, Charles. 2007. "Trust Networks in Transnational Migration." *Sociological Forum* 22(1): 1–25.

Upreti, Bishnu Raj, Sony KC, Richard Mallett, Babken Babajanian and Safal Ghimire with Kailash Pyakuryal, Anita Ghimire and Sagar Raj Sharma. 2012. "Livelihoods, Basic Services and Social Protection in Nepal." London, UK: Secure Livelihoods Research Consortium.

Upreti, Bishnu Raj, Pravat Uprety, Jessica Hagen-Zanker, Sony KC and Richard Mallett. 2014. "Surveying Livelihoods, Service Delivery and Governance: Baseline Evidence from Nepal." London, UK: Secure Livelihoods Research Consortium.

Uprety, Tulasi Prasad. 2008. "Policy and Regulatory Issues in Microfinance." Paper presented at the Micro-Finance Summit Nepal, 16 February, Kathmandu, Nepal.

Von Pischke, J. D., Lynn Bennett and Mike Goldberg. 1993. *Sustainable Financial Services for the Poor: Building on Local Capacity, Main Report, Vol. 1*. Kathmandu: The World Bank.

Wagle, Udaya R. 2012. "Socioeconomic Implications of the Increasing Foreign Remittance to Nepal: Evidence from the Nepal Living Standard Survey." *International Migration* 50(4):186–207. doi: 10.1111/j.1468-2435.2011.00727.x.

Waterfield, Chuck. 2008. "Explanation of Compartamos Interest Rates", Lancaster, PA: Microfinance Transparency. (www.microfinancetransparency.com/evidence/PDF/5.6%20Explanation%20of%20Compartamos%20Interest%20Rates.pdf).

Woodruff, Christopher. and Rene Zenteno. 2007. "Migration Networks and Microenterprises in Mexico." *Journal of Development Economics* 82(2):509–28.

World Bank. 2006. "Global Economic Prospects 2006: Economic Implications of Remittances and Migration." Washington, DC: The World Bank.

World Bank. 2012. "Migration and Development Briefs 19: Remittances to Developing Countries Will Surpass $400 Billion in 2012." *Migration and Development Briefs*. Washington, DC: The World Bank.

World Bank. 2015. "Annual Remittances Data." Washington, DC: The World Bank.

Zarate-Hoyos, German A. 2004. "Consumption and Remittances in Migrant Households: Toward a Productive Use of Remittances." *Contemporary Economic Policy* 22(4):555–65. doi: 10.1093/cep/byh042.

Zhong, Raymond. 2015. "Nepalese Migrants Return Home to Face Havoc." *Wall Street Journal*. (https://www.wsj.com/articles/nepalese-migrants-return-home-to-face-havoc-1430522131).

ABOUT THE CONTRIBUTORS

Kevin R. Beck is a Ph.D. candidate in the Sociology Department at the University of California–San Diego. His research focuses on housing, neighborhoods, and social policy.

Ernesto Castañeda is Assistant Professor of Sociology at American University in Washington, D.C. He is the coeditor with Cathy L. Schneider of *Collective Violence, Contentious Politics, and Social Change: A Charles Tilly Reader* (Routledge 2017) and coauthor with Charles Tilly and Lesley Wood of *Social Movements 1768–2018* (forthcoming, Routledge 2018). He has also published on social movements, immigration, borders, and homelessness. He holds a Ph.D. in Sociology from Columbia University.

Guangqing Chi is an Associate Professor of Rural Sociology and Demography and Director of the Computational and Spatial Analysis Core at the Pennsylvania State University. Trained as an environmental and spatial demographer, he pursues two interwoven areas of research: climate change, land use, and community resilience and critical infrastructure/transportation, population change, and population health within the smart cities framework.

Nadia Y. Flores-Yeffal is an Assistant Professor of Sociology at Texas Tech University. She is the author of the book *Migration-Trust Networks: Social Cohesion in Mexican U.S.-Bound Emigration*. She has also published on human capital transferability, rural and urban differences, and the impact of the media on immigration rhetoric. Her more recent research is focusing on the educational aspirations of undocumented youth and on the social networks of Salvadoran immigrants in the United States. She holds a Ph.D. in Sociology from the University of Pennsylvania.

Josiah Heyman is Professor of Anthropology and Endowed Professor of Border Trade Issues, as well as the Director of the Center for Interamerican and Border Studies, at the University of Texas at El Paso. He is the editor of *States and Illegal Practices* and author of *Life and Labor on the Border* and *Finding a Moral Heart for U.S. Immigration Policy* as well as more than 120 scholarly articles and book chapters on borders, migration, engaged scholarship, and social theory.

Bishal Kasu is a Ph.D. candidate in the Department of Sociology and Rural Studies at South Dakota State University. His areas of research include microfinance, remittances, livelihoods, transportation, and social demography.

Douglas S. Massey is the Henry G. Bryant Professor of Sociology and Public Affairs at Princeton University, where he directs the Office of Population Research. He has published widely on issues of race, immigration, segregation, and social stratification.

Randa Serhan is Assistant Professor of Sociology at American University in Washington, D.C. She is the coeditor of *American Democracy and the Pursuit of Equality* (Routledge 2013). She is interested in urban ethnography, immigrant communities, nationalism, and citizenship. She holds a Ph.D. in Sociology from Columbia University.

Pau Serra del Pozo works at the Bureau for Diversity, Community, and Civic Participation of the Barcelona county. He has taught geography and sociology in Spain, the United States, and France (Ph.D. in Geography, University of Navarra). In 2010 he created the municipal Immigration Observatory of Badalona, Spain. He is the author of *Ethnic Commerce in the Old Town District of Barcelona* as well as articles, book chapters, and reports on the urban insertion of businesses owned by foreign immigrants.

Hwaji Shin is Associate Professor of Sociology at the University of San Francisco (Ph.D. in Sociology from SUNY–Stony Brook). She is the author of "Colonial Legacy of Ethno-Racial Inequality in Japanese Society" (*Theory and Society*, 2010) and also coauthor of an ASA award–winning article, "Global Norms, Local Activism, and Social Movement Outcomes: Global Human Rights and Resident Koreans in Japan" (*Social Problems*, 2008). Her research focuses on nationalism, citizenship, immigration, race and ethnicity, colonialism, and globalization.

INDEX

activation, boundary 14
African/African American migration: forced 16, 34; from the South to northern cities 17, 29, 50, 55
al-Assifa 104
Alba, Richard 9
American Social History Project 50
Arizona S.B. 1070 law 60
Aysa-Lastra, Maria 91

Barcelona 140-1, 165-6; data about businesses in Catalonia and 141; geographical distribution of foreign residents in the metropolitan area of 141; locational strategies of small businesses owned by immigrants in 141-3; multiethnic centralities in 151-7
blurring, boundary 12-13
Border Patrol, U.S. 38, 68
boundaries: activation 14; blurring 12-13; categories and 29-34; shifting 12-13; social 9-14, 67-8; -spanning processes 11-12; symbolic 67-8
bounded solidarity 87
Bourdieu, Pierre 9
cloned businesses, business cloning 140, 159, 161-2, 163-4, 165, 190

Bracero Program 58, 85
Brubaker, Rogers 9

Cainkar, Louise 106, 110-11, 116n19
Calavita, Kitty 51
Calhoun, Craig 110
Cannadine, David 112
career migration 8
caste 19, 137n2, 171, 177-8, *179*, 181, 182, *183-4*, 185, 188
Castro, Fidel 32
categorical inequality 1-2, 9; creating 34-9; Tilly's contribution to our understanding of 2-3
Categorically Unequal: The American Stratification System 9
categories: boundaries and 29-34; groups 1-2; imperative to classify people socially into 26; social relations and 15-16
Central American migration to the U.S. 36-7, 39, 67
chain migration 7-8; family reunification through 14
Chatterjee, Partha 110
Chavez, Mario 94
Chicago School of Sociology 8
cities: manufacturing of ethnicity in destination 7-8; migration and 6-7

citizenship 44–6; nationalism and 16, 44–5; workers and migration in the U.S., 1800–1965 50–6
civil rights movement 35
coethnic diverse centralities 150–1
coethnic specialized centralities 149–50
Collins, Jane 51
colonialism 122
colorblind racism 68
Cowie, Jefferson 51
Cubans 32–3, 36

Darwish, Mahmoud 105
Davis, Mike 68
day labor 65–7, 79–80; consequences of stigmatized status of 77–9; employment and safety at Huntington Station 69–71; experiencing exclusion 78–9; flash hirings of 65, 74–6; homelessness and 77–8; observations and interviews at hiring site for 68–79; resident concerns over 72–4; social boundaries and illegality affecting 67–8; wage theft from 76–7
De Albuquerque, Catarina 135
discrimination, racial 34–6
Distinction: A Social Critique of the Judgment of Taste 9
Dominican Republic 32–3
durable inequality 133–5
Durable Inequality 9
Durand, Jorge 51

Edwards, Richard 50
Ellis Island 85
Emancipation Proclamation 34
ethnic centralities 140–1; coethnic diverse 150–1; coethnic specialized 149–50; explaining business 143–4; in the metropolitan area of Barcelona 144–9
ethnic cleansing 27
ethnicity: manufacturing in destination cities 7–8; race and 16–17; symbolic 99–100, 114n4; Tilly's contribution to our understanding of 2–3
ethnitization 8

Fateh 104
First Great Migration of 1916–1930 17, 50, 55
flash hirings 65, 74–6
Flores-Yeffal, Nadia Y. 88, 89, 90–1, 92, 93, 95–6
Forbes 130

Gannon, Megan 1
Gans, Herbert 85
genocide 27
German immigrants to the U.S. 52–3
Gold, Steven 121
Gordon, David M. 50
Great Depression, the 57
Gutman, Herbert 50

Hamas 110
Han, Chang-woo 127–8, 130
Han, Jaehyang 127
Harvey, David 46
hennas 107–13, 116n15
Higham, John 51
high warmth/high competence categorization 27
high warmth/low confidence categorization 28
Hobsbawm, Eric 100
homelessness 77–8
Hulme, David 173
Huntington Station *see* day labor

ideal-type model of state formation 46–8, *49–50*
Ijichi, Noriko 134
illegal immigration *see* unauthorized/illegal migration
Immigration and Nationality Act of 1965 37
individual boundary crossing 11–12
inequality, durable 133–5
in-group membership 27
Irish immigrants to the U.S. 51–3, 86

jornaleros 66, 68, 69

Khalidi, Rashid 104
Korean immigrants in Japan 135–7;

declining significance of trust networks among 128–33; historical background 122–4; trust network and durable inequality 133–5; trust networks among 124–8

Lamont, Michele 67
Latino immigrants to the U.S. 31–3, 36–9; *see also* day labor
locational strategies of small businesses owned by immigrants 141–3
low warmth/high competence categorization 27–8
low warmth/low competence categorization 28

Malone, Nolan J. 51
manufactured ethnicity 7–8
Maruhan Group 127
Masayoshi, Son 130
Massey, Douglas 9, 51
methodological nationalism 7
Mexican migration to the U.S. 36–9, 56–61; border between U.S. and Mexico and 38, 67–8; trust networks and 83
Mexican New York 83, 93
microfinance 171, 190–1; approaches to implementing 173; effect on poverty 173; financial services provided by 173; goals of 174; introduction to 171–5; in Nepal 176–91; research data and methods 178–82; research results 182–8; women and 174
migration: career 8; chain 7–8, 14; cities and 6–7; destinations 5–6; as fundamental feature of the human condition 26; ideal-type model of state formation, capitalism, and 46–8, *49–50*; illegal (*see* unauthorized/illegal migration); motivation for 30–1; networks 3–6, 121–2; social cognition and 27–9; Tilly's contribution to our understanding of 2–3; to the U.S., 1800–1965 50–6; to the U.S. after 1965 56–61; workers and citizenship in the U.S., 1800–1965 50–6

Migration-Trust Networks (MTNs) 14–15, 83–4; advantages and disadvantages of 95–7; among Koreans in Japan 124–33; durable inequality and 133–5; functioning of 87–95; risks associated with unauthorized immigration and 85–6; study methodology and limitations 85; U.S. policies and unauthorized immigration and 85
Migration-Trust Networks: Social Cohesion in Mexican U.S.-Bound Emigration 84
Molnar, Virag 67
Mosely, Pul 173
multiethnic centralities 151–7

NAFTA 68
nationalism 110; American 59; methodological 7; relations between citizenship and 16, 44–5
Nation and Its Fragments, The 110
Nepal 171; children's education in 185; explanatory variables in 180–1; food expenses in 182; health expenses in 182–5; housing quality in 185–8; livelihoods in 176; microfinance in 176, 188–90; remittances to 176–8, 188–90; research data 178–80; research methods 181–2; research results 182–8
networks 2, 7–8, 18–19, 35, 56, 58, 62, 67, 83, 85, 87, 91, 93, 101, 113, 116n18, 124, 142, 175; migration 3–6; trust 14–15, 91; *see* Migration-Trust Networks MTN
Nevins, Joseph 68
New Economics of Labor Migration (NELM) 171, 172, 191
Ngai, Mae M. 51
Nishi Nihon Shokusan 134

Omi, Michael 51
opportunity hoarding 129
Orozco, Guillermo A. P. 94
out-groups 27–8

Pachinko industry 126–8

Palestinian Liberation Organization (PLO) 106, 115n10
Palestinian Resistance Movement 110
Palestinian weddings 113, 114n2–3; in America 99–103; films depictions 105–6; hennas 107–13, 116n15; historical background of 103–13, 115n12
political refugees 30–1
Portes, Alejandro 87, 122, 143
Puerto Ricans 31–3, 36

race 16–17; anti-immigration sentiments and 61; colorblind racism and 68; discrimination and segregation based on 34–6
Rana's Wedding: Jerusalem, Another Day 105
Rechitsky, Raphi 94
refugees 30–1
Reich, Michael 50
relational theory of migration 4
relations and categories 15–16
remittances 175, 190–1; to Nepal 176–8, 188–90

Sampson, Robert 91, 95
Sassen, Saskia 58
Second Great Migration of 1940–1970 17
segregation, racial 34–6
Sensenbrenner, Julia 87
shifting, boundary 12–13
slavery 16, 34, 35–6
Small Farmer Development Project 176
Smith, Robert 83, 91, 93
social boundaries 9–14; illegality and 67–8; *see* boundaries
social cognition and migration 27–9, 34
South American migration to the U.S. 36–7, 39
state formation: ideal-type model of 46–8, *49–50*; immigration and 44–5
stereotypes 29
Supreme Commander for Allied Powers (SCAP) 123–4
symbolic ethnicity 99–100, 114n4
symbolic boundaries; *see* boundaries

textile industry 51, 125–6
Thomas, William Isaac 2
Tilly, Charles 44, 85, 88; avoidance of methodological nationalism 7; on boundary activation 14; on categorical inequality 9; on citizenship and nationalism 16, 44–5; contribution to our understanding of migration, ethnicity and categorical inequality 2–3; on destinations of migrants 5–6; on love-hate relationship between cities and migrants 6–7, 7–8; on migration networks 3–6, 136; on migration of African Americans to the North 17; on race 16–17; on social boundaries 9–14; on social relations and categories 15–16; on trust networks 14–15, 83, 84, 92, 93, 94, 95, 121–2, 132, 136–7
transnationalism 116n18
transnational networks 4–6
Trujillo, Rafael 32
Trump, Donald 35, 61
Trust and Rule 83
trust networks *see* Migration-Trust Networks (MTNs)

unauthorized/illegal migration 37–8, 57; risks associated with 85–7; U.S. policies and 85; *see also* day labor
undocumented migrants *see* unauthorized/illegal migration
United States, the: African Americans in 16–17, 29, 34; citizenship, workers, and migration, 1800–1965 50–6; immigration after 1965 56–61; Latino immigrants to 31–3, 36–9; nationalism 59; policies and unauthorized immigration 85
unskilled laborers 8

wage theft from day laborers 76–7
Waldinger, Roger 128
Weber, M. 46
Wedding in Galilee 105
weddings, ethnic 99–103, 113, 114n2–3; hennas as second 107–13, 116n15;

historical background of the migrant-sending communities and 103–13
Weil, Patrick 9
White, Harrison 5
Wilson, K. 143
Winant, Howard 51
Wolf, Eric 46
Woon, Long Litt 9–14

"Work, Culture, and Society in Industrializing America" 50

Yim, Young-Eon 132

Zainichi Koreans 129
Zelizer, Viviana 15–16
Znaniecki, Florian 2
Zolberg, Aristide 9–10, 9–14, 51

Taylor & Francis eBooks

Helping you to choose the right eBooks for your Library

Add Routledge titles to your library's digital collection today. Taylor and Francis ebooks contains over 50,000 titles in the Humanities, Social Sciences, Behavioural Sciences, Built Environment and Law.

Choose from a range of subject packages or create your own!

Benefits for you
- Free MARC records
- COUNTER-compliant usage statistics
- Flexible purchase and pricing options
- All titles DRM-free.

Benefits for your user
- Off-site, anytime access via Athens or referring URL
- Print or copy pages or chapters
- Full content search
- Bookmark, highlight and annotate text
- Access to thousands of pages of quality research at the click of a button.

REQUEST YOUR FREE INSTITUTIONAL TRIAL TODAY

Free Trials Available
We offer free trials to qualifying academic, corporate and government customers.

eCollections – Choose from over 30 subject eCollections, including:

Archaeology	Language Learning
Architecture	Law
Asian Studies	Literature
Business & Management	Media & Communication
Classical Studies	Middle East Studies
Construction	Music
Creative & Media Arts	Philosophy
Criminology & Criminal Justice	Planning
Economics	Politics
Education	Psychology & Mental Health
Energy	Religion
Engineering	Security
English Language & Linguistics	Social Work
Environment & Sustainability	Sociology
Geography	Sport
Health Studies	Theatre & Performance
History	Tourism, Hospitality & Events

For more information, pricing enquiries or to order a free trial, please contact your local sales team:
www.tandfebooks.com/page/sales

 Routledge | The home of
Taylor & Francis Group | Routledge books

www.tandfebooks.com